Adjustment and poverty

The 1980s was a decade of sharp adjustment and rising poverty for much, of the developing world. The oil crises of the 1970s and the recession of the early 1980s set in motion a chain of events which had particularly serious consequences for these areas. In *Adjustment and Poverty: Options and Choices*, the author examines the major causes and results of this situation. The work includes:

- an examination of the relationship between adjustment policies and poverty during the 1980s;
- an analysis of the impact of the IMF and World Bank macro-policies on adjusting countries – both in theory and practice;
- a discussion of government tax and expenditure policies – with particular focus on social sector spending;
- identification and assessment of improved policies for the future.

The book focuses on those areas where poverty increased most, mainly in Africa and Latin America. Experiences here are sharply contrasted with those areas which were able to combine adjustment with protection for the poor.

Frances Stewart is Director of the International Development Centre, Queen Elizabeth House, Oxford. She was Special Adviser on Adjustment Policies to UNICEF and is a Council member of the United Nations University. She has published widely on a range of development topics and is recognised as a leading authority on this subject.

Priorities for development economics
Series Editor: Paul Mosley, University of Reading

Development economics deals with the most fundamental problems of economics – poverty, famine, population growth, structural change, industrialisation, debt, international finance, the relations between state and market, the gap between rich and poor contries. Partly because of this, its subject matter has fluctuated abruptly over time in response to political currents in a way which sometimes causes the main issues to be obscured; at the same time it is being constantly added to and modified in every developed and developing country. The present series confronts these problems. Each contribution will begin with a dispassionate review of the literature worldwide and will use this as a springboard to argue the author's own original point of view. In this way the reader will both be brought up to date with the latest advances in a particular field of study and encounter a distinctive approach to that area.

Adjustment and poverty

Options and choices

Frances Stewart

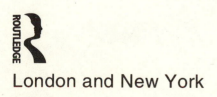

London and New York

First published 1995
by Routledge
11 New Fetter Lane, London EC4P 4EE

Simultaneously published in the USA and Canada
by Routledge
29 West 35th Street, New York, NY 10001

Typeset in Garamond by
Pure Tech Corporation, Pondicherry, India
Printed and bound in Great Britain by
T.J. Press (Padstow) Ltd, Padstow, Cornwall

British Library Cataloguing in Publication Data
A catalogue record for this book in available from the British Library

Library of Congress Cataloguing in Publication Data
Stewart, Frances, 1940–
    Adjustment and poverty: options and choices/Frances Stewart.
        p.   cm.—(Priorities for development economics)
    Includes bibliographical references and index.
    ISBN 0–415–09134–9.—ISBN 0–415–12436–0 (pbk.)
    1. Structural adjustment (Economic policy)—Developing countries.
2. Poverty—Developing countries. 3. World Bank—Developing
countries. 4. International Monetary Fund—Developing countries.
I. Title. II. Series.
HC59.7.S824 1995
338.9′0091722—dc20   94–46809   CIP

ISBN 0–415–09134–9
ISBN 0–415–12436–0 (pbk)

For David

Contents

List of diagrams, charts and tables

Series editor's preface

Development economics has passed through a turbulent decade. Described in widely-cited publications of the 1980s as 'in crisis' (Polly Hill) and 'in decline' (Deepak Lal) its theory has fallen behind its subject-matter, so that both the happiest development of the decade, the massive improvement in growth and equity in the 1980s, and the saddest, the decline of sub-Saharan Africa, are surrounded by controversy rather than consensus about what their cause may be.

The theory of development economics nonetheless has much to be proud of, in particular the transformation of the idea of market failure from a curiosity into a general case and the rigorous application of this idea to a number of real-life situations, including government intervention in foreign trade, capital and labour markets and the appraisal of investment projects. These are not, of course, activities carried out purely in developing countries, but the way they are carried out everywhere owes a great deal to ideas pioneered within development economics. The dust from the disputes of the 1980s is now beginning to settle, and nobody now seriously treats development economics, if they ever did, purely as a Trojan horse designed to undermine the free market in favour of the corrupt operations of government.

At the same time, there remains a lot of doubt about the state of the art in a number of areas, doubt which is magnified by the tendency of theory and practice to remain more separate from one another than in many branches of economics, or other sciences. One dramatic illustration of this has been the introduction of 'structural adjustment lending' by the World Bank and other international financial agencies in the last fifteen years, under which aid money has been offered in return for policy reform. In virtually all cases the justification offered for the policy reforms in question, e.g. privatisation, subsidy removal, trade liberalisation, has not been empirical evidence specific to the country in question but *a priori* theorising often based on an attempt to apply the general theorems of welfare economics without taking note of the conditions which have to be satisfied if those theorems are to apply, for example, perfect knowledge, no externalities, no economies of scale. The absence of empirical support for recommended reforms which often have serious political and social implications has led to justified scepticism, particularly in developing countries, about what development economics has to offer in such a situation.

Accordingly, there would seem to be a need for a set of handbooks which bring development practitioners abreast of theory and practice at the same time, and this is what the *Priorities in Development Economics* series attempts to do in respect of the most important development problems. One possible model, which will apply to some of the early volumes but not necessarily to all, is to spend Part I of the book reviewing the literature and giving reasons for selecting one (or more) approaches to the problem for a detailed empirical test, which then occupies Part II. The essential requirement is that facts and theory confront one another continuously rather than leading an independent existence. As series editor I am proud that this objective has been achieved in the early volumes. Suggestions from readers for problems which could usefully become the basis for future volumes in the series are more than welcome.

Paul Mosley
June, 1995

Preface

I would like to thank Kate Raworth for reading the whole manuscript and making many helpful suggestions and for particular assistance with Chapter 7; Philip O'Keefe for research assistance for Chapter 2; my fellow authors, Giovanni Andrea Cornia, Willem van der Geest and Anuradha Basu for enjoyable and stimulating collaboration and for allowing me to include our joint pieces here. Early drafts of Chapter 2 and Chapter 5 were prepared for the ILO and Chapter 4 was initially prepared for a World Bank symposium; I am grateful for their permission to use the work here. I also thank Denise Watt and Roger Crawford for very good-humoured assistance with preparing the manuscript, especially the tables and charts.

F.S.

Chapter 1

Introduction

The 1980s was a decade of adjustment for much of the Third World – for most countries in Africa and Latin America, and for quite a number of countries elsewhere in the developing world. The decade was also one of rising poverty in Africa and Latin America – a sharp reverse in the previous trend of gradual reductions in the numbers in poverty. In Asia in contrast, poverty was reduced over these years. Between 1985 and 1989 the numbers in poverty in sub-Saharan Africa rose from 191 million to 228 million; in Latin America and the Caribbean the numbers rose from an estimated 91 million in 1980 to 133 million in 1989.[1] The decade also saw rising unemployment, reduced progress in improving human indicators, such as infant mortality rates, and worsening indicators of educational performance in many adjusting countries. Not all adjusting countries had poor performance of this kind: for example, Indonesia succeeded in *reducing* poverty and improving human indicators, while adjusting, as did Colombia. But good performance on human and social indicators among adjusting countries was the exception rather than the rule.

This book aims to review the relationship between adjustment policies and poverty over the decade of the 1980s, focusing particularly on why some countries succeeded in adjusting 'with a human face', while the majority did not. One aim is to assess the performance of adjusting countries with respect to poverty over the decade; another is to identify improved policies for the future. The subject is an important one because of the pervasiveness of the adjustment problem over time and in terms of the numbers of countries affected. By the end of the 1980s, as many countries were seeking adjustment support from the International Monetary Fund (IMF) and World Bank as at the beginning of the decade. Thus the idea that a temporary belt-tightening was all that was needed is no longer plausible, and consequently what happens 'while crossing the desert' (to use a phrase of the World Bank) is important because the crossing has lasted more than a decade already, affecting not only the immediate well-being of hundreds of millions but also their potential for productive activity in the future.

The adjustment policies did not come out of the blue, superimposed on countries whose performance was otherwise progressing satisfactorily. The

policies were adopted – mostly under the auspices of the IMF and World Bank
– because of major imbalances that developed in the early 1980s in many
developing economies. These imbalances, and especially the acute foreign
exchange crisis that emerged, necessitated some adjustment. Countries could
not have carried on as before, because no one was willing to finance them to
do so. It follows that part at least of the cause of worsening poverty was the
imbalances (and the source of these imbalances) that led to the adjustments,
rather than the adjustments themselves. Indeed, in the international financial
institutions (IFIs) the blame for any rise in poverty is laid at the door of
exogenous developments and earlier policy mistakes on the part of governments.[2] However, whether this is so or not – and one conclusion of this book
is that it is only partially true – it remains the case that an alarming and
unacceptable deterioration in human conditions occurred among some adjusting
countries which means that the policies were *not* satisfactory and better
alternatives need to be found. Moreover, the very fact that some countries did
succeed in protecting the poor while adjusting suggests that the deterioration
observed elsewhere may not have been inevitable, but could have been avoided.

SOURCE OF THE ECONOMIC CRISIS OF THE 1980s

The origin of the crisis of the 1980s lay largely in events of the 1970s. In the
1970s, oil-importing countries were faced with very large balance of trade
deficits, following the oil price rise of 1973-4. But at this point there was
abundant financial liquidity in the world, resulting from the liquid balances built
up by the oil producers. Commercial banks lent to deficit countries, with little
hesitation or careful appraisal, in large quantities and at low interest rates.
Oil-importing countries were able to continue to invest and consume as before,
with very little incentive to adjust to the new situation. Non-oil commodity
prices also continued to hold up, albeit with some fluctuations. Naturally this
situation led to a big build-up in debt, which seemed sustainable so long as
interest rates were low, commodity prices buoyant and the commercial banks
were willing to go on lending, at least to rollover the old debt. But at the end
of the decade all these conditions were reversed. In 1979 there was a further
oil-price shock, leading to additional need for foreign exchange on the part of
oil importers. Recession among developed countries in the early 1980s initiated
a downward movement in commodity prices, which continued (with some
fluctuations) for much of the decade. And the era of monetarism began – led
by the Reagan/Thatcher regimes – which ended cheap money. Real interest
rates became positive and remained very high by historical standards for the
whole decade. The prospects of borrowing countries no longer appeared viable
to the commercial banks who ceased virtually all voluntary lending to developing countries by the mid-1980s.

These developments are illustrated in Tables 1.1, 1.2 and 1.3. The terms of
trade worsened for most of the decade, with Africa suffering particularly badly.

Table 1.1 Imbalances among developing countries, 1980s ($m)

	All developing countries	Non-oil exporters	Latin America	Africa	Sub-Saharan Africa	Middle East	Asia
Balance on current a/c $bn							
1975	−11.1	−46.5	−16.4	−6.9	n.a.	−7.0	−8.9[a]
1980	+30.6	−65.7	−29.8	−2.1	−8.6	+76.9	−14.4
1985	−26.6	−24.3	−3.1	−1.2	−3.4	−9.1[b]	−13.2
1990	−11.6	−12.7	−6.0	−3.0	−8.6	−3.7[b]	−2.7
1993	−104.6	−56.2	−43.3	−8.3	−8.4	−27.8[b]	−25.1
Fiscal balance as GDP (%)							
1980	−1.5	n.a.	−0.6	−3.9	−6.5	−2.7	−3.4
1985	−4.8	−4.0	−4.0	−3.3	−5.4	−9.7[b]	−3.0
1990	+3.5	−3.3	−0.8	−3.6	−8.2	−10.6[b]	−2.9
1993	−3.5	−3.6	−0.1	−10.6	−13.2	−6.4[b]	−2.9
Inflation, consumer prices, change per annum (%)							
1974–83	+25.7	+36.8	+58.9	+16.7	+22.7	+18.1[b]	+11.1
1985	+37.8	+47.2	+128.2	+13.0	+18.5	+15.0[b]	+6.8
1990	+65.5	+84.0	+480.2	+16.9	+21.7	+24.6[b]	+7.5
1993	+45.9	+55.1	+236.5	+31.7	n.a.	+24.4	+9.5

Sources: IMF, *World Economic Outlook,* April 1982, April 1986, May 1991, May 1994
(a) Excludes China
(b) Includes developing Europe

Table 1.2 Deteriorating external environment

	All LDCs	Non-oil exporters	Latin American and Caribbean	Africa	Sub-Saharan Africa
Terms of trade					
Change per annum (%)					
1973–82	6.9	−1.0	+2.8	+5.6	−0.3
1983–6	−6.8	+0.8	−3.9	−6.9	−2.1
1987–90	−0.1	−0.7	−1.7	−1.5	−4.0
Debt					
External debt, $bn					
1978	399.1[a]	300.0	155.9	72.4	29.5
1983	889.0	630.5	344.5	126.9	53.3
1986	1,096.3	800.2	382.2	169.7	77.1
1990	1,306.4	971.8	418.7	276.4	118.9
Debt service as % exports					
1978	19.0[a]	17.6	37.9	15.3	15.1
1983	18.4	20.3	42.5	22.7	21.3
1986	22.7	22.1	40.2	28.7	23.5
1990	14.4	14.4	29.3	26.0	24.5
Lending by commercial banks, $bn					
1978	43.9[a,b]	28.4[b]	25.8[b]	6.5[b]	1.6[b]
1983	38.7	23.3	21.4	2.2	−0.1
1986	−0.4	2.3	−4.0	−1.4	−0.5
1990	8.3	11.1	3.5	−1.2	1.9

Sources: IMF, *World Economic Outlook*, April 1986; May 1990; May 1991
(a) Capital importing developing countries
(b) 'Other borrowing' (excludes official)

Rising interest rates plus debt build-up led to a rising burden of debt service, especially in Latin America, where it amounted to over 42 per cent in 1983. These changes led to large current account deficits in most developing countries – which more than doubled in the main regions between 1975 and 1980. Commercial finance from overseas diminished sharply in all areas. Although public lending increased, it did not nearly offset the fall in private finance, and developing countries were forced to curtail their current account deficits sharply between 1980 and 1985.

Table 1.3 Interest rates for developing countries (per cent)

Year	Private creditors	Official creditors
1970	7.2	3.6
1980	12.3	5.6
1983	10.4	7.3
1986	7.4	6.1
1989	8.5	5.6

Source: World Bank, *World Debt Tables, 1990–91* (Washington DC: World Bank)

In Latin America in the latter part of the decade, attempts to reduce the debt burden through the Brady plan and other mechanisms were quite successful and debt service fell significantly in the last years of the 1980s. But in Africa, debt service continued to mount. With some revival of lending – commercial to Latin America and public to Africa – towards the end of the decade, current account deficits again widened. The deteriorating conditions for developing countries, especially in the first half of the 1980s, are indicated by changes in the net transfer of resources, i.e. net lending less interest payments. This had been large and positive at $29 billion in 1980, but by 1986 it was minus $24 billion, a turn around of over $50 billion. Latin America was much the worst affected, with a negative transfer of $20 billion in 1986. Sub-Saharan Africa received a positive net transfer throughout the decade.

In parallel with (and in part a cause of) the imbalances on current account were large deficits on the domestic budget, especially in Africa (Table 1.1).[3] These deficits were often largely financed by printing money, especially in countries with weak financial markets, and were accompanied by high rates of inflation. The data in Table 1.1, however, indicate that there is no simple relationship between government deficits and the rate of inflation; inflation was high and accelerating in Latin America, where public deficits were not very high, and fairly moderate and decelerating in Africa where public deficits were much higher.

It was the imbalance on current account of the balance of payments, together with an inability to secure finance from commercial sources, that led many countries to approach the IMF and World Bank for loans. In the 1980s, twenty-one sub-Saharan Africa countries, seventeen Latin American and sixteen others had IMF programmes of more than two years' duration; twenty-three sub-Saharan, twelve Latin American and nine others had World Bank programmes of more than two years' duration (Table 1.4). Many of the programmes lasted for a number of years, or were renewed again and again. Twenty-three countries had IMF programmes for more than five years and eight countries had World Bank programmes for more than five years. These programmes were invariably conditional on countries introducing certain policy changes – 'adjustment' policies as they are usually termed. Consequently, the Fund and Bank were major policy-makers in the majority of African and Latin American countries throughout the decade. Their influence was not confined to countries to which they lent: some others had 'shadow' programmes (agreed with the Fund, but not financed by them) and others duplicated the main elements of the IFI programmes, without seeking finance or advice.

Table 1.4 Incidence of stabilisation and adjustment policies, 1980s[a]

	Number of countries with programmes			
	5 or more years		*2–4 years*	
	IMF	*WB*	*IMF*	*WB*
Sub-Saharan Africa	13	2	9	21
Latin America and Caribbean	5	2	12	10
Rest of the world	5	4	11	5
Total	23	8	32	36

Sources: World Bank, 1990a; Khan, 1990
(a) Data from IMF for 1989 incomplete

There has been much debate on whether the origins of countries' problems in the 1970s and 1980s were exogenous or endogenous. For example, Dell and Lawrence (1980) argued forcibly that there was a strong exogenous element, while Wheeler (1984) found statistical support for this view among African countries. In contrast, most Bank and Fund authors tend to place the burden of blame on domestic policy mistakes.[4] The data clearly support the view that exogenous events played a role – in particular the fall in commodity prices and the high interest rates were outside any single country's control. But the heavy borrowing of the 1970s was largely due to government decisions during the decade, although these were not seriously criticised by outsiders, including the IFIs, at the time. The sizeable budget deficits were also governments' responsibility; while domestic policies often discriminated against tradables, encouraging import-substituting industries with biases against agriculture and manufacturing exports.

The origins of the problems thus lie in both exogenous and endogenous developments. Irrespective of *cause*, countries had no alternative to adjusting, although the extent and speed of the required adjustment was partly the responsibility of the international community. Had the IFIs and others been quicker in finding a solution to the debt crisis and in accelerating official financial flows to Africa, adjustment could have been more gradual. Less adjustment would have been needed had interest rates been brought down sooner. More radically, had the problem of falling commodity prices been tackled effectively, instead of compounded by the policies advocated, the need for adjustment would have been significantly moderated.

In the event, countries were required to adjust rapidly, sharply and (in many cases) continuously. The IMF and the World Bank became the major policy-makers for many countries. The stabilisation and adjustment policies they designed were intended to reduce the twin imbalances on external and domestic account, and correct policy biases against tradables and market forces, in order to establish the basis for sustainable growth. The adjustment programmes were adopted – with more or less effective implementation – in many countries almost continuously throughout the 1980s, dominating policy-making and displacing most long-run development policies.[5] Because of the pervasiveness, dominance and prolonged nature of the stabilisation and adjustment policies, they had wide-ranging medium-term consequences, not only for the macro-economy but also for incomes of the poor and for the social sectors.

For the first half of the decade, little attention was paid to the plight of the poor by the international community, although quite early in the decade UNICEF drew attention to some early indicators of negative trends.[6] But at this stage both the World Bank and the IMF regarded the issue of poverty in relation to adjustment as solely a domestic one, on which they had, and should have, little to contribute.[7] As the years passed, it became apparent that poverty was increasing sharply in quite a large number of countries, social expenditures were being cut and there was a slowdown in progress on human indicators with some worsening in a few cases. In 1987, UNICEF advocated 'Adjustment with a Human Face' – i.e. an alternative set of policies designed to protect the poor during adjustment.[8] Soon after the IMF and the World Bank acknowledged the need to take into consideration the social consequences of adjustment.

Since 1987, the World Bank's staff guidelines have required Policy Framework Papers for low-income countries to include 'a brief description and assessment . . . of the social impact of the government's intended adjustment program', and all President's Reports supporting structural adjustment to pay particular attention to 'the short-term impact of the adjustment program on the urban and rural poor, and measures proposed to alleviate negative effects'.[9]

A joint Bank/Fund Study prepared for the development committee in 1989 pointed to

declining per capita incomes accompanied by worsening social indicators, particularly in sub-Saharan Africa and Latin America. . . . Some of the poor did benefit, but many vulnerable groups were hurt by measures associated with adjustment. By the mid-1980s, it became clear that 'given the time and effort required to turn deeply troubled economies around, it would be morally, politically and economically unacceptable to wait for resumed growth alone to reduce poverty'.[10]

In 1990 Camdessus, managing director of the Fund, acknowledged

> the recognition that macroeconomic policies can have strong effects on the distribution of income and on social equity and welfare. A responsible adjustment program must take these effects into account, particularly as they impinge on the most vulnerable or disadvantaged groups in society.
>
> (Speech to US Chamber of Commerce, 26 March 1990).

Each IMF country Mission is now required to report on the poverty implications of country programmes. Fund Missions often discuss welfare consequences with governments when preparing programmes, and Policy Framework Papers prepared for the SAF/ESAF programmes[11] are required to 'identify measures that can help cushion the possible adverse effects of certain policies on vulnerable groups'.[12]

One aim of this book is to assess how far the changed attitudes of the international financial institutions towards adjustment and the poor, as evidenced by their public declarations, have been effectively translated into policies.

THE CONTENT OF STABILISATION AND ADJUSTMENT POLICIES

Stabilisation policies are those policies designed to correct the imbalances in the economy in the short run. They are the policies mainly associated with the Fund. The content of Fund stabilisation programmes is, by now, well known.[13] There are three elements: demand restraint, with emphasis on public expenditure reductions, credit control and real wage restraint; switching policies, especially emphasising exchange rate reform and devaluation; and long-term supply policies including financial reform and trade liberalisation. The long-term supply measures are designed to increase efficiency, with the emphasis on an increased role for the market and a reduced role for public intervention. Analysis suggests that demand restraint policies have dominated Fund programmes, being a universal feature, while over half the programmes include switching policies and a somewhat lower proportion long-term reforms (Table 1.5). But the importance of devaluation has grown, and it is now included in almost all programmes.[14]

The WB structural adjustment policies contain the same three elements of demand restraint, switching and long-term supply, but the first two categories form a relatively small proportion of the total, as the main elements of macroeconomic stabilisation are left to the Fund. Thus Bank policies are predominantly adjustment policies, not stabilisation policies, although there is some

Table 1.5 Characteristics of fund-supported programmes, 1980–4, (ninety-three agreements)

	Percentage, including
A. Demand restraints	
1. Limit on credit expansion	100.0
2. Restraint in public expenditure	92.4
3. Deficit reduction	82.8
B. Switching policies[a]	
Increase prices of specific sectors/price decontrol	62.4
Exchange rate reforms	50.6
Wage restraint/guidelines	47.3
C. Long-run efficiency[b]	
Sectoral restructuring	68.9
Financial reforms	51.6
Trade liberalisation	48.4

Source: IMF, 1986, Table 12
(a) Also have demand restraint and efficiency effects
(b) May also have switching effects

overlap between the two institutions, with programmes of the Fund containing elements of adjustment and those of the Bank elements of stabilisation. Almost every country has a Fund package as a necessary prerequisite to WB structural adjustment loans. Moreover, for Africa the two institutions very often form joint programmes. Seventy-eight per cent of Bank adjustment conditions from 1980–8 related to efficiency and 72 per cent, 1989–91 (Table 1.6). In these reforms, the Bank shares the market-oriented philosophy of the Fund. Policies include trade policies (generally import liberalisation), industry, energy and agricultural policies (with emphasis on reforming and deregulating the price system), reforms of the financial sector (reducing financial repression), rationalisation of government and administration, public enterprise reforms (with emphasis on privatisation) and social policy reforms.[15] The dominant conditions were trade policies, sectoral reforms, reform of government administration and fiscal policy reform, all included in over half the agreements, 1979–89.[16] Social policy reforms accounted for only 3 per cent of the total conditions, 1980–8, rising to 7 per cent 1989–91.[17]

SOME USEFUL CATEGORISATIONS

Before proceeding to analyse the impact of adjustment policies on poverty, it is helpful to make some distinctions with respect to types of income and types of policy which will be used throughout the book.

Types of income: primary and secondary

Primary incomes are the incomes generated by the economic system before taxes and benefits. They thus include income from assets (land, capital), from

Table 1.6 World Bank: loan agreement conditions (as a percentage of all conditions)

	1980–8	1989–91
A. *Demand restraint*	38	42
Deficit reduction (fiscal policy)	36	39
Monetary policy	2	3
B. *Switching policies*[a]	4	5
Exchange rate policies[c]	2	3
Wage policy	2	2
C. *Long-run efficiency*	78	72
Trade policies[b]	16	10
Sectoral policies,[b] of which	25	23
–industry	3	2
–energy	3	7
–agriculture	18	10
Financial sector reform	10	11
Rationalisation of government administration	10	15
Public enterprise reforms	17	13
D. *Social policy reforms*[c]	3	7
E. *Other*	4	5

Source: World Bank, 1992a, Table A2.1
(a) Also have demand restraint effects
(b) Also have switching effects
(c) Also have efficiency effects

self-employment and employment. *Secondary incomes* are the incomes people receive after taxation and benefits (including private as well as government transfers and public goods).

The extent of poverty depends on secondary incomes, so that poverty can be reduced either by improving primary incomes of the poor (assuming these are not then taxed away), or, for any given primary income distribution, by secondary transfers. Private secondary transfers have an important role to play – children for example, depend almost entirely on transfers within the family and during crises family transfers can play a critical survival role. Private pension schemes, in rich societies, are an important source of (secondary) income for the old. In traditional societies, private transfers (remittances etc.) can also play a vital role in preventing destitution. But there are limits to the extent of private transfers, especially in situations when the whole family or community suffers simultaneous deprivation. Public transfers include the provision of goods and services free or at subsidised rates. The social income so created can form a large proportion of the incomes of the poor. For example, food subsidies in Egypt accounted for 13 per cent of the total expenditure of the urban poor and 17 per cent of the rural poor in 1980–1.[18]

In principle, public transfers can be very large, and thus can be important in protecting the incomes of the poor. But it must be recognised at the outset, that it is unusual for public transfers to be large enough to transform the situation as compared with the primary income distribution. The limits to secondary transfers arise from four sources: first, political constraints – usually once people have acquired primary incomes, they form powerful political obstacles to substantial redistribution. Secondly, there can be efficiency/incentive reasons for limiting redistribution, as it is difficult to devise and administer tax systems which effectively transfer incomes from rich to poor without acting as a disincentive to effort. Thirdly, administrative constraints may limit redistributive policies. Fourthly, excessive reliance on secondary distribution can be unsatisfactory for the poor, because it involves heavy dependence on the state, which may be undesirable in itself and which makes the poor vulnerable to economic crises or changes in political stance (as was the case, for example, in Sri Lanka). It seems that the decisive problem is political, as in societies which have overcome this problem – either through revolution, or because the richer groups are politically weak and the poor are politically powerful – substantial secondary redistribution has occurred.[19]

For most societies, however, while secondary distribution can do a lot to reduce poverty, considerable emphasis has to be given to improving primary incomes of the poor because of the limits on the likelihood, possibility and desirability of secondary redistribution.

Types of policy

It is helpful to distinguish between three types of policy – *structural, macro-* and *meso-*. Macro- and structural policies mainly relate to the determination of primary incomes, while meso-policies, which concern transfers of primary incomes through taxes, subsidies, and public goods mainly relate to secondary incomes, although some meso-policies can affect primary incomes of the poor – for example, special credit schemes to extend access to the poor, and education and training directed towards the poor.

Structural policies and primary incomes

These are policies that influence the primary income distribution generated by the economic system by directly affecting asset distribution and entitlement rules. They include, for example, land reform, industrial asset redistribution and credit reform. Structured markets – in which governments impose constraints on the operation of markets by requiring them to allocate resources to certain objectives (for example, to credit for small-scale enterprises) – are also a form of structural policy.[20]

Macro-policies and primary income distribution

Macro-policies are policies towards the broad aggregates in the economy, for example the level of taxation and public expenditure, the total level of monetary expansion and the exchange rate. These policies have effects both on the level and the distribution of primary income. The most effective macro-policies, from the perspective of poverty elimination, are those that lead to egalitarian economic growth. For any given income distribution, the change in primary incomes of the poor depends on the change in national income, so that the impact of adjustment policies on economic growth and distribution are both important in analysing their impact on the incomes of the poor.

Meso-policies

Meso-policies consist in taxation and expenditure policies.[21] The poor are affected by some indirect taxes (and subsidies), but rarely by direct taxes. But the main ways in which poor households are affected by meso-policies are through public provision of goods and services to which they have access, when supplied free or at below-cost prices.

There are three critical ratios which determine the extent to which government meso-policies succeed in affecting the situation of the poor through expenditure: the *public expenditure ratio*, the ratio of public expenditure to GDP; the *social allocation ratio*, the proportion of total government expenditure going to social sectors (broadly defined to include any expenditure which may benefit the poor, including on food subsidies and employment schemes); and the *social priority ratio*, which is the proportion of expenditures on the social sectors which go on priority services reaching the poor.

Social funds are a type of meso-policy specifically designed to provide compensation for those adversely affect by adjustment. The Bolivian Emergency Social Fund was the first, and since then a large number have been initiated with the support of the World Bank and other donors. After the IFIs recognised the importance of protecting the poor during adjustment, social funds and redirection of public expenditure were the two main policy instruments the World Bank adopted to meet this objective.[22]

The well-being of the poor may be affected by changes in structural, macro- or meso-policies; structural and macro-policies broadly determine the growth and distribution of primary incomes, while meso-policies determine the government services they receive.

There are no necessary connections between structural, macro- and meso-policies: it is conceivable, for example, that there could be pro-poor structural policies with macro- and meso-policies adversely affecting those on low incomes. There are, however, political connections which make it likely that in the long run the three sets of policies will be consistent. This is because governments which are concerned about income distribution and poverty are likely to use all the policy instruments they have to reduce poverty, while governments representing elites will be unlikely to adopt strong meso-policies to offset inequalities in primary incomes. There are, however, some exceptions to this rule. First, during adjustment, the macro-policy package may have adverse consequences for the poor which, in some circumstances, are unavoidable, but governments may still be able to adopt pro-poor meso-policies. Secondly, élite-dominated governments may support progressive meso-policies because they are long-sighted and see the importance for their own long-run welfare of investing in human resources in order to sustain economic growth and maintain political stability. Thirdly, during an economic crisis, governments may lose sight of their long-run goals and adopt short-term policies which are harmful to the poor despite their pro-poor long-run objectives. This happened in Costa Rica, for example, in the early part of the 1980s. Fourthly, radical regimes with pro-poor structural and meso-policies may be unsuccessful in their macro-policies with consequent suffering for the poor.

The adjustment policies briefly described above contain elements of structural, macro- and meso-policies, although structural policies are least in evidence. Privatisation is one type of structural policy which often forms part of the adjustment package; the short-term effects are quite minor, but it is likely to increase inequality of asset ownership and income distribution in the longer term. Other structural policies include schemes to define and bestow property rights; these have been introduced in some countries alongside the adjustment programmes – also tending to increase inequality in the longer run. Land reform – which has been established as one of the most effective ways of reducing rural poverty[23] – does not form part of the programme; nor do 'structured' markets. In the case of land reform, it could be argued that this is a long-run policy for the government to decide upon, and not a matter for negotiation with the IFIs for the purpose of adjustment. Structured markets are disliked by the IFIs as reintroducing 'distortions' into markets, in direct opposition to the broad intention of the adjustment programmes.

Policies of the IMF are mainly directed towards macro-policies, with the two main components being demand restraint (tax increases, expenditure reductions and credit restraint) and switching policies (devaluation and price reform). Fund and Bank policies have both direct and indirect implications for meso-policies. But this is an area – to a greater extent than macro-policy – where governments may make independent choices, subject to influence and constraints imposed by the IFIs.

DEFINING POVERTY

In order to analyse how adjustment policies affect poverty, it is essential to know the main characteristics of those in poverty. This depends in part on how poverty is defined. There is a huge debate on the appropriate definition of poverty, and some (albeit brief) consideration of it is necessary here, since the impact of policies on poverty depends on who the poor are. The following are some relevant definitional issues.

(i) *Absolute versus relative poverty*: there are two overlapping questions here. First, whether there is a clear-cut distinction between absolute and relative poverty; and secondly, whether it is absolute or relative poverty that is under consideration. Discussion about the absolute versus relative question has shown that absolute poverty unavoidably has a relative dimension, since the amount of income needed to achieve given objectives (e.g. education, nutrition) is greater in richer societies because of the nature of the commodities available and relative price changes.[24] In this book, consideration of the impact of adjustment on poverty is largely concerned with absolute poverty – i.e. with increases in absolute deprivation, with changes in income distribution being relevant mainly as one mechanism affecting absolute poverty. Elsewhere there seems to have been more attention paid to income distribution (or relative poverty) during adjustment, the implicit implication being that as long as the income distribution does not deteriorate, there need be no cause for complaint about the impact of policies on poverty.[25]

(ii) A major issue is the *dimension* in which poverty is to be measured, i.e. whether it is a question of deprivation of *income*, of access to specific *basic needs, goods and services*, to a *quality of life*, or to the *capability* of achieving a particular quality of life. The appropriate dimension depends partly on the fundamental view taken of assessing and evaluating economic and social progress, and partly, more pragmatically, on the feasibility of measures in terms of data availability. Most measures of poverty use an income line, partly for theoretical reasons and partly because of data availability. From a theoretical perspective, a utilitarian or preference-based approach to economic welfare is sometimes used to justify the use of income as being the best available proxy for consumer utility, allowing consumers to maximise welfare within the income constraint. But there are some major problems with such an approach to well-being – the assumption that individual consumer choice leads to welfare maximisation is incorrect in the presence of consumption externalities, implicit social objectives which can influence consumer choice[26] and maldistribution of income within the family; moreover, many of the basic goods and services are publicly provided and may not be available in adequate quantities, so that private income alone may not guarantee a minimum level of well-being.

(iii) A critical question concerns the *cut-off* point, or *poverty line*, in each dimension. Whether and how much poverty increases can be sensitive to the line chosen. This is illustrated by the large differences between different estimates of numbers in poverty for Latin America.[27] The most common way of defining and deriving income-based poverty lines is by estimating the income needed to buy sufficient food to meet calorie requirements, given consumption habits, food availabilities and distribution within the household. But there is much debate about whether there is a unique amount of calories needed given physiological adaption and variations in food needs between individuals.[28] A poverty-band rather a line is then a more legitimate food-based poverty approach, with the lower limit representing the level below which malnutrition would certainly occur, and the upper limit being the level above which there would certainly not be malnutrition (See diagram 1.1). This roughly corresponds to the distinction between 'ultra-poor', or 'destitution', and poverty.[29]

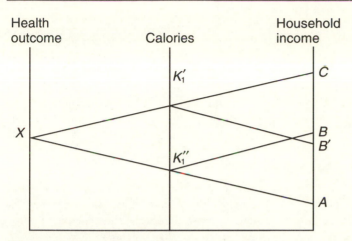

Diagram 1.1 The poverty band

The diagram illustrates some of the difficulties in defining a unique poverty line. The left-hand axis represents the health outcome of an individual, where any point below X represents an unsatisfactory state of health. Because of physiological variations between individuals the amount of calories needed to attain X can vary betweeen K' and K'', shown on the middle axis. The level of household income (right-hand axis) required to attain a given calorie consumption per person can vary according to family income distribution and expenditure patterns, with a range of AB to attain K'' calories and a range of CB' to attain K' calories. Consequently, household income level A may be just enough to attain the minimum health standard, X, but in other circumstances C may be required. Hence a poverty line of C would ensure that everyone received adequate nutrition for health; and income below A would be inadequate in all circumstances.

It should be noted that generally people within a certain range above any chosen poverty line (e.g. the poverty line income plus 25 per cent) are also poor, and benefits they receive from interventions (e.g. food subsidies) should not be regarded as leakages or costs in the way that subsidies received by the upper 25 per cent of the income distribution may be. For other dimensions of poverty (health, education, etc.) the cut-off point defining adequacy is rather arbitrary. It is often easier to determine in terms of access to goods and services (e.g. access to primary health care, primary education, water) than achievement (i.e. attainment of health, or education), even though it is achievement that is the objective. Like income poverty, these dimensions also have a relative element, with higher standards expected in better-off societies. But there are some absolute or universal standards to be required, whatever the income of society, below which people would be defined as poor in these dimensions, or *socially* poor.[30] These standards include universal primary education and access to primary health care.

(iv) Whatever, the line, a further problem is how to count those below the line. Should one adopt the headcount measure, or differentiate those below the line according to how far they fall below it? Obviously, the latter is more satisfactory. Several indices have been suggested for developing a measure of poverty that weights incomes according to the distribution of income below the poverty line. The simplest is the poverty gap measure: this multiplies the number of people below the poverty line, H, by the average income shortfall, i, expressed as a percentage of the poverty line income, or:

$$Pi = H(p - y_p/p)$$

where Pi is the poverty gap measure of poverty, p is the poverty-line income, y_p is the average income of those below the poverty line. This index has the advantage of being larger the greater the average income shortfall, but it is not sensitive to the distribution of incomes around that average.

The Sen index and the Foster, Greer and Thorbecke (FGT) are more complex indices which are both sensitive to the distribution of income below the poverty line.

The Sen index weights the incomes of those below the poverty line by the Gini coefficient of income among the poor. i.e.

$$P_s = H[i + (1 - i)G_p]$$

where i is the average income shortfall as defined above, H the number of people below the poverty line, and G_p the Gini coefficient measuring the distribution of income among those below the poverty line.[31]

The FGT index weights income of those below the poverty line more, the lower their income,[32] i.e.:

$$P_{fgt} = \frac{1}{n} \sum_{j=1}^{q} q \left(\frac{[p - y_j]}{p} \right)^\alpha$$

where n is the size of the whole population, q is the number of people below the poverty line, p, y_j represents the income of individual j (income below the poverty line) and α is a parameter which reflects the weight given to the degree of poverty in the population; the higher α the greater the weight given to the poorest people. The weight usually adopted (e.g. in Psacharapoulos *et al.*, 1993) is for a value of $\alpha = 2$.

An alternative simpler approach, advocated by Lipton, is to divide the poor into two groups – the poor and the ultra-poor.[33] Data availability dictates what measure we can use, but clearly a richer disaggregation permits a more sensitive analysis.

Empirical evidence suggests that for the most part the various poverty measures move in the same direction.[34] While aggregate measures indicate the magnitude of the problem, for policy analysis it is essential to decompose the poor into social and economic classes, by region and location, and by gender and age. As we shall see below, the impact of various adjustment policies on the poor depend critically on whether the poor are mainly urban or rural, self-employed or wage-earners, etc.

World Bank analysis of poverty during adjustment has made a further distinction between the 'old/chronic' poor and the 'new' poor. The former include all those that fell below the poverty line before adjustment was initiated, while the 'new poor' are those previously above the poverty line who are pushed below it as a result of the adjustment policies (e.g. those who are sacked from the civil service). In practice, the 'new poor' are often defined to include all those who lose their jobs as a direct result of adjustment policies, irrespective of savings or incomes. The 'new poor' are frequently much better off than the 'old poor', which is ironic since compensatory measures are frequently targeted mainly towards them (see Chapter 5). The distinction between old and new poor draws attention to the importance of a time dimension in assessing poverty. In principle, it should be permanent income that classifies people as poor or not poor. In practice, the only available measure is current income, and no distinction is made between those whose incomes have fallen below the poverty line for a short period, and those who have been below the poverty line for many years. Adding a time dimension is particularly relevant during adjustment.

(v) In principle, when a multi-dimensional approach to poverty and deprivation is adopted, the question of *weighting* the various aspects arises, if a single holistic measure of poverty is to be presented. The *Human Development Index* (HDI) has provided a method of aggregating three indicators at the national level – income, life expectancy and literacy. But the measures of incomes and life expectancy do not take into account the distribution of population around the average, while the adding-up procedure is essentially arbitrary.[35] Nonetheless, the index has important advantages – notably in providing a single indicator and focusing attention away from conventional GNP per capita as a measure of welfare.[36]

In this book, the main focus is on absolute deprivation; poverty is taken to be multi-dimensional with changes to be measured (wherever possible) by changes in income deprivation, access to basic needs, goods and services and changing human indicators (literacy rates, health, etc.). Measures of the various dimensions of poverty are presented separately, as little is to be gained by adding them up.

SOME METHODOLOGICAL ISSUES

Two methodological issues are pervasive in analysing the relationship between adjustment and poverty, which therefore merit some early discussion.

First, is the question of how to differentiate 'adjusting' and 'non-adjusting' countries for the purposes of comparing performance. Adjustments of some kind take place in every country at all times. What was different about the 1980s is that countries undertook specific 'adjustment' policies, negotiated with the

Fund and the World Bank. The most obvious way of differentiating countries is between those with or those without negotiated programmes. But there are difficulties with this. Many countries had on–off relationships with both institutions. Those with agreed programmes did not necessarily carry out all the conditions fully.[37] Moreover, countries without agreed programmes sometimes introduced similar changes to those in the agreed programmes. For all these reasons a comparison between countries with adjustment programmes negotiated with the IFIs at any point in time and those without, even if one could deal satisfactorily with the counterfactual question, may not capture the effects of adjustment packages.

Evaluations of programmes have adopted different approaches to this issue; some simply look at whether a country has a programme or not; others differentiate according to the duration and intensity of the programmes; others assess, the policy changes directly.[38] In this book, we rely on the distinction made by the World Bank between 'intensive-adjustment-lending countries' (IALs), 'other-adjustment lending countries' (OALs) and other countries not receiving adjustment loans (NALs). Countries are categorised according to whether and when they negotiated structural adjustment loans (SALs) or sectoral adjustment loans (SECALs), as follows:

'Intensive-adjustment countries are those that have received two structural adjustment loans or three or more adjustment operations effective by June 1990, with the first adjustment operation effective in June 1986.... Other adjustment lending countries are those that have received at least one adjustment loan effective by June 1990.

(World Bank, 1992a, p.15).

To some extent this classification is arbitrary, depending on precisely when loans were negotiated. However, it is a useful consistent way of rapidly differentiating between countries according to their adjustment lending history, so we adopt it for some purposes in what follows.

Secondly, there is a fundamental methodological question concerning causality. Suppose we observe that certain events – e.g. a rise in poverty – accompanied adjustment. How can we tell whether this was caused by adjustment or by some other event (e.g. a worsening in the external situation)? The only way this question can be answered is by an appeal to the *counterfactual* or what would have happened in the absence of an adjustment programme. Yet, by definition, the counterfactual is not observable and any estimate of it is bound to be partly speculative. The next chapter will discuss various methods that have been used to estimate the counterfactual. All have some defects. Consequently, it is not possible to make conclusive arguments about causality on that basis. Yet, arguments based on the counterfactual have been used by some to justify developments in the 1980s: the claim is made that even though poverty rose in many adjusting countries this was not 'due' to adjustment, but was the consequence of other events.[39]

Undoubtedly, there is truth in the claim that the adjustment policies were not wholly responsible for the observed deterioration in human conditions, as we shall see from the analysis of the evidence that follows. Yet an appeal to the counterfactual cannot exonerate the policies entirely, not only because of the impossibility of knowing what the counterfactual would have been: but also because policy-making should protect the poor from a sharp worsening in their condition *irrespective of the cause*. This is a debate which will occur repeatedly in this book and to which we shall return in the last chapter.

STRUCTURE OF THE BOOK

This book reviews changes in the three types of policy considered earlier – structural, macro- and meso- – paying especial attention to macro- and meso-policies, since structural policies have played only a small role. Chapter 2 reviews theoretical analysis of the effect of macro-policy changes on income distribution and poverty, and it also presents a brief review of some empirical assessments of effects of macro-policies. Chapter 3 looks at evidence on changing meso-policies and the impact on the poor during adjustment. Chapter 4 analyses changes in food subsidies, which were a component of many adjustment packages. Chapter 5 reviews social funds and other employment schemes. Two regional chapters – Africa (Chapter 6) and Latin America (Chapter 7) – follow, reviewing developments in the two regions most affected by the debt and commodity price crisis. Chapter 8 contrasts some successful and unsuccessful country experience in protecting the poor during adjustment drawn from all over the developing world, and comes to some general conclusions.

NOTES

1 Estimates of Ravallion *et al.*, 1992 for sub-Saharan Africa; and Psacharapoulos *et al.*, 1993, for Latin America and the Caribbean.
2 E.g. IMF, 1986; Heller *et al.*, 1988; World Bank, 1990a; Srinivasan, 1988.
3 The absorption approach to the deficit identifies a likely relationship between a budget deficit (excess of public expenditure over public saving) with a trade deficit (excess of national expenditure over national saving).
4 This is also the view of Killick in an analysis of African economies (Killick, 1992).
5 World Bank and UNDP, 1989, documents how prevalent policy change was in Africa, and Williamson, 1990, in Latin America. But Mosley *et al.*, 1991 question how effective implementation was in some cases.
6 Jolly and Cornia, 1984.
7 The 1990 *World Development Report* comments: 'When structural adjustment issues came to the fore little attention was paid to the effects on the poor' (p. 103).
8 See Cornia *et al.*, 1987.
9 Zuckerman, 1989.
10 IMF/World Bank, 1989. Report quoted from *IMF Survey*, 3 April 1989.
11 Structural Adjustment Facility and Extended Structural Adjustment Facility Loans, which are given to low income African countries by the IMF and World Bank jointly.

12 IMF, *Annual Report 1991*; quoted in Killick, 1994.
13 See, e.g., Killick *et al.*, 1991, Cornia in Cornia *et al.*, 1987; Williamson, 1983.
14 Polak, 1991.
15 See World Bank, 1990a; Mosley, 1987; Mosley *et al.*, 1991; World Bank, 1992c.
16 World Bank, 1990a.
17 The above expresses social policy conditions as a proportion of total conditions. Loans containing social policy conditions accounted for 11 per cent of total loans over the decade 1979–89. Data from World Bank, 1990a.
18 Alderman and von Braun, 1984.
19 For example, in Malaysia, where the Chinese are a rich minority and the Malays are poorer and politically in control, there has been significant redistribution achieved through meso-policies.
20 See Stewart, 1995, for further explanation and illustration of a 'structured market'.
21 This definition has been adopted for simplicity in this book. Meso-policies can be interpreted to extend to all policy influencing the distribution of resources in a given macro-context – for example, policies affecting the distribution of credit, differential tariff policies, etc. See Stewart, Chapter 7 in Cornia *et al.*, 1987.
22 See Ribe *et al.*, 1991; Ribe and Carvalho, 1990.
23 See El-Ghonemy, 1990; Griffin, 1989.
24 See Sen, 1984, Chapter 14, for enlightening discussion of the relative/absolute question.
25 For example, Demery and Addison, 1987; IMF, 1986.
26 Sen, 1977.
27 See Chapter 7.
28 See Sukhatme, 1977; Dasgupta, 1993.
29 A distinction between 'destitution' or 'indigency' and 'poverty' is quite common – see, e.g., Psacharopoulos *et al.*, 1993; Lipton, 1983.
30 This is the term used in IADB, 1993, to describe those people whose access to social goods and services falls below a minimum line.
31 See Sen, 1981, Chapter 2.
32 See Foster *et al.*, 1984.
33 Lipton (1983) claims (although this has been challenged) that there is a natural dividing line, with the ultra-poor having quite distinct characteristics.
34 See, e.g., the evidence on Latin America in Psacharopoulos *et al.*, 1993.
35 There is a natural limit to the dispersion of life expectancy, but this is not so for per capita incomes where the same average figure may be associated with very different distributions and incidence of poverty.
36 The method of calculation of the index and various developments and refinements are discussed in successive issues of the UNDP's *Human Development Reports*.
37 The World Bank claimed a high rate of compliance in RAL II, but the recent Africa Report (World Bank, 1994) finds variable rates of compliance, as does Mosley *et al.*, 1991.
38 Most evaluations of the IMF programmes take the first approach; the World Bank has specified length of time of programme adoption in RAL II and RAL III; but World Bank, 1994, looks at a combination of policy changes and outcomes.
39 Srinivasan has been especially forthright in advancing this position – e.g. Srinivasan, 1988.

Chapter 2

The impact of macro-adjustment policies on the incomes of the poor – a review of alternative approaches

Conflicting hypotheses have been advanced about the effects of adjustment on income distribution and poverty. Reviews of IMF programmes conducted by staff members have concluded that 'in general, Fund programs have improved rather than worsened income distribution'.[1] This view is supported by Srinivasan: 'Adjustment measures by eliminating imbalances and attaining a sustainable and efficient development path are likely to have a positive impact on the welfare of the poor.'[2] In contrast, inegalitarian effects have been suggested by some analysts, stemming largely from the falling wage share associated with devaluation.[3] Others have taken an agnostic position arguing that the effects will depend on the nature of the economy, and on the policy package adopted.[4]

This chapter reviews some of the theoretical arguments and empirical evidence in order to reach some conclusions on the question of the macro-impact of stabilisation and adjustment policies on income distribution and poverty.

As noted in the last chapter, the well-being of the poor depends on both their primary and secondary incomes, where primary incomes are the incomes generated by the economic system before taxes and benefits, while secondary incomes are incomes people receive after taxation and benefits. Stabilisation and adjustment policies affect both: primary incomes are changed mainly as a result of macro-policy changes, while secondary incomes are changed mainly as a result of meso-policy changes. This chapter is concerned with the impact of macro-policy changes on primary incomes.

The primary incomes of the poor depend on the level of aggregate income and their share of the aggregate – in other words, on growth and income distribution. The two may move in the same direction, but need not. For example, an unchanged income distribution can be accompanied by worsening poverty if GNP per capita is falling; and conversely, with rapid growth, poverty may diminish despite worsening income distribution. For the poor, what matters, especially at very low levels of income, is absolute poverty, rather than the distribution as such. But in analysing the impact of policies on the poor, it is helpful to differentiate between the effects on aggregate incomes (or growth) and the effects on income distribution, noting that poverty can decrease despite a worsening of income distribution and conversely as will be illustrated later.

As noted in the previous chapter, stabilisation and adjustment packages contain many policy changes in varying combinations, with some policies present in almost every adjustment programme. Stabilisation policies – mainly associated with the IMF – are those policies designed to reduce major macro-imbalances in the economy, while adjustment policies – mainly associated with the World Bank – are concerned with restructuring the economy so as to increase its long-run efficiency. In practice there is considerable overlap between stabilisation and adjustment policies since some policies (e.g. exchange rate changes) are designed to contribute to both objectives. To avoid long-windedness, this chapter will use the term 'adjustment policies' to encompass both stabilisation and adjustment policies.

In this chapter we shall focus on demand-reducing and switching policies; the former include reduced government expenditure, increased taxation, credit controls, reduced real wages and, in certain circumstances, devaluation;[5] the latter include policies which alter the internal terms of trade, such as devaluation and increased agricultural prices.

The first part of the chapter reviews theoretical approaches to assessing the impact of adjustment policies on income distribution and poverty. The second part considers some empirical evidence.

WHAT CAN WE LEARN FROM THEORY?

Assuming that countries undertaking adjustment initially suffer from major imbalances in balance of trade and budget, then an appropriate policy package would contain both switching and deflationary policies, as illustrated in Diagram 2.1. Deflation alone (in the absence of prices which are flexible downwards) would lead to under-utilisation of resources, while switching alone *could not* achieve the required adjustments. Initial production is at *a*, the tangent of the relative price line and the production possibility frontier. With initial consumption at *b*, there is a balance of trade deficit, *ab*. Deflation alone (assuming prices are not flexible) would eliminate the deficit at *d* (on the income consumption curve), involving a large drop in income (*AD*) and considerable under-utilisation of resources, both tradable and non-tradable. Switching policies change the relative price of tradables and non-tradables so as to secure a resource movement towards tradables and improve the trade balance. Switching policies alone could not eliminate the deficit because more resources are being consumed than can be produced. Consequently what is needed is deflation to bring resource consumption in line with production, and switching policies to lead to a new price line, *Pn'Pt'*, with equilibrium at *e*, no trade deficit and full employment. Diagram 2.1 is drawn to indicate that such an ideal exists; the diagram is also timeless, suggesting that the ideal could be achieved instantly.[6] Whether these implicit assumptions are valid are important issues, to be discussed later. But first the impact of the two main policy instruments on income distribution and poverty will be considered.

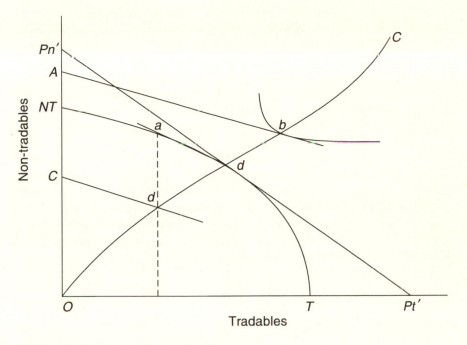

Diagram 2.1 Macro-adjustment options

Demand-reducing policies

Demand restraint has unambiguously negative effects on the poor. As Helleiner puts it, 'contraction of overall spending is almost certain to lower the well-being of both [labour and the poorest]'.[7] Demand-reducing policies include cuts in government expenditure, rises in taxation, reductions in real wages and credit restraint. The policies cut into real incomes by reducing employment and real wages of those in employment and raising the prices of consumption goods, as indirect taxes are raised and prices liberalised. Public sector employees are usually most immediately affected by reduced employment, but this has knock-on effects for the rest of the economy as the number of people seeking a living in the informal sector increases. Initially, opportunities in the informal sector may expand as lower incomes lead to a switch to the cheaper goods produced in this sector; but linkage effects with the formal sector depress markets for the sector, while earnings per person are further reduced as a result of the expansion in numbers seeking a living there. All groups suffer from increased prices brought about by increased indirect taxes and reduced subsidies, the poor being especially hurt by reduced food subsidies.

In principle, demand restraint could be borne proportionately by all groups in society, and while it would then increase poverty, it need not worsen income distribution. The precise distributional effects depend on which elements of expenditure are affected – consumption or investment, public sector or private sector – and within each sector how the cutback is effected, as well as on the distribution of poverty within the economy.

In general, if demand is restrained by holding back consumption dispro-portionately, then one would expect the burden to fall more heavily on people with high propensities to consume – i.e. lower income groups. Some policies are clearly designed to achieve a cutback in consumption – e.g. policies to hold down money wages while allowing prices to rise, policies to reduce public sector employment, raise indirect taxes and reduce consumer subsidies. As argued below, devaluation also has the effect of reducing the real wage in the modern sector. Other policies tend to reduce investment, such as credit restraint, high interest rates, cuts in public sector investment. These policies also affect wage-earners adversely by creating unemployment, but to the extent that they lead to a fall in investment they allow consumption to be higher. In practice in the 1980s, although probably not by design, consumption was sustained relatively to investment in most adjusting countries, thereby protecting con-sumers to a limited extent.[8]

Workers employed in the public sector are those most immediately affected by restraints on government expenditure and reduced real wages. But the credit restraints lead to cutbacks in the private sector, which also suffers from reverse multiplier effects as the public sector contracts. Wage restraints frequently apply to the large-scale private sector as well. The informal sector suffers as a consequence of the cutback in the formal sector from two directions: an increased labour supply as the formal sector contracts (or fails to expand in line with the expansion of the labour force) and reduced market outlets as formal sector markets diminish.

Most of these negative effects are, at least in the first instance, *urban* and, to start with, particularly among those employed in the formal sector. People in the rural sector are relatively insulated, especially, of course, those whose main activities are for self-consumption. But the many links between urban and rural sectors, via migration, markets and remittances, mean that some negative effects are felt there. The distributional implications and the effects on poverty levels depend partly on the location of poverty. Modern sector urban wage-earners are sometimes thought of as a relatively privileged group, and thus concentration of hardship on this group might be thought to be less damaging than other distributions of hardship. But the relevant question is how much *additional* poverty is created, in terms of numbers (i.e. how many extra people are pushed below the poverty line) and in terms of the extent of poverty (i.e. the change in the average income gap of those below the poverty line). If the policies push urban wage-earners below the poverty line and increase the extent of poverty among those in the urban informal sector, the total extra poverty may be just as much as if it were more evenly distributed across the poor population. This tendency for an *urban bias* in the adverse distributional implications of demand restraint is the counterpart of a previous urban bias in the location of modern sector employment. Since the switching policies also exhibit an adverse bias against the urban sector (see below), urban poverty is particularly likely to rise as a consequence of the adjustment package.

In the 'ideal' policy combination shown in Diagram 2.1, the economy would remain at full employment, and deflationary policies would reduce real incomes but not employment. But this ideal is rarely, if ever, realised, for reasons to be discussed later; 'overkill' deflationary policies are typically adopted, leading, at least in the short run, to a rise in unemployment along with the reduction in real wages.[9]

Analysis of adjustment policies by economists in the IMF suggests that the deflationary policies need not hurt the poor.[10] They note three types of effect – an aggregate effect on GNP, an aggregate effect on inflation and an effect on the distribution of access to resources.[11] The first is argued to be possibly negative for the poor for two to three years, with falling output and employment following monetary contraction.[12] But in the longer term, allowing for the positive effects of supply-side policies, there is 'no clear presumption that Fund-supported programmes adversely affect growth' (Heller *et al.*, 1988, p. 16). Empirical evidence on this issue is ambiguous according to the studies reviewed below. No systematic growth effects were apparent from analysis of Fund programmes in the 1970s; in the 1980s, on balance, Fund programmes appear to have had negative effects on growth in the short term while compensating medium-term effects have not appeared.

Second, it is argued that the programmes will reduce inflation and this will help the poor: 'one expects the poor to benefit from reduced inflation because they typically pay most of the inflation tax' (Heller *et al.*, 1988, p. 15). The argument is that the poor lack assets which act as hedges against inflation and also hold a disproportionately large amount of cash because they lack other means of exchange, such as credit cards. No empirical evidence is adduced.

The effects of inflation on the poor depend on whether the goods consumed by the poor rise in price more quickly than do other categories of goods; the extent to which the poor have assets which can act as a hedge against inflation; and on time lags between price and income increases for the poor. For each mechanism, the effects vary according to who the poor are. For example, subsistence farmers will be little touched by inflation, while urban workers could be badly hit, unless their earnings keep pace. In general, debtors are likely to gain relative to creditors, and debtors can be expected to be poorer than creditors.

There is little empirical evidence on these effects. Long-term evidence for Latin America suggests that income distribution was not affected by the rate of inflation, while evidence for the USA shows inflation to be mildly progressive and unemployment strongly regressive.[13] For the Philippines, Blejer and Guerrero found the inflation tax to be regressive, but less so than under-employment.[14] In the inflation of the 1980s, food prices exhibited some tendency to outstrip other prices in most countries,[15] but this might also have happened with a lower rate of inflation. As with other effects, the impact on the poor depends in part on what the alternatives are: if a lower rate of inflation is attained at the cost of lower output and employment, the poor might well lose more than they gain from lower inflation. In any case, of twenty studies of the effects of adjustment programmes on inflation, only five showed unambiguous improvements in the inflation rate (see Table 2.2). So the theoretical argument that lower inflation would help the poor is not of much practical significance.

Third, it is suggested that financial repression helps large firms and deprives the poor of access to credit; reduced financial repression, therefore, might lead to an improved distribution of credit. The poor, however, are limited in their access to formal sector credit by lack of collateral, and this has not been changed by reduced financial repression. Indeed, by making the formal sector more attractive as a repository of funds, the change might actually reduce access of the poor to informal sector credit, with little change in their access to the formal sector. More evidence is needed on this issue.

In summary, demand-reducing policies are likely to increase poverty, especially urban poverty, although they may not worsen income distribution. The offsetting effects suggested by the IMF do not seem very plausible.

Exchange rate changes and other switching policies[16]

Switching policies aim to produce a change in the relative price of tradables. Devaluation is the main policy instrument used for switching (occurring in nearly all IMF programmes at the end of the 1980s and 85 per cent in a sample of World Bank SALs from 1981–8[17]). Changes in government-controlled prices may complement or substitute for devaluation, but here we shall confine analysis to the effects of devaluation.

A nominal exchange rate change (devaluation) does not necessarily lead to a proportionate real exchange rate change or even, in the extreme case, *any* real change in the exchange rate, since it may lead to subsequent domestic price changes which knock out (partially or fully) the initial change in exchange rate. The more strongly organised groups are (e.g. when there are strong trade unions) and the greater the degree of indexation, the more likely it is that a nominal exchange rate change will fail to bring about a significant real exchange rate change. The presence of lax monetary policy may also maks it more likely that devaluation leads to internal inflation. These were the conditions present in some Latin American economies in the 1970s. But in many cases in the 1980s, there is evidence that nominal devaluation was accompanied by some real devaluation in the short run. The adjustment programmes often included strict monetary policy and wage controls which made the devaluation more effective.[18] Devaluation is likely to have a greater effect on the real exchange rate in the short run, while its effects may be eliminated by domestic inflation in the medium to long run.[19]

The analysis below assumes that a real change in the exchange rate occurs, defined as a rise in the price of tradables (T) relative to non-tradables (NT).

The effects on income distribution and poverty depend, then: on the nature of the economy, in particular on whether there is factor mobility between sectors; on the factor intensity in T and NT; on the degree of poverty in the two sectors; and on how prices are formed. The discussion that follows considers how devaluation affects income distribution under different assumptions about the nature of the economy.

We shall start by assuming a 'neo-classical' economy, with well-behaved production functions, complete factor mobility and competitive pricing. Then the well-known Stolper–Samuelson theorem applies and the effect of the devaluation will be to increase returns to the factor that is used intensively in T relative to that used intensively in NT. This apparently straightforward result does not, however, lead to simple conclusions concerning income distribution because of the heterogeneous and varied nature of T and NT, in terms of factor-intensity, in developing countries.

The tradable sector in developing countries consists of some combination of:

Ti   –   mineral primary products which make intensive use of natural resources and capital;

Tii   –   plantation primary products which make intensive use of land and (usually) labour;

Tiii   –   primary products produced by peasant agriculture, making intensive use of land and labour;

Tiv   –   labour-intensive manufactures;

Tv   –   manufactured goods produced for the home market with low (or zero) levels of protection – typically labour-intensive.

The non-tradable sector consists of some combination of:

NTi   –   capital-intensive, highly protected, import substitutes (IS);[20]

NTii   –   labour-intensive services;

NTiii   –   locally produced food for own or local consumption, intensive in labour and land.

Income distribution would improve (become more equal) if returns to labour and peasant-owned land increase, and worsen if returns to capital and capital-ist-owned land and natural resources increase. It is apparent from the classi-fication above that no simple conclusions can be drawn in general. At one extreme, a country which specialises in minerals (Ti) and has few import-substituting manufactures (NTi) could expect a devaluation to *worsen* income distribution; at the other extreme a country specialising in the export of peasant agriculture (Tiii) or labour-intensive manufactures (Tiv), where food production is also traded, might expect a devaluation to *improve* income distribution. In many cases, the direction of the effects may be ambiguous depending on the relative significance of the different types of T and NT and their factor use.

Second, we may assume a neo-classical set of assumptions except that there is *no* factor mobility between tradable and non-tradable sectors, then devaluation will raise the returns to *all* factors in T and reduce the returns to *all* factors in NT. The net effects will then depend on the balance of factor-use and returns to factors in the two sectors. Assume two factors, L and K, in each sector, a devaluation which raises the returns to factors uniformly in the traded sector by d and reduces returns in the NT sector by $1/d$, then wages and profits in T become $d \cdot W^t$, $d \cdot P_t$, while wages and profits in NT become W^{nt}/d, P^{nt}/d. Assume that the share of output of each is y^t, y^{nt}. If the share of wages initially is the same in both sectors, then after devaluation the wage share will go up (or down) according as $y^t \gtrless y^{nt}$ (since where $y^t > y^{nt}$, the rise in wages in T will exceed the fall in wages in NT and conversely). But if the wage share differs in the two sectors, then the effect will depend on the wage share in each sector, and the relative magnitude of incomes in the two sectors.[21]

Let w^t, w^{nt} be the initial share of wages in the two sectors, then the aggregate wage share will be

$$w^o = w^t \cdot y^t + w^{nt} \cdot y^{nt}$$

After devaluation, which raises the share of income in T to $(1 + d) \cdot y^t$ and reduces the share of income in NT to $(1 - d) \cdot y^{nt}$,

$$w^d = (1 + d)y^t \cdot w^t + (1 - d)y^{nt} \cdot w^{nt}$$

The wage share will therefore increase or decrease according as $w^t \cdot y^t \gtrless w^{nt} \cdot y^{nt}$. Thus an increase in wage share is more likely, the larger is the T sector relative to NT and the higher is the share of wages in T relative to NT.

An increase in wage share, however, is not necessarily the same as an improvement in income distribution, nor as a reduction in poverty. If wage rates were the same in both sectors, and below the poverty line, then an improved wage share would mean both an improved income distribution and reduced poverty. But if wages differ between the sectors (which is likely in this case of non-mobility), and are greater in the T sector than the NT (also plausible), then the wage share could rise, but the income distribution and the magnitude of poverty worsen. Suppose a large proportion of those in NT were below the poverty line and none in T, then the change would increase poverty, irrespective of what happened to the wage share. Again, this is plausible given that NT includes the informal and subsistence sector.

A third type of economy is one where the assumption of no factor mobility applies as between urban (U) and rural (R) sectors. Both U and R produce tradables and non-tradables and factor mobility is assumed within both U and R. This case combines some of the features of each of the two earlier cases; factor-prices can be assumed to be equalised within U and R, but not between them. Within each sector, returns will rise to the factor used intensively in T relative to that of NT. Again the net effects depend on the nature of the economy, but it may reasonably be expected that the results will go in different directions in the two sectors. In U, tradables may be relatively labour-intensive because of the importance of non-tradable import-substitutes in that sector;

within R, T may be relatively more capital- and land-intensive (e.g. agriculture using some fertiliser and machinery) than the highly labour-intensive services in the rural informal sector or non-traded food sector.

Devaluation is often argued to improve the rural/urban terms of trade, the implicit assumption being that R contains more tradables than U does. When devaluation is accompanied by reduced import controls and/or tariffs (usually levied on urban manufactured products), often another element in the adjustment package, it becomes more likely that the terms of trade will change in favour of the rural sector. If they do, and there is factor immobility between sectors, then the returns to all factors in the rural areas will rise, and those to all factors in the urban areas will fall. In addition, there will be changes within each sector favouring the factors used relatively intensively in that sector. Since rural incomes, on average, are usually lower than urban, the change in the sectoral terms of trade would tend to improve income distribution; intra-sector income distribution may improve in the urban areas (assuming tradables are labour-intensive manufactures) and worsen in the rural areas (assuming Ts are more land- and possibly more capital-intensive, favouring richer farmers). Again the net effect depends on the relative significance of these individual effects.

Aggregate income distribution can be interpreted as the sum of inter-sector inequality and a weighted average[22] of intra- sector inequality:[23]

$$A_y = A_b + [x_u \cdot A_u + x_r A_r] \tag{1}$$

where A_y is a measure of aggregate inequality, A_b is the between-sector inequality, A_u, A_r are measures of inequality within U and R, and x_u, x_r are the appropriate weights of the two sectors.[24]

The aggregate effects of a change in the exchange rate, dE, can be decomposed into the effects on inter-sectoral inequality and intra-sectoral inequality, or for shorthand,

$$dA_y/dE = f(dA_b/dE, \ dA_u/dE, \ dA_r/dE) \tag{2}$$

Since average rural incomes are almost always below average urban incomes, an inter-sectoral change in the terms of trade favouring the rural areas will contribute to decreased inequality, $dA_b/dE > 0$. No firm generalisations can be made about the intra-sectoral changes, but it is plausible to expect that in the neo-classical model, urban income distribution may improve as resources shift to labour-using exports (but note that the non-neo-classical model discussed below suggests urban income distribution will worsen). Rural income distribution can be expected to worsen as the returns to badly distributed land increase, and exportables tend to be concentrated among richer farmers. Thus an agnostic conclusion emerges for the impact on total income distribution.

We have so far assumed competitive pricing. For the urban/modern sector, especially the IS sector, this is unrealistic. Assume this sector adopts mark-up pricing, while prices of exports are determined by world prices.[25] Then a devaluation redistributes income from wages to profits and rent in two ways. First, assuming wages are fixed in nominal terms, real wages decline as IS goods' prices rise in line with the increased cost of imported intermediate inputs plus proportionate mark-up. Real profits are sustained by the mark-up pricing adopted. Hence both the level and share of wages falls. Secondly, the domestic currency realised from exports rises (while the foreign currency price remains constant), increasing the share of profits and reducing the share of wages in the export sector. These effects, therefore, worsen income distribution in the modern sector. This seems to have been the pattern of behaviour in Latin America over the 1980s, where the real wage and the wage share fell.

In some contexts, devaluation will change the revenue received by the government rather than factor rewards: this applies where the foreign price is determined on the world market and the government determines domestic prices, as with some agricultural products and minerals. The distributional implications then depend on the use the government makes of the additional resources – which could be to reduce deficit financing, to reduce other forms of revenue raising or to raise expenditure compared with what it would have been. These alternatives are best discussed along with the other meso-effects to be considered in the next chapter.

So far we have considered the effects on the primary distribution of income of different groups, *as producers*. A further complication is introduced by analysing what happens to the prices faced by particular groups as consumers. *All* consumers lose real income as a result of devaluation, as the price of imports rise in relation to domestic incomes. Consumers whose consumption is heavily weighted to *NT* will gain relative to consumers whose consumption is weighted to *T*. From this perspective, it is helpful to analyse urban and rural consumers separately. The distinguishing characteristic of poor households is the high proportion of their income spent on food. Among urban consumers, this is often a tradable commodity and consequently the price index they face may become more unfavourable relative to richer consumers who spend proportionately more on *NT*s such as services and IS goods. (In practice, this effect is often compounded, during adjustment, by the removal of food subsidies.) Among rural consumers, food is often *NT* (especially and completely for subsistence farmers), and they may therefore do no worse, and possibly better than richer rural consumers.

The effects of devaluation on *poverty* as against income distribution depend on: what happens to total incomes; the precise distributional changes, in relation to the poverty line; how poverty is measured (e.g. by the headcount measure or some distribution-sensitive measure). Kanbur has developed a formula for measuring the change in poverty, assuming only wage-earners are poor and intra-sector income distribution is unchanged. Changing prices in favour of *T*, following devaluation, by assumption raises income in T by d and reduces income in *NT* by d, and results in a change in poverty given by the following (simplified) formula:[26]

$$DP/DE = Dd/DE[x_{nt} \cdot H_{nt}(1 - I_{nt}) - x_t \cdot H_t(1 - I_t)] \qquad (3)$$

where DE represents the devaluation, Dd the consequent increase in aggregate returns in T and decrease in NT, x_{nt}, x_t sector weights of wage employment of the two sectors, H_{nt}, H_t, the proportion of people in each sector who fall below the poverty line, and I_{nt}, I_t the average income shortfall below the poverty line.

Whether or not poverty increases then depends on the relative size of the two sectors and the extent of poverty in each sector. Consumption effects are not allowed for. This case follows the pattern of factor immobility between T and NT discussed above. It could also be interpreted in terms of changes in the terms of trade between the rural and urban sectors, with the impact on poverty depending on the change in terms of trade that occurs and the extent of poverty in each sector. Changes in intra-sectoral distribution are not allowed for.

With mobility between the sectors – i.e. the Stolper–Samuelson model – the formula becomes more complex. Now there is a change in wages, Dw, as a result of changed factor use. A simplified formula for the change in poverty is:

$$DP/DE = - Dw/DE[x_{nt} \cdot P_{nt} + x_t \cdot P_t] + Dx_t/DE(P_t - P_{nt}) \qquad (4)$$

where x_t, x_{nt} are the initial shares of T and NT in employment, and Dx_t is the change in the share of T following devaluation; Dw is the change in wages, assumed the same for each sector; $\dot{P}_t$, P_{nt} are the poverty indices of the two sectors.[27]

In this case, the change in poverty depends on the change in wages (which could be positive or negative in the longer term according to the relative factor intensity of the sectors), and the change in the share of employment accounted for by the sectors weighted by the difference in the extent of poverty in the two sectors. An increase in the share of employment in the tradable sector may be expected to reduce poverty given the heavy concentration of poverty in the (largely NT) informal sector.

Combining the two cases presented in equations (3) and (4) permits analysis of what happens to poverty when there is factor immobility between rural and urban sectors, intra-sector mobility, and a change which brings about improved rural/urban and T/NT terms of trade.

Let

$$DP/DE = [DP_s/DE + DP_i/DE]$$

where DP_s represents the change in poverty due to changing rural/urban terms of trade between sectors, and DP_i represents the change in poverty due to changes in intra-sectoral income distribution. Adapting Kanbur's approach in equation (3) to denote the urban and rural sectors, and assuming devaluation produces a change in the terms of trade, raising returns in R by Dr and reducing them in U by Dr, equation (3) can be interpreted to show the effect of the change in the inter-sectoral terms of trade on poverty.

$$DP_b/DE = Dr/DE[x_{nt} \cdot H_{nt}(1 - I_{nt}) - x_t \cdot H_t(1 - I_t)] \qquad (5)$$

where Dr/DE represents the change in terms of trade between the sectors following devaluation. The total effect on poverty also includes the intra-sectoral effects on poverty, both in U and in R, following the devaluation, i.e.

$$DP_i/DE = -Dw^u/DE[x^u \cdot (x^u_{nt} \cdot P^u_{nt} + x^u_t \cdot P^u_t) + Dx^u_t/DE(P^u_t - P^u_{nt})]$$
$$- Dw^r/DE[x^r(x^r_{nt} \cdot P^r_{nt} + x^r_t \cdot P^r_t) + Dx^r_t/DE(P^r_t - P^r_{nt})] \quad (6)$$

depicting the intra-sectoral effects of devaluation in urban and rural sectors (derived from equation (4) above). Note that the wage effects, Dw^u, Dw^r, may differ between the urban and rural sectors (since it is assumed there is no mobility between these sectors), but are uniform within each sector. The wage effects represent the effects of changed factor-use from shifts between T and NT, and do not include the general income effects of changing terms of trade between U and R, which are already included in DP_s. Of course, in actuality, observed changes in wages will include both changes due to changing terms of trade and changes due to factor-intensity shifts, so Dw^u, Dw^r are not the same as observed changes in wages.

A further complication is that whereas one may assume that changes in profits are irrelevant to poverty, as most poor people do not receive profits, this assumption cannot safely be made about rent. Many of the rural poor own very small pieces of land, so a full account of changing poverty should also allow for the change in rent received by the poor.

DP_s will be negative (poverty-reducing) in those countries where the magnitude of poverty (numbers below the poverty line multiplied by the average income gap) is greater in the rural areas than the urban. This includes all African countries, and many Latin American countries. But the direction of the intra-sectoral effects is less clear-cut, given the unequal distribution of land (especially in Latin America) and the uneven distribution of T/NT in peasant agriculture. On balance it seems probable that rural intra-sectoral effects may be negative (increase poverty) especially in Latin America. The direction of urban intra-sectoral effects is also ambiguous because labour-intensive manufactures may gain, but even more labour-intensive services will lose.

None of these cases allows for consumption effects; nor for general reductions in the real wage in both T and NT resulting from Krugman–Taylor mark-up price effects analysed earlier. Allowing for these effects would make it probable, especially in the short run, that the change in real wages was negative in equation (4) above, making it extremely likely that in the short run at least, the effect of devaluation would be to increase poverty (although not necessarily to worsen income distribution).

Some conclusions from the review of theoretical considerations

It is clear from this discussion that the effects of devaluation on income distribution are not straightforward and will vary with the type of economy.

This was the conclusion of Knight: 'The circumstances of developing countries are too diverse... to provide any more than a theoretical framework for application to particular countries'.[28]

However, while the summary of arguments presented here would support this conclusion *vis-à-vis* income distribution, there seem to be stronger reasons to expect negative effects on aggregate incomes and therefore, unless income distribution improves significantly, increased poverty in the short run. Moreover, we can go further in coming to some more definite conclusions about the effects on income distribution if we apply the arguments advanced so far to different *types* of economy.

To start with it is helpful to consider which of the assumptions considered earlier are likely to be applicable. Complete factor mobility between *T* and *NT* is not realistic in the short run, but nor is complete factor immobility. Even in the short run some factor mobility is likely, and this will increase as time proceeds. Immobility of factors between urban and rural sectors is more realistic even in the longer run. Land cannot move and labour moves more readily from rural to urban sectors than the other way round. Finally, the mark-up model is probably applicable to a large part of the modern sector, but not to the traditional (nor rural) sectors. We are then dealing with some combination of (A) the Stolper–Samuelson model, (B) a rural/urban factor immobility model and (C) a modern sector mark-up model. Finally (D) consumption effects are also relevant.

A. Following the Stolper–Samuelson approach, the effects depend on the nature of *T* and *NT*. Economies in which income distribution may improve because there is likely to be increased labour-use and/or peasant incomes as a result of devaluation include exporters of labour-intensive manufactured exports; and exporters of products of peasant agriculture, especially if these are evenly distributed among peasant households and not concentrated on richer peasant households. Economies in which income distribution is likely to worsen, as rents and profits increase, include exporters of minerals and of agricultural products produced by plantations/large farmers.

B. Rural/urban sectors with immobility between and mobility within sectors. According to our earlier analysis, the net effects in such economies will depend on the change in terms of trade between the sectors, the initial income distribution and the change following devaluation in each sector. No generalisations are possible because the net effects could go in different directions; while the shift in inter-sectoral terms of trade would generally act to improve income distribution and reduce poverty, this could be offset by worsened intra-sectoral distribution, especially rural distribution.

In this model the conditions in which *more equality* and reduced poverty following devaluation are likely include that:

- devaluation leads to improved rural/urban terms of trade, not offset by other changes (e.g. by reduced subsidies to agriculture);
- rural incomes on average are significantly below urban;

● the magnitude of rural poverty is greater than urban;
● Ts are labour-using relative to NTs;
● in rural areas, Ts are more evenly spread among households of different incomes than NTs.

The main conclusion that arises from consideration of this model which was not obtained from the discussion of the Stolper–Samuelson case is that when rural poverty is significantly greater than urban, devaluation will tend to be poverty-reducing so long as the rural distribution of Ts is relatively equal. The terms of trade effect is therefore more likely to be poverty-reducing in African agricultural exporting economies (more peasant agriculture, more rural poverty) than among Latin American agricultural exporters or mineral exporters from any region.

C. In the mark-up model, real wages are not determined by factor-use, as in the neo-classical models, but by a mark-up over costs. The share of profits rises and the wage share falls following devaluation. The model applies only where there is a sizeable modern sector consisting of oligopolistic firms, a feature of a number of Latin American economies. This type of pricing behaviour is a reason to expect devaluation to worsen income distribution and poverty in the urban areas, especially in the short run. In the medium term the effects could be offset by increases in money wages and/or by strong expansion in employment in labour-intensive exports.

D. Consumption effects. Some generalised negative effects are likely, with average prices rising in relation to wages, thereby making a rise in poverty likely. In addition, the change in T/NT prices may alter income distribution. As suggested above, the net effects are likely to worsen urban income distribution because of the high proportion of urban wage-income spent on traded food; moreover, the effects are often accentuated by reduced food subsidies. Rural income distribution may not be affected.

Putting these conclusions together, we find – subject to many qualifications noted above – that income distribution is likely to worsen following devaluation in economies:

(i)   specialising in mineral exports or agricultural products whose production is unequally distributed;
(ii) where urban poverty is high in relation to rural poverty;
(iii) where there is a large oligopolistic modern sector, specialised in import-substituting production – this will affect urban incomes in particular.

Income distribution is most likely to improve where:

(iv) tradables are labour-intensive relative to non-tradables (i.e. in economies specialising, especially at the margin, in labour-intensive manufactures or labour-intensive agriculture);
(v)   rural poverty is high in relation to urban poverty, and rural incomes (and tradable production) are fairly evenly distributed.

In general, devaluation tends to reduce real domestic incomes in the short run, even when it does not worsen income distribution. Consequently, the negative effects on poverty are greater than any negative effects on income distribution.

Balance between demand-reducing and switching policies

The negative impact of demand-reducing policies on poverty is much more definite than that of switching policies, so the poverty-increasing effects of adjustment packages are likely to be smaller the more switching occurs and the less deflation. As noted earlier, the ideal policy combination allows for continuous full employment of resources, as resources shift from tradables to non-tradables, with deflation just sufficient to release resources for use in tradables. This ideal is rarely realised, as shown by the loss in output and employment in many adjusting countries. One reason is lack of flexibility of the economy, especially in the short run. Institutional deficiencies are a major cause.

An IMF paper argued

> The unquestioned difficulty of devising and implementing successful growth-oriented adjustment programs derives, however, from the fact that expenditure switching policies often involve greater structural change, are less certain in their effect, and may take longer to implement and to achieve desired results, than expenditure reducing policies.[29]

Diagram 2.1 implied instantaneous flexibility; but in most economies, moving out of *NT* to *T* involves a major transformation which requires investment and is not possible to any very significant extent in the short run. Diagram 2.2 shows what happens in a rigid economy where resources cannot move between sectors: in this case, deflation is the only way of achieving the required adjustment and serious under-employment is the inevitable result as incomes have to be cut-back to *d*, where consumption of tradables equals production and there is considerable unused capacity in the non-tradable sector (*ad*). In the medium term, more flexibility may be assumed so that resources may be switched from *NT* to *T* and output of tradables can expand, but for this to occur investment may be necessary. But both public and private investment are typically cut during the adjustment period, reducing potential flexibility in the medium term too.

Flexibility is partly a matter of time and investment, but it also varies among economies. Countries still specialising heavily in primary products are likely to be more rigid than countries with large manufacturing sectors, especially if these are export-oriented and accustomed to reacting to international changes. We might therefore expect countries with higher proportions of manufactured exports to be able to rely more on switching and less on deflation as an adjustment mechanism, and therefore to suffer a lesser increase in poverty during adjustment.

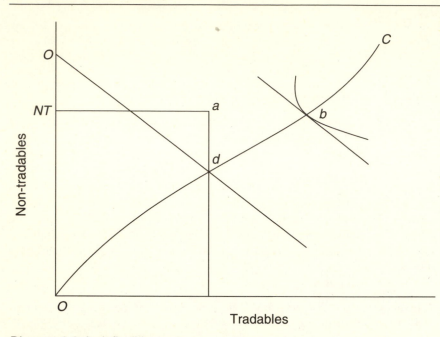

Diagram 2.2 An inflexible economy

Another obvious factor is external finance: more generously financed pro-grammes permit less short-run adjustment (and less poverty creation), and also may provide the resources for investment which allows for more medium-term flexibility.

EMPIRICAL EVIDENCE ON THE IMPACT OF ADJUSTMENT POLICIES ON INCOME DISTRIBUTION AND POVERTY

Actual rates of economic growth were poor in the adjustment period of the 1980s in most adjusting countries in Africa and Latin America, although much better in Asian adjusting countries, with a few exceptions such as the Philip-pines (Table 2.1). Data on levels and changes in poverty are scarce, and data on income distribution are even more deficient. But what there are suggests rising rates of poverty in most African and Latin American countries, while most Asian countries experienced reductions in poverty, with notable success in Indonesia and Malaysia. The limited data show that income distribution worsened in most adjusting countries in Latin America, showed mixed perform-ance in Asia, while there is virtually no evidence for Africa. More detailed support for these generalisations is provided in later chapters of this book.

The combination of change in poverty and in income distribution for some period during the 1980s for twenty-three (mainly adjusting) countries is shown

Table 2.1 Growth performance of adjusting countries, 1980–9 (percentage change in GNP per capita)

Sub-Saharan Africa Early-intensive adjusters[a]		Latin America Early-intensive adjusters		Other areas Early-intensive adjusters	
Côte d'Ivoire	−3.0	Bolivia	−3.5	South Korea	+8.8
Ghana	−0.8	Brazil	+0.9	Morocco	+1.3
Kenya	+0.4	Chile	+1.0	Pakistan	+2.9
Madagascar	−2.6	Colombia	+0.9	Philippines	−1.8
Malawi	−0.1	Costa Rica	+0.4	Thailand	+4.5
Mauritania	−2.2	Jamaica	−1.7	Turkey	+3.0
Mauritius	+5.3	Mexico	−1.5		
Nigeria	−3.6				
Senegal	+0.3[b]				
Tanzania	−1.6				
Togo	−2.4				
Zambia	−3.8				
Average	−1.2	Average	−0.5	Average	+3.1
Other adjusting	−0.7[b]	Other adjusting	−1.9[b]	All Asia	+7.5[b]
Whole Sub-Saharan Africa	−1.7	Whole Latin America	−0.4	All Middle East	+0.5

Sources: UNDP, Human Development Repoprt 1992; Human Development Report 1991
(a) As defined by World Bank, 1990a
(b) 1980–8

	More equal income distribution	
Côte d'Ivoire	Indonesia South Korea Paraguay Colombia Costa Rica	

More poverty   Morocco   Malaysia   Less poverty

| Sri Lanka (1979–81)
Brazil
Bolivia
Guatemala
Argentina
Philippines (1980–5)
Ecuador
Honduras
Mexico
Panama
Peru
Venezuela | Chile
Uruguay

Less equal
income distribution |

Diagram 2.3 Adjustment in the 1980s
Sources: Bourgignon and Morrisson, 1992; Cornia *et al.*, 1987 (Vol. 2); Stewart, 1992; Psacharopoulos *et al.*, 1993
Note: Many countries cannot be placed on the diagram because of lack of data on income distribution

in Diagram 2.3. Over half the countries showed worsening poverty and income distribution, while a minority (five) showed an improvement in both. Very few African countries appear because of lack of data.

Taking actual performance, it seems that in Africa and Latin America, but not Asia, the adjustment programmes were mostly associated with poverty creation. Looking at what actually happened is important – the poor have to live and die in the actual world, and whether the policies that were carried out were adequate and successful must be judged by actual events. But the policies cannot only be judged by these actual developments, since what the policies achieved also depends on the counterfactual, or what would have happened in their absence, as noted in Chapter 1. The adjustment policies were almost always introduced because of major and unsustainable imbalances and consequently some adjustment was unavoidable, which itself would have had implications for output, income distribution and poverty. The problem is that, by definition, we cannot observe the counterfactual. So once we introduce this, the analysis inevitably becomes speculative.

Various attempts have been made to identify an appropriate counterfactual including: comparing performance of countries before and after the adjustment policies were introduced; comparing adjusting countries as a group with a control group of non-adjusting countries; making pairwise comparisons between adjusting and non-adjusting countries in a similar position; using multiple regression techniques to allow for the impact of exogenous events on a sample of adjusting and non-adjusting countries; and developing computable general equilibrium models (CGEs) for particular countries, which permit a simulation exercise comparing different types of policy.

Each of these methods of arriving at the 'counterfactual' is unsatisfactory in some respects. The before/after comparisons may show some improvement or deterioration for extraneous reasons. Moreover, the previous policies may have been unsustainable over the medium term – hence the adjustment – and may have had effects that occurred in the adjustment period but are not due to adjustment policies. Special circumstances cause countries to seek support from the IFIs and to adopt adjustment policies: thus any 'control' group of countries is likely to differ from the 'adjusting' group. The same is true of pairwise comparisons, though it may be easier here to identify countries in similar circumstances. Multiple regression techniques can include external developments and hence tend to be more reliable than simple comparisons between adjusting and non-adjusting countries, but much depends on how these effects are measured.[30] Some differences between countries, including prior history and subsequent availability of finance, are often not brought into consideration.

A further problem, for all these methods, is that the approach differentiates between countries which formally have adjustment programmes negotiated with the IFIs and those that do not. Yet, as noted earlier, most countries adjust in some respects, whether they have IFI programmes or not, so a comparison between those with and those without formal IFI-supported adjustment programmes does not necessarily differentiate correctly between adjusting and non-adjusting countries. There is also a problem about selecting a date when countries adopt adjustment programmes. Often countries make an agreement but only follow it through partially, sometimes they abandon the programme for a year or so, then renew the agreement. These common features of the real world make it difficult (and somewhat arbitrary) to determine which countries should be defined as 'adjusting' and when.

CGE models avoid these problems by developing a model of a particular country and then exploring how a change in a single policy or a combination of policies affects the economy, when it/they are run through the model. The problem with this approach, as we shall see, is that the nature of the model (for example, the assumed elasticities and the closure rules) can make a huge difference to the results. In some respects, therefore, the results reveal the assumptions made in developing the model rather than the actual effects of policies.

These methodological issues need to be borne in mind in assessing the significance of the results reviewed below. If the policies had very strong

Table 2.2 Studies of the macro-effects of adjustment programmes

Author	Period	Sample (progs.)	Prog.	Method	Effects			
					B of P	Inf.	G.	Inv.
1970s								
1. Reichmann and Stillson, 1978	1963–72	75	F	Before/after (two years)	0	–/+	–/+	n.a.
2. Reichmann, 1978	1973–5	21	F	Actual/target	0	–	+	n.a.
3. Connors, 1979	1973–7	31	F	Before/after	0[a]	0	0	n.a.
4. Donovan, 1981	1970–6	12	F	With/without	n.a.	+	0	n.a.
5. Donovan, 1982	1971–80	78	F	With/without	+	+	0	n.a.
6. Killick, 1984	1974–9	38	F	Before/after	0	0	0	n.a.
7. Gylfason, 1987	1977–9	32	F	With/without	+	0	0	n.a.
8. Loxley, 1984	1971–82	38	F	With/without	0	+	0	–
9. Pastor, 1987	1965–81	18[b]	F	With/without } Before/after	+	–	0	
10. Khan and Knight, 1985	1968–75	29	B/F	Simulation	+	–	–	n.a.
11. Goldstein and Montiel, 1986	1974–81	68	F	Generalised[d] evaluation	0	0	0	n.a.
1980s								
12. Zulu and Nsouli, 1985	1980–1	35[c]	F	Actual v. targets	0[a]	–	–	n.a.
13. World Bank, 1988b	1980–7	93	B	With/without	+[a]	0	0	–
14. World Bank, 1990a	1980–8	78	B	Generalised[d] evaluation	+	n.a.	+	–
15. Khan, 1990	1973–88	69	F	Generalised[d] evaluation	+	+	–	n.a.
16. Mosley et al., 1991	1980–7	40	B	Generalised[d] evaluation	+[a]	n.a.	+	–
17. Rodrik, 1990	1982–7	30	B	Before/after	+[a]	n.a.	n.a.	–
18. Faini et al., 1989	1982–6	93	F/B	Generalised[d] evaluation	+[a]	0	0	–
19. Killick et al., 1991	1979–85	38	F	Before/after	+	+/–	0/+[c]	–

Author	Period	Sample (progs.)	Prog.	Method	Effects B of P	Inf.	G.	Inv.
20. Corbo and Rojas, 1992	1981–8	78[f]	B	Generalised[d] evaluation	+[g]	n.a	+	–
21. Mosley, 1994	1980–91	30[e]	B	With/without	n.a.	n.a	–	–
22. Elbadawi et al., 1992	1981–9	41[f]	B	Generalised[d] evaluation	+[g]	0	0	–
23. Schadler et al., 1993	1988–91	85[h]	F/B	Before/after	–[a]	+	+	+

Source: Authors

Notes:

F Fund programmes
B World Bank programmes
0 No or insignificant change
– Deterioration
+ Improvement
0/+ No short-run effect, followed by improvement (or conversely)
(a) Current account
(b) Latin American countries only
(c) African countries only
(d) Generalized evaluation includes both with/without and before/after and takes into account exogenous changes
(e) Sub-Saharan African countries
(f) Countries
(g) Export share
(h) Programmes covering nineteen SAF and ESAF countries – assessment by country

effects, these would show in each of the approaches with sizeable effects. Methodological issues would be of lesser importance. But where the effects are small and ambiguous – as is often the case – the validity of the precise methodology adopted becomes important. But in this situation, we can safely conclude that the total effects are not very significant.

The growth effects of adjustment policies

The empirical evidence on the deflationary effects (defined as negative effects on growth) of adjustment programmes as a whole is mixed, as Table 2.2 indicates. Of twenty-two evaluations, eleven found no effects on growth (or negative followed by positive), four found negative effects, five positive, and two positive after a timelag. It is worth noting that in the evaluations of the 1980s, among studies covering World Bank programmes only, three out of six found small positive effects on growth, while the three evaluations covering IMF programmes only showed more negative effects. Since demand-restricting policies are mainly associated with Fund programmes, this finding is not surprising, confirming the view that the deflationary policies do tend to lead to 'overkill' in the sense that they are associated with loss in output, not just a reallocation of resources and reduced trade deficit. Negative effects on investment were found in all but one study.

The effects on income distribution and poverty

There have been no investigations covering large numbers of countries on the effects of adjustment on income distribution and poverty, attempting to compare adjusting and non-adjusting countries in a similar way to those just reviewed on macro-performance, mainly because of lack of reliable data. Instead, most empirical evaluations have applied CGE models to particular economies. Inevitably, the results are highly dependent on the assumptions behind the models.

A study of the Philippines, however, used multiple regression to assess the impact of adjustment policies on poverty and income distribution for 1980–6.[31] It found that increases in under-employment, inflation and government expenditure worsened income distribution in the Philippines over this period, while productivity gains, increases in the real interest rate and depreciation in the real exchange rate improved distribution, with similar effects on poverty. The most important influences, quantitatively, were productivity and under-employment; the real exchange rate was of lesser significance. The results thus suggest that demand reduction leading to under-employment worsens income distribution and poverty, but if this demand reduction is accompanied by reduced inflation, lower government expenditure and higher real interest rates, these might offset the adverse effects. However, the elasticity of poverty with respect to higher under-employment is greater than the elasticity with respect to reduced inflation. According to this study, in the Philippine case, exchange rate depreciation unambiguously improves income distribution and reduces poverty – this is attributed to the fact that tradables are labour-intensive and that improved rural terms of trade will also help landless agricultural workers. However, Balisacan, using data for 1988–91, and a general equilibrium model, finds that devaluation worsens rural income distribution and poverty because the poorest do not gain from the sale of crops whose prices are favourably affected.

In a study of Kenya, Tyler and Akinboade (1992) use a CGE model based on a social accounting matrix to simulate the effects of a 10 per cent devaluation, 10 per cent increase in investment and 10 per cent increase in agricultural productivity on the macro-economy and on the real incomes of the poor. Alternative assumptions are made about the labour market: first that there is surplus labour and nominal wages are fixed and unaffected by the changes; secondly, that labour is in fixed supply and wages are determined competitively and endogenously, and therefore rise if labour demand increases. Dramatically different results occur under the two assumptions, as might be expected. With surplus labour, and an assumed high elasticity of demand for agricultural exports (3.0), a 10 per cent devaluation leads to an increase in GDP of 10 per cent, exports increase by 15 per cent and there are large increases in employment leading to reduced poverty (although income distribution remains unchanged). But with a competitive labour market, there is increased inflation, a small rise in GDP and a small reduction in poverty. Increases in investment lead to smaller increases in GDP and proportionate increases in the incomes of the poor; again the rise in incomes is greater in the surplus labour case. A rise in agricultural productivity leads to the greatest proportionate rise in the incomes of the poor. One problem with this conclusion – which also applies to the results of Blejer and Guerrero (1990) – is that increasing productivity is not a policy instrument, but the outcome of policies.

The study is valuable in illustrating the importance of assumptions made about the working of the economy to the results of CGE simulation exercises. It also shows that in an agricultural economy like Kenya, devaluation is likely to lead to a reduction in poverty, the extent depending critically on demand-and-supply elasticities.

An OECD study examined the income distribution effects of adjustment policies in the short and medium term in seven countries, using CGE models in five of the seven.[32] Again the effects are shown to be related to the assumed structure of the models used. The critical question is which assumptions are most applicable in the particular economies studied. In general, the studies have not satisfactorily answered this question.

- *Budget cuts:* in Keynesian models with rigid prices, budget cuts lead to unemployment and under-employment and worsening income distribution – this type of assumption was made in the models for Morocco and the Côte d'Ivoire. But where neo-classical assumptions are made, as for Indonesia and Ecuador, and prices and resources are assumed to be flexible, budget cuts lead to crowding-in of private sector activities with reduced negative effects on both income distribution and, especially, poverty. In the neo-classical model, the specific nature of the reduced government expenditure, relative to the private expenditure which is assumed to replace it, becomes important in assessing the income distribution implications. Compensatory crowding-in of private investment occurs. In the Ecuadorian case, deflationary adjustment has more beneficial effects as a result than other forms of adjustment.

- *Monetary contraction*: this was found to be distributionally neutral.
- *Devaluation*: the 'distributive effects of devaluation when compared with those of other stabilization instruments is highly dependent on the structure of foreign trade and the closure of the model'.[33] In each case there were positive distributional effects because the devaluation favoured the rural areas where poverty was greatest. But in some cases there were negative effects on total incomes which led to increased poverty levels – e.g. Morocco and Côte d'Ivoire.

The dependence of outcome on assumptions about the working of the economy is also illustrated by Bourgignon, *et al.* (1991a), in a simulation analysis of the distributional effects of adjustment policies for two 'archetypal' economies, one representing Latin America, the other Africa.[34] In the African archetype, agriculture is of greater importance, while demand-and-supply responses are lower than in the Latin American archetype. The African archetype assumes flexible prices throughout the economy, while the Latin American model has mark-up prices in the modern sector. The assumed 'standard' adjustment package contains depreciation of the currency and an increase in interest rates, but no contraction in fiscal or monetary policy, and thus is not actually 'standard'. The outcomes are radically different in the two cases. In the African case, poverty and income distribution improve as a result of switching policies which raise the incomes of the rural poor. But in the Latin American case, poverty and income distribution worsen significantly as a result of wage and price rigidity which slows growth and leads to unemployment, successful resistance to cuts by richer groups, and investment in foreign-denominated assets by large asset holders.

General equilibrium models (neo-classical models, assuming flexible response) applied to four African economies showed that devaluation improves the rural/urban terms of trade, improves intra-urban income distribution, but worsens intra-rural distribution (as the earlier theoretical analysis suggested). Average incomes of both urban and rural poor rise in each case (see Diagram 2.1).[35]

The results of the simulation exercises broadly endorse – but in a sense add little to – the conclusions from the theoretical discussion, viz.: that the impact of adjustment measures on income distribution will vary according to the nature of the economy; that real exchange rate depreciation tends to improve income distribution and reduce poverty in economies where the rural sector dominates tradables, but can worsen it where mark-up pricing prevails; deflation is poverty-creating unless neo-classical macro-assumptions are made; and the net effect on poverty depends on the balance between deflation and switching in policy response.

The reason the CGE approach adds rather little to theoretical discussion is because, as we have seen, the results of the models depend critically on the assumptions made in the models, and these assumptions are themselves derived from theory.[36] Moreover, the CGE models provide 'results on the mean income of different socio-economic groups, but to measure their impact on poverty, some estimate of how this income is distributed within the groups is needed.'[37] Where the models can be shown to track actual experience closely, they help validate the theory on which they are based, but where, as with poverty and income distribution, data is grossly inadequate this validation does not occur. Moreover, the level of disaggregation is often inadequate – for example, the peasant farming sector is typically not disaggregated, yet one would expect larger and higher-income peasant farms to specialise more in exports and to gain by the changes, while poorer smaller farms, specialising in non-traded crops, would lose. These effects cannot be captured in studies which examine what happens to a typical peasant household.[38]

The lack of a well-defined counterfactual, as well as data deficiencies, make it impossible to come to definitive conclusions on the effects of adjustment policies on income distribution and poverty. Nonetheless, the empirical evidence is consistent with the conclusions suggested by the theoretical analysis, viz.: the results depend on the type of package adopted and the nature of the economy. More deflationary packages appear to have been associated with rising poverty, as the Philippine evidence indicated. Latin American countries, with oligopolistic import-substituting industrial sectors, typically showed worsening income distribution and rising urban (and total) poverty. In contrast, in more flexible economies, such as Indonesia, the switching policies led to expansion of tradables, income distribution improved and poverty lessened.

CONCLUSIONS

This chapter started by presenting three views on the macro effects of adjustment policies on income distribution and poverty: that adjustment improves income distribution and helps the poor; that it worsens income distribution and increases poverty; and the agnostic view. The discussion above has broadly supported the agnostic view with respect to income distribution, but comes to more negative conclusions with respect to poverty – in typical cases, some increase in poverty is likely to be associated with adjustment policies. It has also identified conditions in which adjustment is likely to be associated with worsening income distribution and poverty and those in which it is likely to be associated with improvements in income distribution and poverty.

The main source of an aggregate increase in poverty lies in the deflationary part of the adjustment package; the greater this is the more is poverty likely to increase. Deflation may be greater for one or other of the following reasons:

- because this is what is recommended by the IFIs and/or chosen by the government;
- because real depreciation cannot be brought about because of restrictions on movement in the nominal exchange rate (as was the case in the franc zone), or because of indexation and wage resistance;
- because of inflexibility of the economy, which is likely to be made greater by primary product specialisation; low past and present rates of investment;[39] and lack of external finance, requiring more rapid adjustment and leading to cuts in investment rates.

The lengthy discussion of devaluation suggested that it was likely to improve income distribution and reduce poverty in economies where tradables were agricultural products produced on peasant farms, and there was more rural than urban poverty; but even in this context the poorest farmers might not be positively affected, while urban poverty would be likely to increase. In economies where urban poverty was greater than rural, and the modern urban sector was inflexible and adopted mark-up pricing, devaluation would worsen urban income distribution and increase poverty. However, countries which export labour-intensive manufactures might experience improved income distribution in the medium term as labour absorption expands. Mineral exporters would tend to show negative distributional effects.

The aggregate effects combine those of deflation and devaluation. The reason the typical adjustment package is poverty creating is that the deflation effects overwhelm the other effects. But countries can fall into one of four categories, with varying combinations of effects on poverty and income distribution (see Diagram 2.3). It is noteworthy that most actual examples fall into the worst quadrant of deteriorating income distribution and poverty, although it is possible that if we had data for more African countries they would appear in the north-west quadrant.

Chart 2.1 presents these conclusions schematically. Countries which systematically follow the negative part of the schema (Part B) will unavoidably experience a poverty increase during adjustment, and countries having all the positive elements (Part A) will experience poverty reduction. But mixed experience is also possible, making prediction difficult. Chart 2.2 presents a typology of countries derived from Chart 2.1, with some country examples. Mixed cases are possible. A common combination is shown by many African economies: inflexibility derived from all three sources (primary specialisation, low investment and weak human resources, and financial crisis) but a type of export (peasant agriculture) and high levels of rural poverty which make it

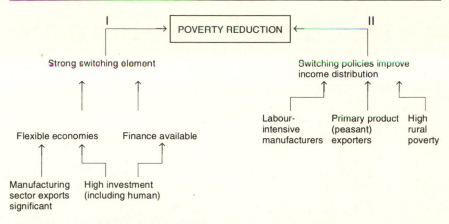

Chart 2.1A Conditions in which adjustment is poverty reducing

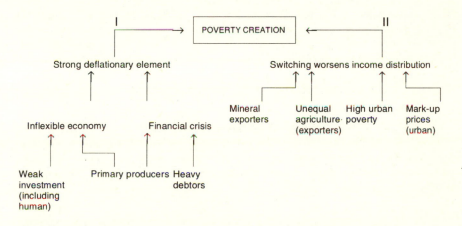

Chart 2.1B Conditions in which adjustment is poverty creating

probable that switching policies improve distribution. This may explain Sahn and Sarris's findings, in a five-country study in sub-Saharan Africa, that there is 'no unequivocal pattern of increase or decrease in the real welfare of the rural poor.'[40]

In much of the discussion of income distribution effects we have not explicitly considered the counterfactual, except to the extent that much analysis of the effects of a policy change implicitly takes no policy change as the counterfactual. It is, of course, possible that the alternative to the adjustment package would have been worse in terms of deflation and income distribution, as is vehemently argued by some observers.[41] But others have identified adjustment packages that would have been more pro-poor.[42] However, one of the aims here in identifying the poverty impact of adjustment is not to prove that it was better or worse than some possible alternative, but to assess whether they were good enough in terms of protecting the poor during adjustment, or

A. Poverty-reducing adjustment	Country examples
A1 – flexible economies	South Korea
– labour-intensive manufactured	Indonesia
exports and/or egalitarian agriculture	Malaysia
A2 – well-financed adjustment	Turkey
	Ghana
B. Poverty-creating adjustment	
B1 – inflexible economies	Malawi (and much of
	sub-Saharan Africa)
B2 – mineral exporters	Zambia
B3 – unequal agricultural exporters	Ecuador
B4 – moderate sector oligopolistic, urban poverty	Argentina
significant	

Chart 2.2 A typology of countries undergoing adjustment

whether improvements should be sought. It is in these terms that many (but not all) of the packages fail.

NOTES

1 IMF, 1986, p. 3; similar conclusions emerge from Heller *et al.*, 1988.
2 Srinivasan, 1988, Abstract.
3 See, e.g., Taylor, 1983; Pastor, 1987: 'Usually income distribution against labour and the poor is implicit in stabilisation attempts' (Taylor, 1983, p. 200).
4 Demery and Addison, 1987; Helleiner, 1987; Kanbur, 1987; Bourgignon and Morrisson, 1992.
5 Krugman and Taylor, 1978, elucidate the conditions under which devaluation is deflationary.
6 This diagram is much used in discussions of these issues, usually with little qualification about its realism: the analysis is derived from Salter and from Corden and used, for example, by Knight, 1976; Demery and Addison, 1987; Kanbur, 1987; Bourgignon *et al.*, 1991b.
7 Helleiner, 1987, p. 1504.
8 See evidence in Chapters 6 and 7.
9 See Dell, 1982.
10 IMF, 1986, Heller *et al.*, 1988.
11 IMF, 1986; Heller *et al.*, 1988.
12 Heller *et al.*, 1988, drawing on the conclusions of Khan and Knight, 1985.
13 Blank and Blinder, 1985.
14 Blejer and Guerrero, 1990.
15 See Cornia, 1987.
16 The issue of how the exchange rate affects income distribution has been explored by, among others, Krugman and Taylor, 1978, Knight, 1976, Demery and Addison, 1987, and Kanbur, 1987. This section draws heavily on these sources, and especially Knight's clear and comprehensive account.
17 Evidence from Polak, 1991; World Bank, 1990a.
18 The real exchange rate depreciated significantly in both Africa (over 40 per cent, 1978–81 to 1986–8) and Latin America (13 per cent same period). Data from Bourgignon *et al.*, 1991b.

19 Kaldor questions whether devaluation will change the real exchange rate in the medium term: 'this approach assumes devaluation is capable of changing critical price and wage relationships that are the outcome of complex political forces and that could not be changed by domestic fiscal and monetary policies' (Kaldor, 1983)

20 Whether IS manufactures should count as NT or T is ambiguous. If surrounded by heavy import controls or prohibitive tariffs, then the sector is NT; but if the tariffs are low, then a devaluation will increase the protection of the sector encouraging resources to move into it, and the sector should be classified as T (i.e. it becomes Tv in the above classification).

21 Discussion of 'wages' should be understood to include labour-income among the self-employed.

22 The weights may be population shares and/or income shares, according to the measure of inequality adopted. For some measures of inequality the weights do not necessarily add to one – Anand, 1983, p. 92.

23 This decomposition can only be done with a limited class of inequality measures. The mose popular measure, the Gini coefficient, cannot be decomposed in this way. See Anand, 1983, pp. 86–92. Anand shows that both the Theil indices (the entropy index, T, and the second Theil index, L, which measures the logarithm of the ratio of tthe arithmetic mean of income to the geometric mean) can be decomposed in this way.

24 Population share in each sector in the case of the Theil index.

25 The argument here follows that of Krugman and Taylor, 1978.

26 This is a very simplified version, which adopts the headcount measure of poverty combined with an average income gap. Kanbur himself adopts the class of poverty indices of Foster et al., 1984. But the more sophisticated approach does not alter the basic result.

27 That is, $P_{nt} = H_{nt}(1 - I_{nt})$; $P_t = H_t(1 - I_t)$.

28 Knight, 1976, p. 226; also see Demery and Addison, 1987: 'There are several mechanisms involved, not necessarily working in the same direction as far as poverty and inequality is concerned, it being impossible analytically to derive unambiguous conclusions', pp. 1488, 1490.

29 IMF, 1987.

30 For example, Corbo and Rojas include change in interest rate as an exogenous variable, but not change in the terms of trade (Corbo and Rojas, 1992).

31 Blejer and Guerrero, 1990.

32 See Bourgignon and Morrisson, 1992, for an overview.

33 Bourgignon and Morrisson, 1992, p. 64.

34 See also Adelman and Robinson, 1988, who show that functional income distribution is very sensitive to 'closure' assumptions of the model, but size distribution is much less so.

35 Dorosh and Sahn, 1993.

36 See Robinson, 1991, for a discussion of some of the limitations of the models used.

37 Maasland, 1990.

38 For example, Sahn and Sarris, 1991.

39 Bourgignon and Morrisson, 1992, attribute much of the success of the Indonesian and Malaysian adjustments to prior investment.

40 Sahn and Sarris, 1991, p. 259.

41 E.g. Srinivasan, 1988; IMF, 1986; Heller et al., 1988.

42 E.g. Bourgignon et al., 1991a; Bourgignon and Morrisson, 1992, passim.

Chapter 3

Meso-policy choices and the poor[1]

INTRODUCTION

Macro-policy choices form the major policy influence on the *primary* incomes of the poor, as discussed in the last chapter. Meso-policy choices – in particular with respect to taxation and public expenditure – may compensate for or accentuate the effects of macro-policy, through their influence on *secondary* incomes. Well-designed meso-policies can largely protect the poor from adverse effects on their primary incomes arising during temporary recession.

Fiscal changes have some impact on each of the three main ways in which the poor may be affected by adjustment – first, they can have an impact on disposable incomes as a result of direct taxes or transfers and government-financed schemes designed to generate employment or help raise productivity; secondly, the fiscal system influences the prices of the goods and services consumed by the poor, especially food, through indirect taxes and subsidies; and thirdly, government expenditure affects the availability (and price) of publicly provided goods and services consumed by the poor, notably health, education and water.

The extent to which changes in the fiscal system affect the poor depends not only on the nature of the fiscal system, but also on *who the poor are*, since, for any given fiscal system, the poor will be affected differently according to their sources of income and patterns of consumption. It follows that it is difficult to generalise on how a particular fiscal system will affect the poor because the impacts are likely to differ across societies, just as sources of poverty differ.

This chapter is primarily devoted to an analysis of the impact of the fiscal system on the absolute conditions of life of the poor, rather than on their position relative to other groups in society. The primary aim is to show that the impact on the poor of fiscal changes during adjustment, while frequently negative in practice, *is not unavoidably negative*, but rather that there is a series of choices which governments are able to make that can accentuate or reduce the negative effects. The choices will be presented in general terms, but they will be illustrated by actual choices made in different countries in the 1980s. This chapter deals with meso-policies generally; the subsequent two chapters look at two aspects of meso-policy which were particularly relevant to the adjustment experience – food subsidies (Chapter 4) and social funds (Chapter 5).

Meso-policies and secondary incomes

Meso policies influence the distribution of primary incomes both through taxation and through expenditures. On the tax side, if taxation of the type paid by lower-income groups is increased (either through a general increase in tax rates or a redistribution of the tax burden) this can worsen the secondary incomes of the poor. Although the poor usually do not pay direct taxes, in most societies they pay some indirect taxes (e.g. often on beer, tobacco and fuel, and sometimes on some other basic commodities) and they also bear other taxes indirectly (because the items they consume include some inputs on which tax has been paid). However, in general, the main effect of meso-policies on the poor is through public expenditure on goods and services consumed by the poor, not taxation.

As noted in Chapter 1, there are three critical ratios which determine the extent to which government meso-policies succeed in improving the situation of the poor through expenditure:

1 The *public expenditure ratio*, the ratio of public expenditure to GDP. Assuming that deficit finance is limited, this depends on the tax effort. There is a large variation among countries both in tax ratios, ranging, for example from 7.3 per cent for Sierra Leone to 74 per cent in Botswana, and in public expenditure ratios, ranging from 10.3 per cent in Uganda to 50.9 per cent in Botswana; data are for 1988.

2 The *social allocation ratio*, the proportion of total government expenditure going to social sectors (which should be broadly defined to include any programmes which may support the poor, including food subsidies and employment schemes). The social allocation ratio (including here, for statistical reasons, only education and health sector expenditures) varies from 13 per cent in Indonesia to 50 per cent in Costa Rica.

3 The *social priority ratio*, the ratio of expenditures on the social sectors which go on priority services which reach the poor. It is difficult to arrive at precise estimates of the priority ratio. In the first place, the definition of a priority service will vary according to the level of social achievement of the society: for example, universal secondary education is a priority only in societies which have already achieved universal primary education. But in all societies some secondary and some tertiary education is needed. A second problem is that it is not normally possible to identify which public goods go to deprived groups and which go to well-off groups. Thirdly, there are usually statistical problems in arriving at intra-sectoral breakdowns. Consequently, estimates of the priority ratios are inevitably somewhat controversial. But so long as the

same basis is used across societies, variations in the ratio are indicative. Defining the priorities as including primary health care and primary and secondary education, the ratio varies sharply across societies from a high of 77 per cent in South Korea and 68 per cent in Malaysia to a low of 13 per cent in Sierra Leone.

These three ratios are then used to calculate the human expenditure ratio (HER), the proportion of national income going to social priorities:

$$\mathrm{HER} = E/Y \times S/E \times P_r/S$$

Human expenditure per capita (HER/N) can be derived from the HER:

$$HE/N = E/y \times S/E \times P_r/S$$

where HE = expenditure on human priorities; HER = ratio of HE to GNP; Y = GNP; E = public expenditure; S = expenditure on the social sectors; P_r = expenditure on priorities for the poor in the social sectors; N = population; y = income per head.

Given that each ratio may differ substantially across countries, the total impact of meso-policies on government expenditure on priorities can show very great variations as indicated in Table 3.1, ranging from a human expenditure ratio of over 12 per cent in Zimbabwe to less than 1 per cent in Pakistan and Indonesia.[2] Human expenditures per head show even greater diversity because of differences in per capita incomes: in this sample of countries they vary from $453 in Singapore to $9 in Bangladesh.[3]

The efficiency of use of human expenditures also varies. Consequently, the impact on the poor is given by $I_p = E_p \times f$, where I_p is the impact on the poor, E_p, expenditure on human priorities and f is a measure of the efficiency of resource use, or the inverse of the human expenditure impact ratio (HEIR) in the priority sectors. The HEIR is akin to the capital output ratio for capital expenditure. But it is more difficult to measure because the 'output' is less easy to quantify, since it consists in 'more healthy', 'better nourished' people and so on. A very crude measure is life expectancy; the ratio of purchasing power parity (PPP) dollars spent on human priorities to life expectancy is shown for the sample in Table 3.1.[4] It varies from 6.1 in Singapore to 0.17 in Bangladesh. But this is a highly misleading indicator of efficiency for a number of reasons: first, a certain minimum life expectancy can be expected irrespective of human development expenditures; secondly, high-income countries tend to have high wages in the human development sectors (partially but not totally corrected for by the PPP adjustments), so that higher expenditures may reflect higher wages and not a greater quantity of resources; thirdly, one may expect diminishing returns to additional expenditure (in terms of extra years of life expectancy) as life expectancy rises especially because there is a natural upper limit to life expectancy; fourthly, there are many other determinants of life expectancy besides human development (HD) expenditure – including for example nutrition

Table 3.1 Analysis of public social spending, 1988

Country	Human expenditure ratio (%) (1)	Public expenditure ratio (%) (2)	Social allocation ratio (%) (3)	Social priority ratio (%) (4)	Income per capita $ PPP (5)	Life expectancy 1990 (6)	Human expenditure per person (1) × (5) $ PPP (7)	Human expenditure impact ratio (7) ÷ (6) (8)
High levels of human expenditure – above 5%								
Zimbabwe	12.7	52	49	50	1,370	59.6	174	2.9
Botswana	7.7	51	37	41	2,510	59.8	193	3.2
Malaysia	6.3	32	29	68	5,070	70.1	319	4.6
Morocco	6.3	29	42	52	2,380	62.0	150	2.4
Jordan	5.5	50	25	44	2,570	66.9	141	2.1
Costa Rica	5.4	41	50	26	4,320	74.9	233	3.1
Medium levels of human expenditure – between 3% and 5%								
Singapore	4.3	35	35	35	10,540	74.0	453	6.1
Kuwait	4.0	36	42	26	9,310	73.4	372	5.1
South Korea	3.7	16	30	77	5,686	70.1	210	3.0
Mauritius	3.1	27	40	29	5,320	69.6	165	2.4
Chile	3.1	33	50	19	4,720	71.8	146	2.0
Low levels of human expenditure – below 3%								
Thailand	2.5	16	37	42	3,280	66.1	82	1.2
Sri Lanka	2.5	31	43	18	2,120	70.1	53	0.76
Philippines	2.4	21	22	53	2,170	64.2	52	0.81
Tanzania	2.4	29	15	55	570	54.0	14	0.26
Colombia	2.1	15	40	36	3,810	68.8	80	1.16
Sierra Leone	1.5	13	39	31	1,030	42.0	16	0.38
Bangladesh	1.2	12	24	42	720	51.8	9	0.17
Pakistan	0.8	25	21	14	1,790	57.7	14	0.24
Indonesia	0.6	25	13	18	1,820	61.5	11	0.18

Source: UNDP, *Human Development Report 1991*
Note: The social priority is the expenditure on primary health care and basic education as a percentage of total social sector expenditure

standards; fifthly, current life expectancy is likely to depend on past HD expenditures over a number of years, not current HD expenditures; sixthly, an average increase in life expectancy may, in part, reflect improvements in the longevity of the rich rather than improvements in the conditions of the mass of the people.

To avoid some (but by no means all) of these problems, Table 3.2 compares the HEIR for countries with similar life expectancies and similar per capita incomes. The variation is then much reduced, but remains significant:[5] for example, Colombia appears to be more than four times as efficient as Malaysia; Sri Lanka's HEIR is less than half that of Jordan; and the Philippines' HEIR is a quarter that of Botswana.[6]

Table 3.2 Human expenditure impact ratios

Life Expectancy		
Below 55	55–65	Over 65
Very low income countries (<$1,500 per capita)		
Sierra Leone 0.38	Zimbabwe 2.9	
Bangladesh 0.17		
Tanzania 0.09		
Low income countries (<$3,000 ≥ $1,500)		
	Botswana 3.2	Jordan 2.1
	Morocco 1.5	Sri Lanka 0.76
	Philippines 0.81	
	Pakistan 0.24	
	Indonesia 0.18	
Middle income countries (<$6,000 ≥ $3,000)		
		Malaysia 4.6
		Korea 3.0
		Mauritius 2.4
		Chile 2.0
		Colombia 0.97
High income countries (≥ $6,0000)		
		Singapore 6.1
		Kuwait 5.1

Source: Table 3.1

It follows from this analysis that meso-policies to support the poor can consist in reducing taxes paid by the poor, raising the three ratios and raising the efficiency of resource use in priority expenditures. In addition, an improvement in macro-performance, by raising per capita incomes, will, of course, increase expenditure on priorities for any given set of ratios. Conversely, a *decline* in per capita income, which, as we have seen, occurred in many adjusting countries in the 1980s, will require an increase in the human expenditure ratio, to be brought about by an improvement in at least one of the three ratios – the public expenditure ratio, the social allocation ratio or the priority ratio. The remainder of this chapter considers changes in these ratios in adjusting countries.

FISCAL CHOICES AND THE PUBLIC EXPENDITURE RATIO

Public expenditure can be seen as the sum of total revenue, R, and the budget deficit, B, or

$$E^t = R^t + B^t$$

where t denotes the time period. Let e, r, b represent the expenditure, revenue and budget ratios, or E, R and B expressed as a proportion of GNP. Then,

$$e^t = r^t + b^t$$

The level of public expenditure per head can then be seen as depending on the revenue ratio, the budget deficit ratio and income per head:

$$E^t/N^t = e^t \cdot y^t = (r^t + b^t)y^t$$

where $y^t = $ income per head at time t. The change in real expenditure per head over time then depends on the change in per capita income, changes in the proportion of GNP collected in taxation and changes in the budget deficit. i.e.

$$\frac{\varepsilon^{t+1}}{\varepsilon^t} = \frac{[r^{t+1} + b^{t+1}] \cdot g^t}{r^t + b^t}$$

where ε^t, ε^{t+1} represent public expenditure per head at time t and $t+1$, and g^t is the growth rate between time t and $(t+1)$.

For any given allocations of government expenditure, the poor are likely to benefit when the choices *avoid aggregate expenditure cuts and, where possible, permit expenditure increases*. IMF stabilisation policies are invariably associated with a target reduction in B, with the prime emphasis on the attainment of this reduction through expenditure cuts, rather than through tax increases. Thus, from 1980 to 1984, a reduced budget deficit occurred in 83 per cent of Fund programmes, while 93 per cent of the programmes involved restraint on government expenditure. Many of the programmes also included some tax-raising measures. Nonetheless, a detailed study of seven countries following IMF programmes in 1983–5 found that all but two 'focused on expenditure restraint rather than revenue-raising measures'.[7] World Bank SALs also include reduction in budget deficits as a major aim (39 per cent of loan conditions, 1989–91), and also typically require expenditure reductions but the programmes put relatively more emphasis on tax reform: 'tax reform as a component of broader fiscal adjustment is at the heart of the stabilization and adjustment process in many developing countries'.[8]

It is possible, however, to make choices which protect real expenditure levels. Relevant policies are those which:

- avoid falling GNP per capita;
- avoid over-ambitious targets for the reduction of B;

● place more emphasis on the achievement of target improvements in B by raising revenue rather than cutting expenditure.

These policy choices, particularly the first two, come properly into the arena of macro-policy choices and were discussed in the previous chapter. Here we shall consider them only briefly. There are constraints on each of the three types of policy. Governments do not have full control over the factors which determine growth. However, particularly when they are able to borrow (or reduce debt-servicing payments), they do have some control over the speed of adjustment and the extent to which adjustment is stagnationary or growth-oriented.

Budget deficits can also be used to sustain government expenditure, but it is generally believed that they generate inflationary pressures and that 'the poor suffer worst from inflation',[9] although careful empirical evidence is lacking on this. This issue was briefly discussed in the last chapter. We concluded there that much depends on who the poor are; and whether the alternative to inflation is higher rates of un/under-employment. There is little evidence to suggest that moderate rates of inflation will hurt the poor particularly, but accelerating and high rates of inflation may do so, especially when they lead to drastic stabilisation programmes, which invariably have negative effects on employment and wages. In any case, as noted earlier, there is only a loose relationship between the size of the budget deficit and the rate of inflation – depending on how the deficit is financed and non-monetary causes of inflation. The review of evidence in the last chapter showed stabilisation and adjustment programmes have had little effect on the inflation rate (but the effects of the budget deficit as such were not identified).

Where the fiscal deficit is high (over 5 per cent of GNP), some reduction is generally a desirable element in adjustment. However, the question of the speed and extent of the reduction in B is debatable. From the perspective of the poor, a slower and more limited adjustment might be desirable. Where the fiscal deficit is relatively low (below 2 per cent of GNP), reduction may not be necessary.

The third policy option mentioned above is to increase revenue, thus permitting a reduced deficit while maintaining expenditure. There are also limits here, including political constraints on possible changes, especially if taxation is already high. However, in countries with a low tax ratio, this option offers a frequently unexploited potential. In general, the poor are likely to benefit more from macro-policies involving increased R and stable E than from policies which focus on reduced E, because the poor usually pay fewer taxes, while they get some benefits from public expenditure, both direct and in-direct. For example, Alaihima (1984) showed that, in Sri Lanka in 1980, households with the lowest 20 per cent of incomes bore 9.4 per cent of the total tax burden and received 26.8 per cent of the benefits from government expenditure.[10]

Table 3.3 Fiscal changes in the 1980s

| | No. of countries | Expenditure ratio | | | Revenue ratio | | | Budget deficit | | | Growth GNP% | Index of government expend. p.c. |
		1981	1990	Change	1981	1990	Change	1981	1990	Change	1981–9/90	1990 (1981=1)
Africa												
Av. adjusting	15	29.20	25.73	-3.47	22.04	20.79	-1.25	-6.37	-2.56	3.81	-1.27	0.78
Int. adj.	9	32.81	29.41	-3.40	23.70	22.40	-1.30	-9.11	-3.45	5.66	-1.54	0.78
Other adj.	6	29.25	25.10	-4.15	23.50	22.12	-1.38	-3.78	-1.80	1.98	-1.12	0.78
Other	4	33.90	29.63	-4.28	28.95	30.78	1.83	-2.08	2.35	4.43	1.13	0.96
All	19	30.19	26.55	-3.64	23.49	22.89	-0.60	-5.47	-1.53	3.94	-0.76	0.82
Latin America												
Av. adjusting	13	24.75	24.68	-0.07	19.88	21.76	1.88	-3.36	-2.57	0.79	-0.72	0.94
Int. adj.	8	24.39	27.23	2.84	20.95	25.69	4.74	-2.30	-2.85	-0.55	-0.24	1.09
Other adj.	5	25.32	20.60	-4.72	18.16	15.48	-2.68	-5.06	-2.12	2.94	-1.48	0.71
Other	7	22.29	19.16	-3.13	18.76	18.51	-0.25	-2.54	-1.73	0.81	-3.20	0.64
All	20	23.89	22.75	-1.14	19.49	20.63	1.14	-3.08	-2.28	0.80	-1.59	0.83
Other regions												
Av. adjusting	9	23.67	23.77	0.10	20.93	20.37	-0.56	-5.53	-2.60	2.93	2.80	1.29
Int. adj.	6	20.10	21.30	1.20	18.50	18.70	0.20	-5.40	-2.60	2.80	3.20	1.41
Other adj.	3	30.80	28.70	-2.10	25.80	23.70	-2.10	-5.80	-2.60	3.20	2.00	1.11
Other	3	21.10	26.00	4.90	13.37	15.60	2.23	-5.40	-6.80	-1.40	0.77	1.32
All	12	23.03	24.33	1.30	19.04	19.18	0.14	-5.50	-3.65	1.85	2.29	1.30
All countries												
Av. adjusting	37	26.29	24.88	-1.41	21.01	21.03	0.02	-5.11	-2.57	2.54	-0.09	0.96
Int. adj.	23	26.57	26.54	-0.03	21.39	22.58	1.19	-5.77	-3.02	2.75	0.15	1.05
Other adj.	14	28.18	24.26	-3.91	22.09	20.09	-2.00	-4.67	-2.09	2.85	-0.58	0.83
Other	14	25.35	23.62	-1.74	20.52	21.39	0.87	-3.02	-1.65	1.37	-1.11	0.88
All	51	26.50	24.98	-1.52	21.26	21.45	0.25	-4.60	-2.37	2.23	-0.40	0.95

Source: World Development reports (various)
Notes: Adjusting, intensively adjusting and other adjusting as defined by World Bank, 1992. A number of countries are omitted, especially in Africa, because of lack of data

Fiscal choices in adjusting countries in the 1980s

In practice, adjusting countries made a variety of fiscal choices in the 1980s as shown by changes in the three key fiscal variables, e, r and b.

Tables 3.3 and 3.4 indicate the changes by region, for a sample of countries for which data are reasonably complete, dividing the countries into IALs, OALs and NALs. As noted earlier, the division is somewhat arbitrary. Moreover, the coverage is not complete because of lack of detailed expenditure data for many countries. For example, in sub-Saharan Africa, Madagascar, Benin, Burundi, Guinea, Guinea-Bissau, Côte d'Ivoire and Gabon are 'adjusting' countries which have been omitted from the analysis for lack of data. The 'other country' category is even more deficient in coverage.

Bearing these cautions in mind, the following broad conclusions emerge. For all countries, on average, there was a small rise in the revenue ratio and a

Table 3.4 Proportion of countries increasing fiscal ratios over the 1980s

	Expenditure ratio	Revenue ratio	Budget deficit (reducing)	GNP per capita 1980–9	Government expend. p.c. 1981–90
Africa					
Av. adjusting	0.40	0.40	0.53	0.20	0.40
Int. adj.	0.33	0.44	0.67	0.11	0.44
Other adj.	0.50	0.33	0.33	0.33	0.33
Other	0.25	0.25	0.25	0.50	0.25
All	0.37	0.37	0.47	0.26	0.37
Latin America					
Av. adjusting	0.46	0.54	0.73	0.38	0.54·
Int. adj.	0.75	0.75	0.57	0.50	0.75
Other adj.	0.00	0.20	1.00	0.20	0.20
Other	0.14	0.43	0.57	0.00	0.00
All	0.30	0.50	0.67	0.25	0.35
Other regions					
Av. adjusting	0.40	0.40	0.67	0.89	0.89
Int. adj.	0.50	0.50	0.67	0.83	0.83
Other adj.	0.33	0.33	0.67	1.00	1.00
Other	1.00	1.00	0.67	0.67	0.67
All	0.58	0.58	0.58	0.83	0.83
All countries					
Av. adjusting	0.43	0.46	0.68	0.43	0.54
Int. adj.	0.52	0.57	0.65	0.43	0.65
Other adj.	0.29	0.29	0.71	0.43	0.36
Other	0.36	0.50	0.57	0.29	0.27
All	0.41	0.47	0.59	0.39	0.45

Source: As Table 3.3

significant reduction in the budget deficit, with the net effect of a small fall in the expenditure ratio. Expenditure per head therefore fell, 1981–90. Adjusting countries' performance as a whole was similar to non-adjusting, but within the adjusting group, the IALs showed a bigger rise in the revenue ratio and were therefore able to maintain a near constant expenditure ratio while showing a reduced budget deficit, while the OALs experienced a fall in both revenue and expenditure ratios. The net effect allowing for better performance on growth among the IALs was that they showed a small rise in per capita government expenditure over the 1980s, while the OALs had a large fall.

There were considerable differences between regions. In Africa, on average the expenditure ratio fell quite significantly for each category of country, whether adjusting or not, falling in twelve out of nineteen countries. This was accompanied by a small fall in the revenue ratio and a significant reduction in the budget deficit. Thus the fiscal policies in Africa reinforced the negative growth performance leading to a fall in aggregate expenditure per capita for most countries. The fall on average was much bigger than in Latin America. The one exception was the small non-adjusting group, where growth in per capita incomes offset most of these effects and there was only a small fall in government expenditure per head. In contrast, in Latin America, the expenditure and revenue ratios rose among IALs. These countries also experienced a smaller fall in per capita income. The consequence was that government expenditure per head rose by nearly 10 per cent among intensive adjustment-lending countries in Latin America, falling quite sharply among other adjustment-lending countries; the biggest fall in government expenditure in Latin America was in the non-adjustment lending category.

In the rest of the world, growth in per capita incomes was more positive and this, rather than changes in fiscal policies, was the main factor behind the growth in government expenditure. There was little change, on average, in expenditure and revenue ratios. Some countries – the Philippines and Thailand – achieved large increases in the revenue ratio. Other adjusting countries reduced revenue and expenditure ratios sharply, e.g. Morocco, South Korea, Indonesia and Sri Lanka.

Large variations were to be observed between countries within each region and within the different categories: for example, among the IALs Mexico reduced expenditure and revenue ratios and had negative growth in per capita incomes leading to a large fall in government expenditure, while Costa Rica increased revenue and expenditure ratios and government expenditure per head. Within-region comparisons will be discussed in detail for Africa and Latin America in Chapters 6 and 7.

By analysing the fiscal choices made by adjusting countries with respect to the main factors determining changes in government expenditure per head, it is possible to pick out types of 'good' and 'bad' experience, from the perspective of maintaining government expenditure per head during adjustment (Table 3.5).

Table 3.5 Summary of experiences with fiscal choices in adjusting countries in the 1980s

	Good			Bad			
	G1	G2	G3	B1	B2	B3	B4
Growth in per capita incomes	+	+	–	–	–	–	+
Change in real government expenditure per head	+	+	+	–	–	+	–
Expenditure ratio	+/–	+/–	+	–	+	+	–
Revenue ratio	+/–	+/–	+	+/–	+/–	+/–	+/–
Budget deficit	Reduced	Increased and sustainable	Reduced or sustainable	Reduced	+/–	Increased and unsustainable	+/–
Examples	Mali Mauritius Indonesia South Korea Sri Lanka Thailand	Chile Turkey Tunisia Costa Rica	Philippines Bolivia Ghana Zimbabwe Colombia Uruguay	*Large cuts in expenditure* Argentina Zambia Zaire Sierra Leone Tanzania Venezuela *Moderate cuts* Malawi Mauritania Togo Mexico	Gabon Nicaragua	Brazil Nigeria Kenya	Morocco Jamaica

Sources: Tables 3.3, 3.4

Good Experience

In general, as one would expect, economic growth facilitates growth in public expenditure, although in some cases, cuts in government expenditure mean that growth is accompanied by falling expenditure per head. Countries which succeeded in combining growth with rising expenditure per head and a falling budget deficit during adjustment include Mali, Indonesia, Mauritius, South Korea, Sri Lanka and Thailand (category G1).

More fundamental fiscal problems arise where growth is negative. In the 1980s, 'bad' experience (i.e. falling government expenditure per head) predominated among negative growth cases. Nonetheless, countries *can* raise expenditure per head if they increase the expenditure ratio, and they can do so without greatly increasing, or even while reducing, the budget deficit so long as they raise the tax ratio sufficiently (category G3). Good examples in the 1980s included Bolivia, Colombia, Ghana, Uruguay and Zimbabwe. In Ghana, this was achieved as a result of the recovery from a very weak tax position of only 6.9 per cent of GNP in 1980. Bolivia's experience was similar, although from a higher starting point. On the other hand, Zimbabwe succeeded in raising the tax ratio by 9 per cent of GNP, even though taxes already accounted for over 30 per cent of GNP, showing that it is possible for non-mineral countries in Africa to raise their tax ratio significantly. Brazil, Costa Rica and Ecuador also raised their revenue ratio substantially over the 1980s.

Bad experience

Some countries compounded the effects of negative growth by lowering expenditure ratios, thereby producing large cuts in expenditure per capita (category B1). In a number of cases, the cuts in the expenditure ratio and in expenditure per head were severe. For example, Argentina, Sierra Leone, Tanzania, Zambia and Zaire each experienced cuts in expenditure per head of over 30 per cent. In Sierra Leone, this was due to the collapse of revenue because of the contraction of the formal sector of the economy. In Tanzania, the 'informalisation' of the economy likewise reduced tax potential. The 'classic' IMF stabilisation package, with prime emphasis on expenditure reduction rather than revenue raising, encourages the negative pattern observed in this category. It is noteworthy that this is the largest single category of adjusting countries.

Some countries experienced such severe drops in GNP per capita that expenditure per head fell, despite rising expenditure ratios. This occurred in Gabon and also Nicaragua (category B2). Many countries have revenue and expenditure ratios which are low compared to those achieved elsewhere, and, for these countries, an increase in the tax and expenditure ratio represents an important policy option. However, it is more difficult to do this where the tax ratio is already high, as for example in Gabon and Mauritania. In these countries, more reliance has to be placed on policies regarding the *allocation* of

Table 3.6 Allocation ratios in the 1980s

| | Share of | | | | | | | | | | | | | | | Index of 1990 (1981) |
| | Defence | | | Health and education | | | Economic | | | Other, inc. interest | | | H+E as % GNP | | | |
	1981	1990	Change	1981	1990	Change	1981	1990	Change	1981	1990	Change	1981	1990	Change	
Africa																
Av. adjusting	9.48	7.83	−1.65	21.49	18.09	−3.40	23.09	21.95	−1.14	40.88	47.50	6.62	5.87	4.49	−1.38	0.68
Int. adj.	8.18	5.93	−2.25	22.34	19.73	−2.61	26.80	27.09	0.29	37.20	41.14	3.94	5.75	4.83	−0.92	0.73
Other adj.	11.58	10.88	−0.70	20.14	15.48	−4.66	17.16	13.74	−3.42	46.76	57.68	10.92	6.06	3.95	−2.11	0.59
Other	8.68	8.35	−0.33	23.30	22.90	−0.40	24.98	30.90	5.92	37.18	32.03	−5.15	8.03	6.85	−1.18	0.94
All	9.29	7.95	−1.34	21.92	19.22	−2.70	23.54	24.06	0.52	40.01	44.60	4.59	6.38	5.05	−1.33	0.74
Latin America																
Av. adjusting	7.56	6.84	−0.72	24.38	22.45	−1.93	19.67	11.40	−8.27	21.18	31.72	10.54	6.18	5.70	−0.48	0.87
Int. adj.	8.01	5.71	−2.30	24.27	20.07	−4.20	18.53	9.76	−8.77	14.17	31.31	17.14	6.10	5.43	−0.67	0.87
Other adj.	6.78	8.80	2.02	21.96	26.63	4.67	21.68	14.28	−7.40	33.45	32.43	−1.02	6.33	6.18	−0.15	0.85
Other	9.39	9.94	0.55	18.16	22.94	4.78	18.96	12.56	−6.40	29.74	25.74	−4.00	4.24	4.50	0.26	0.79
All	8.27	8.04	−0.23	21.96	22.64	0.68	19.39	11.85	−7.54	24.51	29.39	4.88	5.43	5.23	−0.20	0.90
Other regions																
Av. adjusting	16.96	14.86	−2.10	16.58	18.14	1.56	28.46	21.08	−7.38	30.42	38.68	8.26	4.14	4.28	0.14	1.32
Int. adj.	21.65	18.63	−3.02	17.52	19.20	1.68	29.85	19.05	−10.80	24.37	37.40	13.03	3.91	3.95	0.04	1.34
Other adj.	7.57	7.30	−0.27	14.70	16.03	1.33	25.67	25.13	−0.54	42.53	41.23	−1.30	4.60	4.95	0.35	1.29
Other	17.40	15.37	−2.03	9.63	13.27	3.64	36.23	24.97	−11.26	30.00	37.37	7.37	2.15	3.94	1.79	1.12
All	17.07	14.99	−2.08	14.84	16.92	2.08	30.40	22.05	−8.35	30.32	38.35	8.04	3.64	4.20	0.55	1.14
All areas																
Av. adjusting	11.03	9.55	−1.48	21.00	19.51	−1.49	23.55	18.29	−5.25	31.49	39.85	8.36	5.47	4.82	−0.65	0.87
Int. adj.	12.38	9.87	−2.51	21.43	19.67	−1.76	25.15	19.08	−6.07	25.88	36.85	10.98	5.28	4.74	−0.54	0.91
Other adj.	8.98	9.29	0.31	19.39	19.33	−0.05	20.79	16.77	−4.03	41.27	45.15	3.88	5.79	4.94	−0.84	0.95
Other	10.90	10.65	−0.25	17.80	20.86	3.06	24.38	20.46	−3.92	31.92	30.03	−1.89	4.88	5.05	0.18	0.90
All	10.92	9.82	−1.10	20.09	19.96	−0.13	23.71	18.76	−4.95	31.42	37.02	5.60	5.29	4.90	−0.40	0.91

	Share of												H+E as % GNP			Index of 1990 (1981)
	Defence			Health and education			Economic			Other, inc. interest						
	1981	1990	Change	1981	1990	Change	1981	1990	Change	1981	1990	Change	1981	1990	Change	
Proportion countries increasing																
Africa–All		0.47			0.29			0.41			0.71			0.24		0.46
Africa adjusting		0.46			0.23			0.46			0.69			0.23		0.23
Africa–other		0.50			0.50			0.25			0.75			0.25		0.75
Latin America–All		0.50			0.50			0.12			0.73			0.33		0.28
Latin America adjusting		0.45			0.45			0.18			0.80			0.27		0.45
Latin America–other		0.57			0.57			0.00			0.60			0.43		0.00
Other regions–All		0.17			0.83			0.17			0.83			0.58		0.83
Other regions adjusting		0.22			0.78			0.22			0.78			0.44		0.78
Other regions–other		0.00			1.00			0.00			1.00			1.00		1.00
All regions–All		0.40			0.51			0.24			0.75			0.36		0.49
All regions adjusting		0.39			0.45			0.30			0.75			0.30		0.45
All regions – other		0.43			0.64			0.21			0.73			0.50		0.50

Sources: World Bank, *World Development Reports* (various); UNDP, *Human Development Report 1992*

public expenditure, for which the potential is strong because of the high expenditure ratios.

Despite falling incomes, some countries succeeded in raising government expenditure per head by heavy emphasis on deficit finance (category B3). Consequently, their deficits rose to an unsustainable position, as for example Nigeria and Brazil, where the tax base collapsed and the deficit rose to over 10 per cent of GNP. This is not, then, a pattern to be emulated.

A final category of bad experience is represented by countries which exhibited growth in per capita incomes but, because of falling expenditure ratios, failed to translate this growth into increased per capita government expenditure (category B4). Examples were Malaysia and Jamaica.

CHANGES IN ALLOCATION RATIOS IN THE 1980s

There were certain changes in allocation ratios in the 1980s shared by every region (see Table 3.6). There was a general decline in the share of defence expenditure across all regions, and a general rise in the 'other' category which includes interest payments. We shall assume for ease of exposition that this category can be described as interest payments – this is borne out by other analyses measuring interest payments directly, which show a rise in the share of interest in the majority of countries in each region, with an average rise in selected countries of over 10 per cent of government expenditure in Latin America, nearly 6 per cent in Africa and about 5 per cent in Asia.[11] According to our data, the rise in interest payments, as a proportion of government expenditure, greatly exceeded the fall in the share of defence, the latter falling by 1 per cent for all regions, and the former rising by 5.6 per cent.

There was also a near-universal fall in the share of government expenditure going to 'economic' expenditure (which consists largely of expenditure on economic infrastructure) – only sub-Saharan Africa showed little change, while there were large falls in Latin America and other regions.

Changes in social allocation ratios differed across regions, with a fall in Africa, a slight rise in Latin America and a significant rise in other areas. When health and education expenditure is expressed as a share of GNP, it fell on average in both Latin America (LA) and sub-Saharan Africa (SSA), but rose in other areas. Marked regional differences occurred in the change in level of government expenditure per capita on health and education, with a fall of similar proportions (around 15 per cent) in Latin America and SSA, and a big rise (about 65 per cent) in Asia. This difference is due to the combined effect of negative growth in per capita incomes in SSA and LA, compared with positive growth in Asia, together with more favourable meso-policies in Asia.

There was a big difference between adjusting and non-adjusting countries in changes in allocation ratios: the adjusting countries showed a large rise in the share of expenditure going to interest rates (8.4 per cent more of their government expenditure being devoted to this category) and a small fall in the share going to social sectors, while the non-adjusting group showed a small *fall* in the share going to interest payments and a *rise* in the share going to the social sectors. The share of GNP going to the social sectors rose in the case of the non-adjusting countries (by 1.5 per cent points) and fell in adjusting countries (by 3.1 per cent).

The combined effect of changing expenditure ratio and social allocation ratios over the period led to a *fall* in the share of health and education in GNP among adjusting countries, compared with a small rise among the non-adjusting. All categories of countries experienced a fall, on average, in government expenditure per head on the social sectors with little difference between the categories; as noted above, the big difference was between all categories of country in 'other regions' with a positive change, and the negative performance in Latin America and Africa.

Performance was by no means uniform within any category or region – as indicated by the proportions of countries changing their allocation ratios. For example, in Africa over 20 per cent of the adjusting countries succeeded in raising their social allocation ratio, and the same proportion raised expenditure per head on the social sectors.

If we define success as an increase in per capita expenditure on health and education, the following categories can be distinguished:

- Those countries which had positive growth in per capita incomes whose meso-policies were also favourable (raising the proportion of GNP going to the social sectors). An example is Turkey which enjoyed positive growth, increased the expenditure and the social allocation ratios (while cutting the share of defence), experiencing an increase of three-quarters in expenditure per head on health and education. More mixed but still positive meso-policies combined with positive economic growth occurred in Sri Lanka and Cameroon which succeeded in raising the proportion of GNP going to health and education even while experiencing a fall in the expenditure ratio through increasing social allocation ratios. Per capita expenditure on health and education rose by about a quarter in both these countries.

- Those countries which had positive growth in per capita incomes whose meso-policies were unfavourable, but not sufficiently so to offset the effects of rising incomes. A good example was South Korea which showed a small decline in the share of GNP going to publicly financed health and education (owing to a fall in the expenditure ratio), but nonetheless doubled real expenditure per head on health and education.

- Those countries which succeeded in raising per capita expenditure on health and education through meso-policies, despite a fall in per capita incomes, including: Ghana, Zimbabwe, Uruguay and Panama. In all except Panama both the expenditure and the social allocation ratios moved positively, with in each case some fall in the allocation to defence. Ghana, like Panama, was helped by a decline in the share of interest payments, due to arrangements made by the international community to substitute soft for hard loans and rearrange payments obligations. But in Zimbabwe and Uruguay, the share of both the economic and the interest payments categories were maintained or increased and the improved social allocation came entirely at the expense of defence. In Panama, the increase in the social allocation ratio was substantial (10.4 per cent of public expenditure – achieved at the expense of a combination of defence, interest and economic categories) and offset a reduction of 4.5 per cent of GNP in the expenditure ratio.

In contrast, some countries had negative meso-policies throughout with falling expenditure and social allocation ratios, accentuating the ill-effects of negative growth. They included: Ecuador, Mexico, Malawi, Zaire, Zambia, Togo and Tanzania. Some countries' unfavourable meso-policies were such as to lead to a fall in government expenditure per head on health and education, despite positive economic growth, including Jamaica, Morocco and Indonesia.

As can be seen from Table 3.7, the adjustment lending countries (both intensive and other) present examples of both good and bad experiences of meso-policies. In some cases, the net effect was a dramatically large drop in expenditure on the social sectors – as in Zambia and Tanzania, with falls of over 60 per cent, or Mexico and Morocco, with falls of over 30 per cent. In other cases, meso-policies led to a significant increase in expenditure on the social sectors during adjustment – increases of 40 per cent or more in Panama and Ghana.

Table 3.7 Meso-policies in selected adjusting countries

Country	Change in E*	Change in (H+E)/E	Change in (H+E)/Y	Growth in per capita y	Index of expenditure per capita on H + E
'Good' meso-policies					
Sri Lanka	−5.0	+4.6	+0.8	+2.4	1.27
Panama	−4.3	+10.4	+2.2	−1.9	1.40
Ghana[a]	+3.9	+5.7	+2.0	−0.8	1.54
Zimbabwe	+9.2	+4.6	+4.9	−1.1	1.39
Uruguay[a]	+2.6	+0.4	+0.4	−0.6	1.09
'Bad' meso-policies					
Ecuador	−1.5	−8.8	−1.9	−0.6	0.67
Mexico[a]	−11.4	−4.3	−1.3	−1.5	0.61
Malawi[a]	−6.1	−0.1	−1.1	−1.4	0.73
Zambia[a]	−17.9	−2.0	−3.7	−3.5	0.36
Tanzania[a]	−12.1	−11.9	−3.0	−2.4	0.29
Jamaica[a]	−6.3	−1.5	−2.0	+0.3	0.83
Morocco[a]	−10.7	+0.5	−1.9	+1.9	0.64
Indonesia[a]	−6.0	0	−0.6	+3.6	0.82

(a) Intensively adjusting.

PRIORITY RATIOS IN THE 1980s

It is not possible to take a comprehensive view of changing priority ratios in the 1980s because of the scarcity of data on the intra-sectoral allocation of resources. However, the limited evidence available suggests that the priority ratio in the health sector was very low and did not improve, while in the education sector the evidence is more mixed. Health sector data from sixteen African and Latin American countries with relatively complete information on levels of care show that despite the overall decline affecting many countries, hospitals continued to absorb an inordinately high proportion of total health care expenditure, i.e. between 80 and 90 per cent.[12] In countries with a strong focus on primary health care, such as China, this proportion was around 60 per cent. Evidence for thirteen countries in Latin America between 1980 and 1985 shows that the hospital sector received an increasing share of total health sector resources and/or the primary sector a decreasing share in eleven countries.[13] Evidence for five sub-Saharan African countries showed a rise in the proportion of public expenditure devoted to hospitals in three and a fall in two from the late 1970s to the mid-1980s.[14]

Thus, the fiscal crisis did not trigger a systematic redistribution of health care resources towards the subsectors with higher social rates of return, indicating the difficult political and technical problems involved in the process of reallocation. However, there were a few important innovations in the health sector, with the spread of some low-cost, high-impact and pro-poor primary health care interventions, such as child immunisation and oral rehydration therapy, in most developing countries, including those affected by fiscal cuts. With rates of coverage for these activities growing on average by around 20–30 per cent between 1981 and 1989, considerable welfare gains were obtained with relatively modest government financial resources.

In the education sector, there is wide variation across countries in the proportion of educational expenditure going to primary education in 1987–8, ranging from 21 per cent in Venezuela to 83 per cent in Chad, suggesting considerable scope for reallocation of educational expenditures in some countries. Evidence on changes during the adjustment period is mixed. According to Colclough and Lewin 'there is some evidence, . . . that secondary and tertiary systems have been more protected, throughout the years of recession and adjustment, than primary schooling.'[15] They estimate that real public expenditure per pupil declined by about 40 per cent in Latin America, 1980–7, and by about 65 per cent in Africa; primary school enrolment fell, 1980–7, in Africa, while secondary enrolment continued to rise. Moreover, data for 1980–3 show a sharper decline in real recurrent expenditure per pupil in primary schools in Africa than other levels. However, a study of twenty-three African countries showed that primary education secured an increased share in fifteen.[16] Among eight Latin American countries, five increased the proportion going to primary education and only two reduced it.[17] A study of ten adjusting countries from all regions showed that five countries improved the primary share of public expenditure, in two cases there was no change and in three the primary share fell.[18]

To some extent, improvements in the primary school ratio appear to have been at the expense of secondary education, not tertiary. Thus among the African countries reported on by Dougna (1987), more countries decreased their allocation to secondary education (ten) than to tertiary education (eight), and more increased their allocation to tertiary (nine) than secondary (five).[19] Among Latin American countries, six out of seven countries decreased their allocation to secondary schools, while only three out of seven decreased the allocation to tertiary education.[20] While the reallocation towards primary education is desirable, both from the point of view of equity and economic efficiency, the changing balance between secondary and tertiary education is likely to have worked in the opposite direction. Most evidence shows higher returns to primary education than secondary, and secondary than tertiary education.[21] Evidence for Sri Lanka shows that the poorest 20 per cent of the population received 27 per cent of the benefits from primary education, 17 per cent of those from secondary education and 12 per cent from tertiary, while the richest 20 per cent received 14 per cent of the benefits from primary education, 25 per cent from secondary and 32 per cent from tertiary.[22]

There is also evidence for a few countries that *adult* education has been squeezed over these years: for example, in Tanzania, the share of adult education in recurrent expenditure fell from 7.5 per cent (1982–3) to 3.8 per cent (1986–7).[23]

Despite the evidence cited showing that priority ratios improved in the majority of adjusting countries (which relates to the years up to 1987), a review of the implementation of ten World Bank loans between 1987 and 1990 that contained specific recommendations for reallocation of expenditure within the educational sector towards primary education showed that there was no recorded success: project and supervision reports showed five cases of lack of success, with no assessments in the remaining cases.[24] The main reason for lack of success seems to have been resistance to cuts in the tertiary sector; for example, in Senegal scholarships were supposed to fall, but in fact they rose by a third, while growth in expenditure in Dakar University was more than twice the rate intended. Similarly, there was resistance to cutbacks among students in Ghana and in Morocco the slowdown in university entrants was not achieved. In Morocco, the attempt to negotiate a second Education Loan with the Bank failed because of lack of agreement on the need to reallocate funds to basic education.[25]

Like expenditure and social allocation ratios, priority ratios behaved differently in different countries, indicating that this too is an area in which governments can make choices which may protect against or accentuate the effects of macro-changes. For example, in Chile, during a time of considerable expenditure cuts, the priority ratio in education (the share of primary and secondary education) improved markedly as the state retreated from tertiary education, with the tertiary share falling from 34 per cent in 1980 to 3 per cent in 1986. In Zimbabwe, which became an independent country in 1980 determined to correct the inherited inequity in health and education, there was a large rise in the proportion of national income devoted to the social sectors and a rise in the proportion of that expenditure going to primary schools and primary health care over the first half of the 1980s. From 1979/80 to 1985/6 the proportion of expenditure allocated to preventive services rose from 8 per cent of total health expenditure to 14 per cent – this proportion then stabilised for the rest of the decade; the proportion of the education budget going to primary education rose from 64.5 per cent in 1980 to 74.8 per cent in 1986, but there was some decline over subsequent years.[26] Gross enrolment rates doubled in primary schools leading to universal primary education. In contrast, in Venezuela where over half the education budget goes to tertiary education, and there are similar misallocations of health budgets, there were few reforms in the 1980s despite increasing poverty. An increasing proportion of the health budget went to hospital medicine, 1983–8, and the immunisation rate actually fell over the decade, in contrast to developments almost everywhere.[27] In Costa Rica, the social sector expenditure cuts of the first half of the 1980s fell most heavily on priority areas, and the share of the bottom 40 per cent of households in educational expenditure fell from 42 per cent in 1980 to 36 per cent in 1986 as the share of primary and secondary education fell.

Aggregate effects of adjustment on the education sector

Several aggregate cross-section studies have estimated the effects of adjustment policies on the education sector, following similar methodologies to those used for assessing the macro-effects of adjustment described in the previous chapter. The results are summarised in Table 3.8. Two studies showed no clear effects, but the two most comprehensive studies showed negative effects on all educational indicators, including education expenditure as a share of government expenditure, education expenditure per student and the gross primary enrolment rate.

Expenditure cuts by input type

A comprehensive analysis of countries whose overall government expenditure fell over the 1970–84 period indicates that capital expenditure was cut most severely. It fell on average 65 per cent more than overall expenditure.[28] Wages and other recurrent inputs were relatively protected since they fell less than the average and in similar proportions (15 and 18 per cent, respectively), while subsidies declined even less. In contrast, expenditure on interest payments more than doubled, confirming the earlier findings.

Another analysis covering thirty-six countries, whether experiencing expenditure cuts or not, over the 1979–83 period broadly supports these findings, i.e.

Table 3.8 Methodologies to analyse the impacts of adjustment on education

Methodology	Source	Number of countries	Economic indicators	Education indicators	Conclusion
Before and after adjustment	Sahn, 1989	16	Public budget (real and percentage of GDP)	Education spending (real and share of discretionary public budget)	No clear impacts of adjustment
Comparison of countries suffering fiscal duress with others	Gallagher 1990	35	GDP growth	Education spending (share of total and discretionary public budgets) Gross enrolment rates (primary and secondary)	No clear impacts of adjustment
Adjusting versus non-adjusting countries	Kakwani Makonnen and van der Gaag, 1989	86	Public budgets (total and discretionary[a] as percentage of GDP) Per capita pricate consumption	Education spending (share of total and discretionary public budgets, GDP) Per capita spending Primary enrolment rates (gross and net) Growth of primary school teachers Student/teacher ratios	Intense adjustment related to declines in all education indicators
Adjusting versus non-adjusting countries	RAL II (World Bank, 1990a)	78	GDP growth Public debt Public deficit Savinings, investment rates Per capita private consumption	Education spending (percentage of discretionary public budget and GDP) Per capita expenditures (annual change) Gross primary enrolment rate	Intense adjustment related to declines in all education indicators

Source: Noss, 1991
(a) 'Discretionary' means total expenditure less interest payments

capital expenditure was the most severely affected (in 70 per cent) followed by expenditure on subsidies. Wages and recurrent inputs were the least affected.[29] Other detailed analyses confirm this broad pattern of expenditure cuts. A study of health care spending in Central America and the Caribbean in the early 1980s shows that there was a tendency for fixed capital formation to decline sharply, while no or only modest cuts were apparent for wages and inputs (including medicines).[30]

In conclusion, there is some evidence that the ways in which cuts were apportioned limited the short-run negative effects of the decline in overall government expenditure. But marginal populations not yet reached by public infrastructure and future generations will be affected by the resulting lack of services. There are bureaucratic and political advantages in focusing cuts on investment rather than consumption. It may also be a logical procedure if the need to cut expenditure is expected to be temporary. However, in the social sectors the most deprived (those who do not yet have access to basic services) then bear the biggest loss.

Food subsidies and targeting

Reductions in food subsidies are a common element of IMF and World Bank adjustment programmes. In some cases, general food subsidies are replaced by targeted subsidies. Some implications of these changes are discussed in the next chapter. We show there that the replacement of general by targeted subsidies tends to increase the proportion of the total subsidy received by lower income households, but targeted subsidies also typically fail to reach a higher proportion of the poor than general subsidies. In terms of the meso-ratios, the reductions in food subsidies thus are likely to have had the effect of reducing the 'food' social allocation ratio; the targeting probably improved the priority ratio (or the proportion of the food subsidy being received by the poor), but many of the poor were left out, so that the net effect was often a reduction in the welfare of the poor. Of course, those poor households who never previously received food subsidies (particularly many rural households) were unaffected by the changes and in some cases – especially if targeted subsidies were introduced in a situation where previously there had been no general subsidies – the poor were net beneficiaries.[31]

The introduction of user fees

User charges are a common element in adjustment packages. They are justified as improving welfare and reducing waste, as well as providing an additional source of government revenue. Elementary welfare theory suggests that re-source allocation is optimised when people pay the marginal costs of goods or services consumed because they will then only consume the good if the additional utility accruing as a result is at least as great as the extra costs incurred. In the absence of user charges, excess consumption will occur diverting resources from where they would generate higher utility. This simple argument is behind the proposals to introduce user charges in many areas, including water, health and education.[32]

There are a number of flaws in the argument. First, where social returns exceed private returns and/or the consumer is unaware of the returns – as in both health and education – charging marginal cost will deter use to below what is socially optimal. Secondly, in both sectors the person making the choice is frequently not the person enjoying the benefit (i.e. parents decide on behalf of children) so that utility maximisation is an inappropriate approach. For both primary health and education, universal use is generally accepted as a desirable goal, so any measures which lead to reduced use are undesirable. Thirdly, the incidence of primary health and education is progressive, relative to original income and to most other forms of government expenditure.[33] Unless low-income groups are exempt, charges tend to be regressive and to deter the poor from using the services most.

User charges were introduced in many countries in Africa, Latin America and, to a lesser extent, Asia as part of the adjustment process, in some cases with attempts to exempt the poorest. A survey of the large literature on this subject shows that a number of efficiency and welfare problems have resulted from the implementation of these schemes.[34]

First, fees contributed a relatively small proportion to the budgets of the ministries involved. In the case of the health sector in Africa, for instance, fee systems currently yield gross-averages of around 5 per cent of the total operating costs of the sector, with a maximum of 15 per cent in Ghana. If the costs of collecting the fees are included, the yields would be lower and, in some cases, negative. In such circumstances, user fees are not efficient as a revenue-raising device.

Secondly, in a good number of countries, revenues from fees in the health sector go entirely to the ministries of finance. In this way, fees become a mechanism of fiscal policy, rather than an instrument of health policy; while other sectors receive more funds, the health sector may contract because of the decline in demand for health care services induced by the fees.

Thirdly: 'the bulk of the available evidence appears to confirm that, whilst user-charges for health care can generate additional income, they also deter patients at greatest risks. . . . Equity in health care is thus deteriorating, measurably, in access to care terms, and probably also in health status differentials between socio-economic groups'.[35]

One reason is that attempts to exempt poorer groups were frequently largely ineffective. For example, in Zimbabwe in 1991 school fees were introduced for primary schools in the urban areas, and for secondary schools throughout the country. Despite provision for refunds for children from poorer homes, complex procedures for refunds meant that only 3 per cent of the school population, or 12.5 per cent of the target population, were covered. A survey of textile and cloth workers showed that 40 per cent had reduced their children's schooling, including taking children out of school, or not sending them to the next level of education.[36] Similarly, increased health charges were reflected in a fall in use of health care facilities; twenty-one primary health care units showed a drop of a quarter in their caseloads, with a similar decline in clinics and hospitals from 1991 to 1992.[37]

Many studies confirm that the price elasticity of demand declines as income rises. A study of health care financing in Peru, for instance, found just this, implying that undifferentiated fees reduce the access to health care proportionately more for the poor than for the rich.[38] Several investigations of the effects of the introduction of user fees on the utilisation of health systems support these conclusions; country studies include Zaire, Ghana, Kenya, Lesotho, Swaziland and the United Kingdom.[39] In all of these countries, the introduction of fees led to a decline in utilisation rates, which was greater for the poor than more affluent consumers. In education, charges introduced for primary education as part of adjustment loans in the early 1980s led to a decline in use – e.g. in Malawi. Later, the World Bank stopped recommending primary school fees, although they still enter some adjustment packages, as noted above in the case of Zimbabwe.

Taking intra-sectoral issues as a whole, we find that during adjustment there was some tendency for the priority ratio in education to improve and that in health to worsen. Reduced food subsidies and the introduction of user fees for health and education have tended to increase the absolute burden on the poor, as the system of targeting and exemptions has been 'leaky' so that many of the poor faced increased costs for these essential items.

MESO-CHOICES: TAXATION POLICIES

The ways in which the poor are affected by the tax system during adjustment depend on the design of the tax system and the changes which occur with adjustment. Taxes are generally categorised as direct taxes (levied on incomes and profits), indirect (levied on goods and services) and social security contributions (levied on formal-sector employers and employees). Direct taxes are almost invariably progressive and rarely affect the poor. The distributional impact of indirect taxes depends on their design. The main indirect taxes paid by low-income households are those that affect food, the sources of energy and transport used by the poor, and drink and tobacco. Indirect taxes can be designed to fall heaviest on luxury consumption goods and thus can be progressive. Indirect taxes on production (normally in the form of export taxes) may fall on the poor if the poor are involved in production for export. Social security contributions are only paid in the formal sector where, typically, workers are relatively well paid, and thus poor households are not normally affected. However, with large cuts in real wages of formal sector employees, some poor households may be required to pay social security contributions.

In addition to taxation, many countries receive a significant proportion of revenue from publicly-owned enterprises. The distributional incidence of this depends on what the parastatals are producing and who is consuming the production; it is unlikely to fall heavily on the poor.

A precise assessment of the distributional incidence of the tax system in a particular country and of the way changes over time affect the incidence, therefore, requires careful country studies of tax incidence. But these are not available on any scale, nor especially incorporating changes over time. Here we can only record changes in the main categories of taxation, starting with the presumption that the rich pay more direct taxes and the poor pay more indirect taxes.

IMF and World Bank programmes have tended to support a shift from direct to indirect taxes in the tax reforms associated with adjustment. Analysis of Fund programmes, 1980–4, showed increases in taxes which were likely to be progressive occurred in a smaller proportion of the programmes than increases in taxes which were probably regressive (Table 3.9). In WB programmes, a sample of adjusting countries indicates a falling proportion of income tax (except for middle-income countries), a rising proportion of sales taxes, with the remaining categories showing no systematic trends (Table 3.10).

Table 3.9 Fiscal changes in seventy-eight Fund
            programmes, 1980–4

	Programmes (%)
More 'progressive' taxes/subsidies	
Increase in personal income	11.5
Income tax reform or tax extension	17.9
Corporation tax surcharge	12.8
Collection of corporation tax arrears	7.7
Introduce/raise land taxes	5.1
Introduce/raise urban property tax	6.4
Increase tax on petrol	38.5
Reduced petrol subsidies	26.9
More 'regressive' taxes	
Reduce personal income tax	6.4
Reduce corporation tax	14.1
Raise excise taxes	53.8
Raise sales taxes	28.2
Reduced food subsidy	34.6

Source: From IMF, 1986

Changes in tax incidence during adjustment by region are summarised in Table 3.11. In every region there was a fall in the share of direct taxes in total revenue, which was more marked among adjusting than non-adjusting countries. In Africa and Latin America, there was also a fall in indirect taxes – in Latin America, the fall was much bigger than the fall in direct tax share. An increase

Table 3.10 Changing tax structure in sample of countries with World Bank adjustment loans[a]

| | Total tax revenue (%) | | | | | |
| | Low-income countries | | Middle-income countries | | Sub-Saharan Africa | |
	Pre-adjustment	Post-adjustment	Pre-adjustment	Post-adjustment	Pre-adjustment	Post-adjustment
Income tax	38.7	33.7	25.3	27.0	33.8	25.0
Sales tax	27.3	35.4	40.3	42.1	21.1	26.8
Trade tax	28.0	19.4	24.0	23.7	38.8	47.6
Other tax	6.0	10.9	9.7	6.5	6.3	1.2

Source: World Bank, 1992b
(a) Covers ninety-nine adjustment operations, involving forty-two countries

in 'other' revenue makes up the difference. 'Other' includes social security contributions (important only in Latin America), payroll taxes, property taxes, 'taxes not allocable to other categories'[40] and non-tax revenue (e.g. fines, income from state property and parastatals). The share of social security contributions rose in six countries in Latin America and fell in six, with little change on average.

Table 3.11 Changes in tax structure in the 1980s

	Share in current revenue of								
	Direct taxes			Indirect taxes			Other		
	1981	*1990*	*change*	*1981*	*1990*	*change*	*1981*	*1990*	*change*
Africa									
Av. adjusting	31.32	29.82	−1.50	52.01	51.35	−0.66	16.67	18.83	2.16
Int. adj.	31.87	30.18	−1.69	53.98	51.89	−2.09	14.15	17.93	3.78
Other adj.	30.50	29.28	−1.22	49.05	50.55	1.50	20.45	20.17	−0.28
Other	29.48	38.85	9.37	54.88	41.85	−13.03	15.64	19.30	3.66
All	30.93	31.72	0.79	52.61	49.35	−3.26	16.46	18.93	2.47
Latin America									
Av. adjusting	24.14	23.08	−1.06	44.91	37.28	−7.63	30.95	39.64	8.69
Int. adj.	18.20	17.21	−0.99	51.03	43.33	−7.70	30.77	39.46	8.69
Other adj.	37.28	33.35	−3.93	34.20	26.70	−7.50	28.52	39.95	11.43
Other	15.28	14.93	−0.35	56.62	56.82	0.20	28.10	28.25	0.15
All	21.66	20.21	−1.45	49.04	44.18	−4.86	29.30	35.61	6.31
Other regions									
Av. adjusting	27.91	26.67	−1.24	50.57	53.04	2.47	21.52	20.29	−1.23
Int. adj.	25.02	26.47	1.45	52.35	53.88	1.53	22.63	19.65	−2.98
Other adj.	33.70	27.07	−6.63	47.00	51.37	4.37	19.30	21.56	2.26
Other	13.07	12.07	−1.00	61.33	60.23	−1.10	25.60	27.70	2.10
All	24.20	23.02	−1.18	53.26	54.84	1.58	22.54	22.14	−0.40
All areas									
Av. adjusting	28.19	26.89	−1.29	49.41	47.36	−2.05	22.41	25.75	3.34
Int. adj.	25.65	25.04	−0.61	52.60	49.71	−2.89	21.75	25.25	3.50
Other adj.	33.32	30.02	−3.30	44.01	43.40	−0.61	22.67	26.58	3.91
Other	19.14	21.63	2.49	57.17	53.00	−4.17	23.69	25.37	1.68
All	25.96	25.47	−0.50	51.51	48.89	−2.62	22.53	25.64	3.11
Proportion countries increasing									
Africa – All		0.58			0.37				
Africa adjusting		0.47			0.47				
Africa – other		1.00			0.00				
Latin America – All		0.35			0.35				
Latin America adjusting		0.27			0.27				
Latin America – other		0.50			0.50				
Other regions – All		0.42			0.42				
Other regions adjusting		0.44			0.44				
Other regions – other		0.33			0.33				
All regions – All		0.46			0.38				
All regions adjusting		0.40			0.40				
All regions – other		0.62			0.31				

Sources: World Bank, *World Development Reports* (various); UNDP, *Human Development Report 1992*

Contrasting experience is to be observed between countries: a large increase in the proportion of revenue raised by direct taxation occurred in South Korea, the Philippines and Ecuador, while in Bolivia, Venezuela and Indonesia there was a particularly large switch from direct to indirect taxation. Although the IFIs were normally associated with a switch to indirect taxes, in the Philippines, alarmed by the fall in total tax revenue from 1980 to 1985, the government was asked to explore the possibility of introducing a property tax and a capital gains tax as well as being encouraged to introduce a value-added tax.[41]

It is difficult to be definitive about the incidence of taxation over these years, but it seems that the changes were probably on balance regressive, particularly in adjusting countries. It is probable that direct taxes are more progressive than all other sources of revenue taken together. Consequently, the fall in direct tax share would suggest some decline in progressivity. Moreover, tax reform also often modified the progressivity of income taxes (reducing high rates proportionately more) and that of indirect taxes (by reducing tax and tariff differentials). But one cannot say more without detailed country studies.

CONCLUSIONS ON MESO-POLICIES

There are two types of conclusion from this analysis. First, there are some broad tendencies associated with adjustment policies. Secondly, on the basis of the variety of experience observed we can conclude that countries can and do make choices during adjustment which can either make an unfavourable situation worse for the poor, or can protect people from negative tendencies. The broad tendencies observed above are:

1 Fiscal choices in Africa reinforced the effect of declining per capita incomes, leading to a fall in government expenditure per head in most adjusting and non-adjusting countries.[42] Adjusting and non-adjusting countries showed a significant decline in the expenditure ratio in Africa; there was a smaller fall in the revenue ratio and an improvement in the budget deficit. In contrast, in Latin America, intensively adjusting countries succeeded in raising the revenue and expenditure ratios and, as a consequence, achieved a small rise in government expenditure per head. But the other countries, including OALs, had a large fall in expenditure ratios, and suffered a fall in government expenditure per head. In Asia, fiscal policies showed smaller changes, but government expenditure per head rose (in adjusting and non-adjusting countries) as a result of rising per capita incomes.

2 The social allocation ratio fell among adjusting countries and rose among non-adjusting countries. The converse occurred with respect to interest payments, which rose sharply among adjusting and fell among non-adjusting, as a share of total expenditure.

3 The net result of changes in expenditure ratios and in social allocation ratios was a fall in the share of health and education in GNP among adjusting

countries, and a rise in the share among non-adjusting. Thus meso-policies taken together were, on average, unfavourable for the social sectors in Africa and Latin America, with a small favourable change in Asia. Priority ratios showed some improvement in the education sector on balance, and some worsening in the health sector (evidence for Latin America only).

4 Per capita expenditure on the social sectors fell significantly among adjusting countries in Africa and Latin America, by around 30 per cent in Africa and 13 per cent in Latin America. It rose substantially in other regions. There are no significant differences to be observed as between adjusting and non-adjusting countries in any region.

5 Cuts in food subsidies formed part of many adjustment programmes. Although they were sometimes replaced by targeted subsidies, the real value of the subsidies was rarely maintained and the system of targeting generally led to a large proportion of poor people being left out. (Evidence on this follows in the next chapter.)

6 User charges for health, education and other services were also part of the programmes – in principle, in many cases the poor were exempt; in practice, the system of exemption was often imperfect.

7 Changes in the tax system led to a fall in the proportion of direct taxes in the total revenue, which would be likely to mean that the poor pay a higher proportion of the total. But the precise incidence of the changes is not known.

While the broad tendencies of meso-policies were unfavourable to social sector expenditure and the poor during adjustment, there were exceptions, with some countries having favourable meso-policies which protected social sector expenditure even during a time of falling per capita incomes; conversely some countries had particularly unfavourable meso-policies. Examples of the former are Ghana and Zimbabwe; in both, health and education expenditure increased as a per centage of GDP and government expenditure per head rose, despite falling incomes; in Ghana this was accompanied by a reduced government deficit. In Latin America, Panama and Uruguay raised government expenditure per head on the social sectors over these years, despite negative growth, and both slightly improved their budget deficits. (Brazil also raised government expenditure per head on the social services but largely at the expense of a greatly increased budget deficit.) Countries with positive growth, such as Mauritius, Chile and many of the Asian countries, also achieved rising per capita expenditure on the social sectors, but this was due more to successful macro-rather than meso-policies.

In contrast, countries with particularly unfavourable meso-policies included Tanzania and Zaire, with huge falls in the share of national income going to the social sectors, and, in Latin America, Mexico and Ecuador. In each, expenditure ratios and social allocation ratios worsened over the period.

The fact that there were some good performers in a generally adverse environment indicates that countries had some choices. But not many exercised these choices in a way that protected the poor. They were constrained by external influences – notably from the Fund and Bank – by internal bureaucratic and political problems, as well as by their own political objectives and/or indifference to the plight of the poor.

The Fund and Bank programmes pushed countries in certain directions. First, both Fund and Bank strongly opposed deficit financing; while excessive deficits are not desirable, the IFIs pushed further and faster than was desirable, given the social problems. The Fund particularly emphasised expenditure reduction rather than tax increases as a way of reducing the deficit. Secondly, both gave priority to repaying overdue debt and respecting debt service obligations. For much of the 1980s, this was given first call in adjustment programmes, so that the fruits of the considerable success in raising revenue and in improving the trade balance in adjusting countries in Latin America were devoted to debt service payments rather than to protecting social and economic expenditures.[43] Similar emphasis was given in Africa – in Ghana, for example, the first IMF loan required repayment of a large amount of commercial credit; subsequent World Bank loans involved further commercial repayments as well as repaying the IMF.[44] Thirdly, elements of the Fund/Bank programmes, notably policies towards food subsidies and user charges, led to increased burdens for the poor.

Countries, however, were not obliged to follow every letter of the IFIs' programme. They could negotiate about the details and timing of the conditions if not the broad direction, while there was considerable laxity in fulfilling some of the conditions agreed.[45] The variation in choices we have observed among adjusting countries attestifies to this. Mosley has argued that the extent of a country's freedom to depart from the Fund/Bank conditions depends on its bargaining power.[46] Countries which depend critically on the finance the Bank can provide have very little freedom of choice. But countries with alternative sources of finance can be more independent. Contrast the on–off relationship of Nigeria to the World Bank – a large and powerful country with oil revenue – with that of Malawi, for example.

Another constraint countries faced was that emanating from their own bureaucracies. These made it difficult to take 'rational' choices about expenditure cuts. Inevitably, existing programmes had more support than new programmes; hospitals were less severely affected than primary clinics; and, the extent of cuts in defence expenditure were less than outsiders might think was desirable. A further constraint was imposed by local political forces: as we saw above, some of the Education Loan requirements for a switch of resources away from the tertiary sector were unsuccessful largely because of opposition from students. Attempts to remove food and petroleum subsidies often met vocal and sometimes violent opposition – as for example, in Zambia, the Sudan and Venezuela. Neither bureaucratic nor political forces tended to be pro-poor, although the poor might benefit as part of a wider and more powerful group, as in the case of some comprehensive food subsidies which benefited urban workers.

Governments were certainly constrained by external and internal forces; yet freedom remained within these constraints which permitted some countries to adopt meso-policies which were pro-poor, while others compounded the adverse macro-developments by their meso-choices.

NOTES

1 This chapter draws heavily on material from Cornia and Stewart, 1990.
2 But it must be emphasised that these estimates include only central government expenditure, so can be seriously misleading for those countries where expenditure by regional authorities is important. Federal countries have been omitted to avoid gross distortions.
3 The data for income per head is adjusted for purchasing power parity.
4 Purchasing power parity (PPP) estimates of income by country correct money estimates for disequilibrium exchange rates and other distortions, following the methodology of Summers and Heston, 1988. Data come from UNDP, 1992.
5. Some of the variation is likely to be because not all the relevant expenditure has been included because of decentralisation. This is almost certainly why the ratios of Pakistan and Indonesia seem so low.
6 The methodology is very crude and could be greatly improved. Progress might be made by including other variables as well as human development expenditure on the input side; by improving measures of human development 'output'; and by micro-studies of the effects of human development expenditures.
7 Heller et al., 1988, p. 22
8 World Bank, 1992a, p. 51.
9 Toye, 1991; see also Johnson and Salop, 1980; Streeten, 1987.
10 See also Meerman, 1979.
11 Cornia and Stewart, 1990.
12 IMF, 1990.
13 Chapter 7, Table 7.15.
14 George et al., 1994.
15 Colclough and Lewin, 1991, p. 12.
16 Data from Background Paper for World Conference for Education for All, Thailand, 1990.
17 Grosh, 1990a.
18 Noss, 1991.
19 Quoted in Berstecher and Carr-Hill, 1990.
20 Grosh, 1990a.
21 See Schultz, 1989, Table 1; Psacharopoulos, 1980. Knight and Sabot, 1990, have also shown that restrictions on secondary education in Tanzania had inegalitarian consequences, as the shortages of secondary graduates caused high wage differentials, in comparison with Kenya where secondary education was much more widespread.
22 Alaihima, 1984; see Grosh, 1990a, for similar evidence for a number of Latin American countries.
23 Wagao, 1990.
24 Stevenson, 1991, Table 9: 'Intra-sectoral resource allocation measures have been largely unsuccessful'.
25 Stevenson, 1991.
26 Davies et al., 1991.
27 See Angell and Graham, 1994a and b; they note that Venezuela's health budget per capita is more than three times more than those in Chile, Jamaica or Panama, yet infant mortality rates are considerably higher.

28 Hicks, 1991.
29 Pinstrup-Andersen *et al.*, 1987.
30 Musgrove, 1987.
31 Angell and Graham, 1994b, suggest that the Venezuela targeted nutrition scheme which replaced general subsidies was a definite improvement for the poor.
32 For health, see World Bank, 1987.
33 Grosh, 1990a.
34 Creese, 1990; Nolan and Turbat, 1993.
35 Creese, 1990, p. 14; Nolan and Turbat, 1993.
36 Lowenson, 1993.
37 Chisvo, 1993.
38 Gertler *et al.*, 1987.
39 Creese, 1990; Nolan and Turbat, 1993.
40 *World Development Report,* 1992, p. 293.
41 Mosley *et al.*, 1991, Vol. 2.
42 Younger, 1994, establishes that for a sample of twenty-one countries in Africa, the fall in expenditure per head which occurred especially 1982–6, followed a period of very rapid rise in the 1970s, so that the 1980s as a decade showed *higher* expenditure per head in these African countries than the 1970s.
43 The World Bank often refers to 'discretionary' government expenditure, which is total expenditure excluding interest payments, indicating the absolute priority given to debt servicing.
44 Cornia *et al.*, 1987, Vol. 2; Mosley *et al.*, 1991, Vol. 2.
45 This is documented in Mosley *et al.*, 1991.
46 Mosley *et al.*, 1991, Vol. 1, Chapter 3.

Chapter 4

Food subsidies: two errors of targeting

Giovanni Andrea Cornia and Frances Stewart[1]

INTRODUCTION

An important element in the social policies of adjustment packages is the elimination of universal subsidies, sometimes replacing them by targeted subsidies. Although no global estimates are available on changes in food subsidies, several studies have shown that food subsidies were reduced during adjustment, and general subsidies were replaced by targeted subsidies, usually of a lower total value.[2] This chapter considers some implications of these changes for the poor.

In this chapter, we assume that the overriding objective of food interventions is to transfer incomes to poor households. It might appear that universal subsidies are a very inefficient mechanism for achieving this because they unavoidably also cover the non-poor. This is the justification for replacing the universal food subsidies with targeted ones, designed to achieve minimum leakage to the non-poor, so that any given resource transfer will have maximum impact on poor households. A well-targeted programme, then, will be one which achieves minimum leakage. This is a common view in the literature.[3] But this view may be incorrect for a number of reasons, including administrative and efficiency costs, political factors and other general equilibrium effects.[4]

These will be considered only briefly below. An important additional reason why the criterion of minimising leakage may not be the right one lies in the existence of *two errors of targeting*: errors of omission of the poor from the scheme, as well as errors of inclusion of the non-poor. (These two types of error correspond to type I and type II errors in statistical analysis.) These two errors are the main focus of this chapter.

TWO TYPES OF MISTAKE IN TARGETING

In terms of the efficiency of the targeting mechanism, there are two types of mistake to which any intervention may be subject. The first is that of failing to reach the target population. We shall describe this as an *F-mistake*, i.e. a failure in the prime objective of the intervention. The second type of mistake is that made when the intervention reaches the non-target population; this we shall call an *E-mistake* (since what is involved is excessive coverage). A major criticism of nutritional schemes in general, and *a fortiori* of untargeted schemes, is that E-mistakes are high. For example, in a study of targeting, Mateus (1983) argues that total costs are unnecessarily high because of the high number of E-mistakes in a variety of interventions; he notes that in Morocco it was estimated that 80 per cent of the budgetary costs in the rural areas and 70 per cent in the urban areas 'increased the consumption of the already well-nourished' (op. cit., p. 9).

In designing targeted interventions, attention has tended to be focused on mistakes brought about by excessive coverage, with much less attention on mistakes resulting from failures to reach the target group. Narrowly targeted interventions often show apparently favourable cost–benefit ratios.[5] This arises from the smaller size of the target group and the fact that the more the intervention is restricted to groups in extreme deprivation, the greater one would expect the improvements from the intervention to be – measured, say, by gains in weight of malnourished children. But to date, cost–benefit analyses of food interventions have not included any evaluation of F-mistakes, or the costs of failing to cover the whole target population. F-mistakes are particularly serious where it is the ultra-poor who are left out, and are likely to be largest where malnutrition is widespread. The larger the proportion of the population which is malnourished, the higher the potential F-mistakes and the lower the potential E-mistakes. This is one reason why the controversy about the extent of malnutrition is so relevant to the design of nutrition interventions.[6]

For the most part, pursuit of low E-mistakes tends to raise F-mistakes because some of the target group tend to be eliminated from the scheme along with the non-target population, for the following reasons:

- lack of information about the targeted schemes among the target group;
- costs of acquiring entitlements to targeted schemes. These may require travel, registering applications, appearing at a clinic etc. depending on the targeting mechanism;
- qualifications for entitlement, which, while excluding the non-poor, also almost invariably exclude some of the target group (e.g. use of geographical qualification for entitlement);
- social stigma.

Measuring E- and F-mistakes

Given a population N composed of poor people P (who constitute the target of the food intervention) and non-poor people NP, for each intervention one can observe four categories illustrated in Table 4.1.

F-mistakes consist of P^{nc} and may be measured as a proportion of the total population, P^{nc}/N, or as a proportion of the target population, P^{nc}/P. The latter is the measure of F-mistakes which is used in this section. It is a good indication of how far a scheme is failing in its primary intention to reach the target group.

Table 4.1 Classification matrix: E- and F-mistakes of food interventions

	Poor	Non-poor	Total
All covered by nutritional intervention	P^c	NP^c [E- mistakes]	N^c
All non-covered by nutritional intervention	P^{nc} [F-mistakes]	NP^{nc}	N^{nc}
Total	P	NP	N

where

$$P + NP = N^c + N^{nc} = P^c + P^{nc} + NP^c + NP^{nc} = N$$

In the ideal case, E- and F-mistakes are nil, i.e.

$$P^c + NP^{nc} = N$$

while in the case of total mistargeting (i.e. when none of the poor are covered by the intervention and all the non-poor are)

$$NP^c + P^{nc} = N$$

E-mistakes consist of NP^c and may be measured as a proportion of the total population, NP^c/N, or as a proportion of the total non-target population, NP^c/NP. E-mistakes may also be estimated as the money cost of the excess coverage, or vNP^c where v is the average money cost of the subsidy received by the non-target population, and may be expressed as a proportion of the total costs of the subsidy, i.e. vNP^c/S, where S is the total money value of the subsidy. Where the subsidy consists of a given sum, equal for each recipient (as with school meals), this ratio is equivalent to the ratio of $NP^c/[NP^c + P^c]$.

The most common measure of E-mistakes is vNP^c/S as it gives an estimate of the financial costs of the mistake. This is shown below as E′. Where data are available we also show the proportion of the non-target population covered, NP^c/NP, which we describe as E″. Where the non-target population is a small proportion of the total population, as in very poor areas, a high E″ can be associated with low E′; conversely if the non-target population is a high proportion of the total, a small E″ could be associated with a high E′.

THE TWO ERRORS IN PRACTICE

This section reviews evidence from eight countries showing how the two major errors vary with the type of food support scheme. The country studies illustrate that the magnitude of the errors depends not only on the design of the scheme but also on the environment in which it is introduced. The cases examined include countries from each of the three developing regions, and both middle- and low-income countries.

Tamil Nadu – India

A scheme providing free school meals and infant feeding was introduced in Tamil Nadu in 1982. The noon meals scheme is politically very popular, and was one factor behind the re-election of the ruling party, ADMK, in 1984. In addition, people have access to subsidised rice through the public distribution system.

Noonday meals

Coverage in principle: Pre-school children (age two and older) registered at nurseries; all registered school attenders below ten; extended to old age pensioners, ex-servicemen and widows below a poverty line.

Cost: Ten per cent of state budget, which is equivalent to the deficit of the state electricity board, and exceeds the state's annual investment in agriculture. It is financed out of general revenue, additional taxes on luxuries, some voluntary contributions plus compulsory contributions from government salaries.

Mistakes: The most detailed evidence is provided by Harriss (1992) in a study of two villages in North Arcot, a 'richer' village and a poorer village. In both villages, the same proportion (over 80 per cent) of the children from higher income groups attend school, but a lower proportion eat at school in the richer village so that the richer village had a lower E-error. In the richer village, significantly fewer children among poor households attend school than in the poor village because of greater employment opportunities (56 per cent compared with 77 per cent in the poor village). Hence the poorer village had a lower F-error (see Table 4.2). Overall 60 per cent of dropouts were female, so that girls

Table 4.2 E- and F-mistakes in North Arcot (per cent)

	Richer village	Poorer village
Noonday meals		
Pre-school and school		
F-mistake	36.3	20.7
E′	32.0	37.5
E″	53.2	88.6
Pre-school		
F	17.0	
E′	31.2	
E″	76.9	
School		
F	54.3	
E′	33.1	
E″	36.1	

Public distribution system (both villages)	
F (approx.)	0
E′	37
E″ (approx.)	100

Source: Harriss, 1992

F = the percentage of target group (defined as bottom 60 per cent of households) not covered
E′ = the percentage of subsidy going to non-target population
E″ = the percentage of non-target group covered by subsidy

suffered proportionately more F-mistakes. In both villages, there was almost universal uptake of pre-school meals (which could be taken home) and therefore high E- and low F-errors.

In the public distribution system (PDS), the ration of subsidised rice per household had more or less universal uptake. A more general all-India investigation of the PDS found that it did not – as is often suggested – have an anti-rural or pro-rich bias, but was broadly universally accessible.[7] This implies low F-mistakes, and substantial E-mistakes, but the study did not provide data to permit calculation of E-mistakes on an all-India basis.

Jamaica

Jamaica abolished general food subsidies in 1984 and replaced them with a more targeted food stamp scheme and school feeding programme. Some general food subsidies were reinstated in 1986–8. The general food subsidies were again phased out in 1989 and replaced by increased benefits via the targeted programme, but without full replacement in value.

The targeting was to: all pregnant and lactating women; children under five; the elderly; the handicapped; and the poor. The benefits were broadly maintained in real terms. Targeting was of two types: there was a form of self-targeting for mothers and children who had to attend clinics/schools to get benefits; and the rest obtained access by coming forward for income-testing and successful registration.

As shown in Table 4.3, E-mistakes were significantly reduced as a result of the switch to targeting from general subsidies, but F-mistakes were sharply increased. The F-mistakes occurred because not all the poor attended clinics, and because registration was required for the means-tested food stamps and for the elderly. The F-mistakes were high (about half of all households with malnourished children did *not* receive benefits).

Table 4.3 E- and F-mistakes in Jamaica[a] (per cent)

	F Poorest 20%	E′ Top 60%	E″ Top 20%
General subsidies	Very low	66	100
Food stamps	50	43	6
Pregnant and lactating women	25	—	4
Children under five	39	—	11
The elderly	45	—	13

Source: Grosh, 1992a
(a) Data relate to households

On the basis of the traditional approach (i.e. judging only on the basis of E-mistakes), Grosh concludes that 'the targeting of food stamps is much better than the targeting of general food subsidies'.[8]

Pakistan

Pakistan had a system of subsidised rations available only from ration shops. This system was removed in 1987 and replaced by a smaller general subsidy on unlimited quantities of wheat, which was intended to be temporary.

The pre-1987 subsidised rations were for an inferior brand of flour and were available much more readily in urban than in rural areas because of the lack of rural ration shops. The budget share of rationed flour was 0.056 for the poorest group and 0.006 for the richest group. There was considerable diversion because the flour subsidy went to wheat released to mills and a large proportion (an estimated 69 per cent) of subsidised wheat did not reach the ration shops. The general subsidy saved 20 per cent of the costs of the ration scheme. Because of lower cost and greater coverage, the rate of subsidy was lower for each recipient.

Conclusions: The ration shop scheme was much worse in terms of F-mistakes. E-mistakes were probably a little smaller in the targeted scheme because of the diversion problem (Table 4.4). Administrative costs of the new general scheme were lower than the rationed scheme.

Table 4.4 E- and F-mistakes in
Pakistan[a] (per cent)

	Rural	Urban
Ration scheme		
F	65	50
E'		52[b]
		81[c]
E''	20	21
General subsidy		
F		0
E'		78[b]
E''		100

Source: Alderman, 1988
(a) Data relate to families
(b) Percentage leakage to the top two-thirds of the population assuming no diversion
(c) Same as in (b) but assuming a 60 per cent diversion

The more targeted subsidy had low political support and therefore was replaced. ('While the concentration of users of the ration system on low-income users achieved a degree of targeting, it also isolated users from a broader political base.' Alderman, 1988, p. 251.)

Egypt

Egypt has had a generous system of food subsidies with two main elements: a general unrestricted subsidy on coarse and refined flour and bread; and ration cards for other basic commodities. The schemes were very expensive (10 to 15 per cent of total government expenditure in the 1970s and 1980s) and were associated with (and often blamed for – although defence expenditure at 14.4 per cent of government expenditure might equally be held responsible) large budget deficits. The IFIs have devoted considerable efforts to persuading Egypt to move away from the general subsidies to more targeted schemes and plans in this direction have been initiated.

In contrast to many other countries, Egypt had a good network of rural ration shops, and rural coverage was nearly as good as urban. In the urban areas, the total value of food interventions were considerably greater for the poor than the rich (for whom they were negative because deviations from world prices, resulting from government interventions raised the price of some commodities consumed by the rich), but in the rural areas the absolute value was somewhat greater for the top income group (data for 1981–2; see Table 4.5). However, food interventions were strongly progressive for both, when expressed as a percentage of income, being 13 per cent of the total expenditure of the bottom (urban) quartile and minus 4 per cent of the top in urban areas; and 18 per cent of the bottom and 5 per cent of the top in rural areas.

Table 4.5 E- and F-mistakes in Egypt[a] (per cent)

	Urban	Rural
F-mistakes		
Households without ration cards	6.9	8.1
People without ration cards	4.5	7.0
Non-availability of subsidised		
– bread	21.7	74.7
– bread/flour	2.9	12.2
E-mistakes[b]		
E' – top three-quarters	55.7	75.0
E' – top quarter	–5.2[c]	22.9
E' (total, rural and urban)		
– top three-quarters		69.5
– top quarter		14.9

Source: Calculated from Alderman and von Braun, 1984 and 1986
(a) Data relate to households
(b) Data for calculation of E"-mistakes are not available, but the reasons for failure of comprehensive coverage include: (i) head of household working abroad; and (ii) not wanting newly-weds to claim separate ration cards. Both are likely to be greater among the non-poor so that coverage is probably greater among low-income groups, and the true F-mistakes are likely to be lower than shown above
(c) The value of the subsidy is calculated as the effect on food prices of government interventions compared with world prices. Import restrictions on luxuries lead to a negative value for urban upper-income groups

Nutrition: In the early 1980s, Egypt had better standards of nutrition than might be expected for its per capita income. This is likely to be due to the food subsidies as calorie consumption exhibits a high-income elasticity. Alderman and von Braun (1984) calculate that the consumption of poor households is 100 to 200 calories greater per day than it would be in the absence of the interventions.

Mistakes: There was very high uptake of rations in both rural and urban areas (well over 90 per cent of households). In the rural areas, the limited number of bakeries meant that the bread subsidy was often inaccessible and rural consumers relied on the flour subsidy. However, the careful investigation conducted by Alderman and von Braun indicates that for around 12 per cent of households, neither bread nor flour was available.

Conclusions: Egypt's food subsidies showed very low F-mistakes, in both rural and urban areas (slightly higher in the rural areas). E-mistakes were large, when including all subsidies going to the top three-quarters of the income distribution as leakages. Naturally, they were much less when defined to include only subsidies going to the top quarter of the population. Targeting – in terms of E-mistakes – would have been improved if the subsidy on coarse flour and the basic rations had been maintained, while other interventions were abolished. This would have reduced the E-mistakes without raising the F-mistakes. As is well established through the bitter resistance to their removal, the food interventions have had strong political support.

Sri Lanka

Before 1979, Sri Lanka had a universal rice, wheat and sugar subsidy which provided a minimum of two pounds of rice per week to the whole population at highly subsidised prices. From 1977, a new more market-oriented government reduced and then replaced the subsidies. Entitlement was means-tested, and subsequently the subsidy which was administered via ration shops was replaced by food stamps issued to households according to income and number of children. Registration was frozen in 1980. A fixed nominal sum was allocated to the stamps, whose real value declined over time. Changes in June 1986 extended the number of beneficiaries from 6.8 million to 7.2 million, and provided some increases in the value of stamps for children under twelve.

Costs: The universal rice subsidy was expensive, amounting to 15 per cent of government expenditure in the mid-1970s, whereas by 1984 the cost of food subsidies had dropped to only 3 per cent of government expenditure. As a result of the failure to index the value of food stamps, their real value fell severely (by over half per recipient by 1981/2 compared with the rice rations).

Mistakes: The pre-1979 system ensured virtually complete coverage of the target population at the cost of high E-mistakes (Table 4.6). In absolute amounts, per capita receipts were greater among high-income groups than low-income groups because they could afford to buy their full ration. But as a percentage of income, the subsidies were much greater for low-income groups.

Table 4.6 E- and F-mistakes in Sri
          Lanka[a] (per cent)

Pre-1979 rice subsidies	
F-mistakes	Very low
E-mistakes	
E′ (top 80 per cent)	82
E′ (top 60 per cent)	62
E″	100
1981/2 food stamps	
F-mistakes	
(bottom 20 per cent)	29
(bottom 40 per cent)	30
E-mistakes	
E′ (top 80 per cent)	64
E′ (top 60 per cent)	31
E″ (top 60 per cent)	34

Source: Edirisinghe, 1987, Table 45
(a) Data relate to households

Per capita subsidies were equivalent to 25 per cent of expenditure of the bottom quintile compared to 8.7 per cent of expenditure of the top quintile. In contrast, the new programme reduced E-mistakes, although not as much as had been envisaged as a large number of households whose incomes were above the cut-off line nonetheless secured stamps. But there was a large increase in F-mistakes, with 30 per cent of the bottom quintile not covered. These mistakes arose from the complexity of the administrative process, and from the fact that from 1980 registration was frozen.

Nutrition: The change to the targeted food stamp scheme was associated with a significant worsening in nutrition among the bottom 20 per cent of the population, who reduced their calorie consumption by 9 per cent from 1979 to 1981/2. The next quintile reduced calorie consumption per capita marginally, while all other groups increased their consumption. This worsening is attributed by Edirisinghe (1987) to the loss in income associated with the reduced value of (and reduced access to) food subsidies as a result of the introduction of the scheme. Food subsidies contributed nearly a third of the food budget of the bottom 20 per cent in 1978/9; this was reduced to one-fifth in 1981/2.

Politics: Politically, there was strong support for the pre-1979 subsidies, as evidenced by organised protest against their removal on several occasions. ('These subsidies continued in part because a remarkably high degree of active political participation by the population, particularly the organized sector of labor force, provided sufficient pressure to ensure that they did.' Edirisinghe, 1987, p. 11.) Once the change-over was achieved, it appears that there was much less political support for the new scheme, so that the government was able to reduce the value of the stamps without arousing much opposition.[9]

Tunisia

Tunisia is a middle-income country, with malnutrition estimated to affect less than 10 per cent of the population. In the mid-1980s, Tunisia had general unrestricted food subsidies on cereals, oils, milk and sugar, amounting to 8 per cent of government expenditure. High-income groups received three times the absolute amount per capita of low-income groups; nonetheless, the subsidies represented a lower proportion of total income for upper-income groups than for lower.

Mistakes: Since subsidies were universally available and there were very few subsistence farmers, F-mistakes were virtually non-existent. But E-mistakes were high. E-mistakes were significantly worse for the urban population than the rural, mainly because of the greater concentration of high income households in urban areas.[10] As Table 4.7 shows, there is considerable variation according to commodity, with extremely high E-mistakes on milk (over 90 per cent), and much lower ones for hard wheat than for the other commodities.

Table 4.7 E'-mistakes in Tunisia[a] (per cent)

All subsidies					
E' (top 90 per cent)	96				
E' (top 65 per cent)	75				
E' (top half)	65				
By commodity[c]	U	R	Total	Commodity composition of subsidies[b]	
				All groups	Lower-income groups[d]
Milk	93.1	74.3	91.4	3.2	1.6
Soft wheat	87.5	60.8	81.1	29.5	21.9
Sugar	89.0	55.3	74.9	14.4	13.8
Oil	87.6	52.1	72.1	6.2	12.2
Hard wheat	83.5	52.4	64.8	32.2	44.6

Source: Calculated from Yusuf, 1989, Table 10.
(a) Data relate to households
(b) There are also subsidies on meat, eggs, soap and school supplies, so total does not add to 100
(c) Refers to the top 65 per cent of households
(d) Refers to the bottom 35 per cent of households

Thus, E-mistakes could have been significantly reduced, while maintaining negligible F-mistakes, by concentrating the subsidy on hard wheat. If the rate of subsidy on hard wheat had been increased 2.1 times and the remaining subsidies abolished, the poorest 35 per cent would have been as well off while the total cost of the subsidies would be reduced by half. The one doubt about this procedure – which would also have saved administrative costs – is whether it would have been viable politically. There was strong political support for the system of subsidies, as indicated by food riots in 1984, when abolition was proposed.[11]

Mexico

As part of its adjustment programmes, Mexico is replacing general subsidies on maize and maize flour to urban tortilla manufacturers, with targeted subsidies on tortillas and milk, (means-tested using complex administrative procedures) for the urban poor, and the establishment of rural shops to provide subsisized maize flour.

As can be seen from Table 4.8, all the programmes, both general subsidies and targeted ones, had very high F-mistakes. In the case of the general subsidies

Table 4.8 E- and F-mistakes in Mexico (per cent)

	Urban	Rural	Total
General subsidies on maize			
F-mistake	Very low	100	54
E'-mistake (top three deciles)	39	0	
Targeted subsidies			
(a) *Tortilla*			
F – poor families[a]	73	100	88
F – poor pregnant/lactating women; children 0–12	75	100	90
E' – 'better-off'	40	0	
(b) *Urban milk programme*			
F – poor families[a]	56	99	89
F – pregnant/lactating women; children (poor households)	52	99	83
E' – 'better-off'	40	0	
(c) *Rural community stores*			
F – poor families[a]	100	6	49
F – pregnant/lactating women; children < 5 (poor)	100	7	61
E' – (non-poor)	0	46	
(d) *Food supplementation*			
F – poor families[a]	76	84	81
F – pregnant/lactating women; children < 5 (poor)			60
F – children 5–12			88
Magnitude of programmes	Total $m p.a.	Per beneficiary household $ p.a.	
General subsidies	1,652	151	
Targeted subsidies:			
(a) Tortilla	98	91	
(b) Urban milk programme	193	106	
(c) Rural community stores	51	9	
(d) Food supplementation	191	190	

Source: World Bank, 1991
(a) Families with incomes below 1.5 times the minimum wage

this arose from failure to cover the rural poor who accounted for approximately 54 per cent of total poor families, although complete coverage of the urban poor was achieved. The switch to targeting did not reduce E-mistakes, although this had been the main intention of the change. The best targeted programme from the perspective of F-mistakes – the rural community stores – also had the least spent on it, and the benefit per recipient was very small.[12]

The Philippines

In the Philippines a subsidised food ration scheme was introduced – on a pilot basis – for each household in a few villages. This had very high uptake (95 per cent after three months). Because most villagers were poor both E- and F-mistakes were very low *in the villages covered*, but since the scheme was confined to only a few villages, F-mistakes outside the chosen villages were clearly very high – poverty rates in the Philippines being of the order of 50–60 per cent during the 1980s with a high incidence in both rural and urban areas. However, while this is to be expected with a pilot scheme, it does illustrate a common problem associated with geographic targeting – viz. omission of the poor outside the area covered by the scheme (Table 4.9).

Table 4.9 E'- and F-mistakes in the Philippines pilot
scheme (per cent)

F-mistake (in villages covered after three months)	5
E' (those with >80 per cent of recommended calories)	8.8

Source: Garcia and Pinstrup-Andersen, 1987

MAJOR CONCLUSIONS FROM THE STUDIES

1. F-mistakes tend to be low with universal subsidies if they are unrestricted, and usually if they are rationed, if every household is entitled to rations. But where they are rationed, it is essential that the ration shops be widely accessible. In some countries, lack of ration shops in the rural areas has significantly raised F-mistakes – as in the Pakistan case above. But in others, such as in Sri Lanka and Egypt, the ration/subsidy shops were generally accessible and F-mistakes were low.

2. The universal schemes tend to involve significant E-mistakes, varying from 78 per cent (Pakistan) to 31 per cent (Sri Lanka), where an E-mistake is defined as the proportion of benefits that go to those outside the target group. The magnitude of the E-mistakes depends on:

● The level of income. If average incomes are low so that a high proportion of the population falls into the 'target' group, the maximum level of E-mistakes associated with universal schemes is limited. This was the case in the villages in North Arcot, where the public distribution scheme showed E-mistakes of only 37 per cent, and the E-mistake for school meals and pre-school feeding ranged from 32 to 38 per cent. In contrast, where the target population forms only a small proportion of the total, then E-mistakes can be very high, as in Tunisia.

● Consumption patterns among different income groups. If consumption patterns are similar among income groups, then any universal subsidy on a basic commodity is likely to benefit rich as well as poor groups – as with rice in Sri Lanka. But if 'poor people's commodities' can be identified, e.g. hard wheat in Tunisia, then lesser E-mistakes will be associated with universal subsidies.

● How narrowly the target group is defined. If the target group is confined to the severely malnourished, or to particular age groups, then E-mistakes will be higher than if the target group also includes the moderately malnourished and extends to all ages. There is a case for differentiating E-mistakes according to the income of the beneficiaries. For example, benefits that reach members of the bottom half of the income distribution who do not fall into the 'target' population are less serious than errors involving benefits going to the top half of the income distribution.

● The nature of the subsidy. We have used the term 'universal' subsidies, distinguishing these from 'targeted' subsidies. Yet all universal subsidies contain elements of implicit targeting, since their distribution depends on the commodities subsidized and the consumption patterns of different income groups. If the subsidised fall most heavily on poor people's goods, then E-mistakes will be less than if they fall on luxuries. The contrast between the Egyptian case, where the subsidies were mainly on poor people's goods, and the Tunisian case, where a high proportion fell on luxuries illustrates this point: in Egypt, the top three-quarters of the urban population received 56 per cent of the subsidies, while in Tunisia the top 65 per cent (urban) received 88 per cent.

3. Universal unrestricted subsidies can sometimes confer much larger absolute benefits on richer than poorer groups, since the richer groups can afford to consume more. But they may be designed to avoid this. In Egypt, richer groups in the urban areas received much less than poorer groups, while for the country as a whole there was little difference. In contrast, in Tunisia the value of the subsidies received per head in the top 10 per cent of the population was 3.7 times that received by the bottom 10 per cent. But even where they appeared highly regressive – as in Tunisia – they almost invariably *offered much greater benefits to poorer groups as a proportion of income*: in Tunisia the difference in per capita income between top and bottom groups was at least 8:1. Consequently, assuming that they are financed by taxes which are proportionate to income, they should improve secondary income distribution. In countries such as Egypt where they are designed more progressively, they greatly improve secondary income distribution.

4. In a number of countries targeted schemes have replaced universal schemes. In almost every case, as indicated in Table 4.10, the result has been a major

increase in F-mistakes with some reduction in E-mistakes. In Jamaica F-mistakes rose from almost nothing to as much as 50 per cent; in Sri Lanka from very low to 30 per cent; in Pakistan (where the reverse process occurred) they fell from 65 per cent (rural) and 50 per cent (urban) to near zero. The reduction in E-mistakes was usually substantial, but generally not as complete as had been expected as non-target groups managed to secure some of the targeted benefits – e.g. in Sri Lanka the top four-fifths' share dropped from 84 per cent to 62 per cent and the share of the top three-fifths of the income distribution dropped from 60 to 30 per cent; but in Pakistan, diversion of the targeted rations meant there was little difference in E-mistakes between the two schemes.

5. At best, when there was a switch from a general to a targeted subsidy, the real value of the benefits to those who received them was unchanged, but this

Table 4.10 Summary of targeting mistakes in selected countries

Country/region	General subsidies			Food stamps/rations		
	F	E'	E''a	F	E'	E''
Jamaica	Very low (top 60%)	66	100	50	43	n.a.
Pakistan (urban)	Very low (top 66%)	78	100	50	52–80	21
Egypt	7 (top 75%) 15 (top 25%)	70	100		n.a.	
Sri Lanka	Very low (top 60%)	62	100	30	31 (top 60%)	34
Tunisia	Very low (top 65%)	75	100		n.a.	
				Tortilla		
Mexico (urban)	Very low (top 30%)	39	100	73	40 (better-off)	n.a.
				Rural community stores		
				6	46 (non-poor)	n.a
Philippines (villages)	5 (>80% cal. rec.)	9	100		n.a.	
Tamil Nadu (two villages)	Very low	37	100		n.a.	
	Pre-school feeding			*School meals*		
Tamil Nadu ('richer' village)	17	31	77	54	33	36

Source: See Tables 4.2–4.9
(a) E'' mistakes are assumed to be 100 per cent, and F-mistakes to be very low for the universal subsidies. In fact, some people from both rich and poor households are likely to be omitted for various reasons, so E'' may be less than 100 per cent, and F positive but low. Precise data are not normally available

was unusual. Mostly, it seems that the switch also leads to a reduction in the real value of the subsidy over time (as in Sri Lanka). Less strong political support for the targeted schemes probably accounts for this. Sometimes, a reduction in the real value of the subsidy was intended as part of a cost-cutting exercise.

6. The one study of school meals as a mechanism of nutritional support indicates that large numbers of poor children may be excluded if they do not attend school because they are working. School meals would tend to discourage non-attendance,[13] but as Harriss (1992) shows, significant F-mistakes may still occur. Pre-school feeding does not have this problem.

7. Administrative costs are estimated to be higher for the targeted food interventions, ranging from 2 to 5 per cent of the total costs of the schemes. (The Sri Lankan scheme is estimated to cost 2 per cent and the Jamaican scheme 4 per cent of total costs). Evidence for the UK and USA supports this conclusion. In seven UK programmes, administrative costs were estimated at around 3.5 per cent of universal programmes but between 5 and 15 per cent of means-tested programmes, while in the USA administrative costs of universal programmes were found to be 2.5 per cent compared with 12 per cent for two means-tested programmes (and 95 per cent for the means-tested veterans programme).[14] The administrative costs of non-food schemes such as employment or credit schemes tend to be significantly higher than food subsidy schemes, but they also generate other benefits.

8. The political support for general schemes which reach some of the non-poor (i.e. have significant E-mistakes) appears to be higher than that for the more narrowly targeted schemes, according to the evidence reported here. For this reason the value of targeted subsidies is more likely to be eroded over time, as observed in the case of Sri Lanka.

HOUSEHOLDS AND FOOD INTERVENTIONS: A NEW SOURCE OF ERROR

Most individuals – and nearly all children – live in households. The way households function – particularly in relation to allocation of food – therefore mediates between any outside intervention and individual food consumption. This is so whether the intervention is direct (feeding schemes) or indirect (food subsidies, works schemes) because the household can reallocate the resources over which it has discretion to offset the effects of the intervention if it wishes.

Household decisions concerning food can be thought of as a two-stage process (although the two stages may be decided simultaneously): first, how much of total household income is to be allocated to food; and secondly, how food is to be distributed within the household.

If the aim of a food intervention is simply to raise the incomes of poor households, leaving them to decide on allocation and distribution, then we need only be concerned with whether the intervention does raise the incomes of poor households. But if the objective is to improve nutrition of particular categories of people within poor households (e.g. children), then we need also to consider the issues of allocation and distribution.

Different models of how households function lead to different conclusions on the links between food intervention → total food consumption → family food distribution. The main contrast is between the neo-classical and bargaining models of the household. The neo-classical model assumes joint utility maximisation (e.g. through a benevolent dictator at its head), in which decisions on allocation and distribution are taken with 'family' utility maximisation as the objective.[15] In contrast, bargaining models assume differences in objectives within the household, with allocation and distribution being the outcome of the bargaining strength of the various individuals (or bargaining groups) within the family.[16] The two types of model can lead to important differences in conclusions on the effects of food interventions.

Neo-classical model

According to the joint-utility maximisation model, since 'all resources are essentially pooled and reallocated to individuals, it does not make any difference to whom subsidies are given, or, for the most part, whether such subsidies are in cash or kind'.[17] Unless direct feeding of target groups exceeds their total pre-intervention consumption (unlikely except in special intensive programmes), this will be no more effective in raising their food consumption than a general increase in household income of the same magnitude, since the rational neo-classical family will reallocate their resources to achieve the efficient utility-maximising optimum.

In the neo-classical model, the family is a complex maximising entity, adjusting at work and consumption margins to achieve utility maximisation, and an intervention may therefore affect the level and distribution of food consumption through a general equilibrium process, incorporating the productivity effects of food consumption of particular individuals. For example:

- Increased male wages would increase family food consumption, as a result of an income effect, and might increase the share of male members so as to permit higher male workforce participation. Similarly, increased female wages or employment opportunities might increase total food consumption and the female share.
- The share of children in food consumption might be affected by changes in their current and future earnings stream, if this were related to their current nutrition.
- General food subsidies would increase household food consumption as a result of both income and substitution effects, but it would normally not affect distribution within the family.

Bargaining models

These may subsume the neo-classical distributional effects arising from the general equilibrium process just noted, but they also include bargaining effects of food interventions. Various bargaining groups have been distinguished leading to different outcomes. Most common is the male/female distinction; another distinction is generational. In these models, distribution of family food resources depends in part on the bargaining strength of the various categories. Taking the male/female divide, this means that female consumption will vary positively not only with household income, but also with female control over family income (e.g. from outside earnings).

In this context, children may be treated in a variety of ways:

- Bi: as being in the bargaining groups of their mother;
- Bii: as being in the bargaining groups of their same-sex parent;
- Biii: as forming bargaining groups of their own.

In the first type, (Bi), children will fare better if mothers receive income directly (through their own earnings, or subsidies they receive) or if the food support goes directly to them (direct feeding schemes), than if the extra income goes to raise household income via male earnings.

In the second type, (Bii), female children will fare better where extra income/subsidies are directed at the mothers, or at themselves, while boys will benefit from extra male incomes. In the third type, (Biii), food interventions have most effect when directed at children themselves; child nutrition would then benefit from extra child earnings.

What is the reality?

Empirical research is at a very early stage in this area. Moreover, the observed facts are often consistent with more than one model, while one can never directly observe objective functions.[18] But both facts and intuition lend support to the view that no single one of the models is a correct representation of reality, but aspects of each are present – to a varying extent in different contexts.

As far as the neo-classical model is concerned, the altruistic view of the family may contain some (Darwinian) truth but evidence suggests it does not tell the whole story, as it is inconsistent with the observed inequalities, especially between men and women. Inequalities in relation to recommended calorie needs have been widely observed in Asia, for example, in Bangladesh, India and the Philippines;[19] but such inequalities have not been evident in Africa.[20] Although neo-classicists have suggested that this inequality is consistent with joint family utility maximisation because of the greater earning capacity of males, this does not appear sufficient to explain the whole discrepancy in Asia, and Behrman (1988) has suggested there exists a 'pro-male bias' over and above investment considerations.

Consequently, empirical evidence lends support to the existence of elements of bargaining in family structures. There is substantial evidence showing that basic needs consumption rises as a proportion of family income, and child nutrition improves as female bargaining position is strengthened, as indicated by greater female earnings or improved female education.[21] This supports version Bi of the bargaining model. But while child nutrition in general improves with an improved position of mothers in the family, there is some evidence that that of girls rises most (e.g. in the Ivory Coast[22] and the Philippines[23]) giving some support to version Bii. Finally, there is some evidence that girls' nutrition improves as their actual or potential wages rise[24] and that boys' nutrition rises with their earnings[25] giving some credence to the third model (Biii).

Given this rather confused situation about the applicability of alternative household models, we may tentatively draw the following conclusions concerning the effectiveness of alternative food interventions:

- In so far as the whole of poor families are in the target group any intervention which increases family income of poor families will be satisfactory.
- If improved nutrition (of the whole family) is the objective, general food subsidies are preferable to other mechanisms for transferring income because of the substitution effect. Mechanisms which transfer income to women are also more effective than general increases in income because of the greater propensity of women to spend extra resources they control on food.
- If a subset of the family is the target (women or children), then there is enough evidence supporting bargaining-type models to suggest that mechanisms which increase women's and/or children's control over resources will be preferable to those which increase male incomes.

Mechanisms which should therefore be favoured include:

- increasing female wages, employment and credit;
- subsidies paid directly to women;
- direct feeding schemes (pre-school and school meals);
- mechanisms which increase child incomes would also be effective, but most forms of child labour are undesirable for other reasons.

In terms of our classification of mistakes, unravelling the household suggests a new source of E- and F-mistakes arising within the household. These were largely ignored in the earlier discussion. Assuming the target population is a subcategory within poor households, both E- and F-mistakes are likely to be more serious than shown in the earlier data, which treated the whole family as the target. E-mistakes inevitably arise as non-target family members share in additional consumption. F-errors arise if the real target group does not receive extra consumption. But most evidence shows that child food consumption and nutrition rises with family income, so that children are not left out as income rises.[26] Thus F-mistakes may not be larger than suggested in the earlier estimates, but the target group may not benefit to the maximum extent.

VALUING THE E- AND F-MISTAKES

In this section we attempt to value the E- and F-mistakes identified above. Lack of a data-set specifically for this, and therefore the need to rely on secondary sources which often do not provide all the necessary information, prevent us being conclusive. But we can show that incorporating F-mistakes may alter the evaluation of food interventions.

Measuring the total E + F-mistake as the weighted sum of all those 'mistargeted'

The usual approach to comparing the relative efficiency of alternative food interventions focuses on minimising the leakage to the non-target population (or E-mistakes). In our approach, the ratio to be minimised is a weighted valuation of $(NP^c + P^{nc})/N$, or $(aNP^c + bP^{nc})/N$, where a is the weight to be given to E-mistakes and b the weight to be given to F-mistakes. In the conventional approach a is assumed to equal to 1 and $b = 0$. In contrast, we believe that in general $b > a$, since failure to reach the target population undermines the objective of the intervention.

A critical issue, therefore, is the value of a and b. Relevant considerations in arriving at some system of weighting are the costs of E-mistakes; these would be less if there is not a major budgetary problem (e.g. in a revenue-rich country such as Botswana or Saudi Arabia), or if the tax system can be used to claw back E-mistakes; in either case $a < 1$; and how damaging F-mistakes are, which includes both the welfare costs and the efficiency costs of not reaching the target population.

At this stage we simply illustrate how the ordering of schemes changes, as valuation of the errors varies. This is shown in Table 4.11 which values the added-up errors in four ways – E-mistakes only; F-mistakes only; giving both E- and F-mistakes equal weights of 1; and assigning F-mistakes a weight three times that of E-mistakes ($b/a = 3$).

Table 4.11 shows how the ranking alters according to the weighting adopted. General subsidies are invariably inferior to targeted schemes considering only E-mistakes (which here may have been exaggerated, as it is assumed that 100 per cent of upper-income groups are covered). If F-mistakes only are considered, then general subsidies are invariably superior to targeted schemes in the examples considered. When both are incorporated, the outcome depends on the proportion of the population who are in or outside the target group, the magnitude of errors of omission and commission and the relative weight given to the two. For example, in Pakistan the targeted scheme is superior to the general subsidies if the two errors are given equal weight, but the general subsidies are superior when the F-mistakes are weighted at three times E-mistakes. For Jamaica, if only the top 20 per cent are regarded as causing E-mistakes, the general subsidy is superior if E- and F-errors are weighted equally (but this would change if one extended E-mistakes to a wider section of the population).

Table 4.11 A comparison of the efficiency of alternative interventions on the basis of alternative measurements of the targeting mistakes

Mistakes/weighting	E only	F only	E + F [a = b = 1]	E + 3F [a = 1, b = 3]
Measure adopted	NP^c/N	P^{nc}/N	$(NP^c + P^{nc})/N$	$(NP^c + 3P^{nc})/N$
Sri Lanka[a]				
General subsidy	0.60	0	0.60	0.60
Food stamps	0.20	0.12	0.32	0.56
Jamaica[b]				
General subsidy	0.20	0	0.20	0.20
Food stamps	0.12	0.10	0.22	0.42
Pakistan[a]				
General subsidy	0.60	0	0.60	0.60
Food rations	0.12[d]	0.24[c]	0.36	0.84
Tamil Nadu (richer village)[e]				
General subsidy	0.39	0	0.39	0.39
School meals	0.14	0.32	0.46	1.10
Pre-school meals	0.30	0.12	0.42	0.66

Source: See Tables 4.6, 4.3, 4.4 and 4.2
(a) Poor and non-poor: bottom 40 per cent and top 60 per cent of the population
(b) Poor and non-poor: bottom 20 per cent and top 20 per cent of the population
(c) Assuming 40 per cent of the poor are covered
(d) Estimate
(e) Poor and non-poor are defined as the bottom three classes and top three classes

Measuring the total E + F-mistake as the sum of the programme leakage, welfare cost and future forgone income due to mistargeting

In this section we consider valuing F-mistakes not only in welfare terms but also as income forgone, i.e. W, welfare costs, and Y^*, future income forgone. E-mistakes are valued here in the usual way, i.e. as the leakage (L) of financial resources to non-target groups.

In principle the welfare costs depend on the poverty of those not reached and therefore the gains from reaching them, which, according to most approaches to welfare measurement would differ according to the poverty of the non-recipient. If data permitted, we could adopt an Atkinson utility index to measure the welfare costs at different income levels.[27] But for data reasons this will rarely be possible; moreover, we do not know the value e, representing societies' valuation of inequality.

Valuing the present value of the forgone income (Y^*)

There are three important relations relevant to assessing the value of the forgone income: that between adult nutrition and labour productivity; that between growth retardation at an early age, IQ scores, school achievements and long-term labour productivity; and that between maternal malnutrition, low birth weight (LBW) incidence among female infants, and their reproductive efficiency during their adult life. Empirical studies support the view that each relationship leads to a significant loss of productivity arising from malnutrition.

Adult nutrition and labour productivity

A review of evidence shows:

● Calorie intake and micro-nutrient supplementation are positively correlated with the labour productivity of manual workers (Table 4.12).

Table 4.12 Estimates of the elasticity of the nutrition–productivity relation

Study	Kilocalories[a]		Productivity gains (%)	Elasticity of			
	Initial level	Increase		Wages wrt. Calories	Labour productivity wrt.		
					Calories	Weight-for-height
Kraut and Muller, 1946	2,400	600	47	—	1.88	—
Railway workers	2,800	400	37	—	2.60	—
Mineworkers	3,200	400	7	—	0.56	—
Steelworkers	—	400	22	—	—	—
Keys *et al.*, 1950	3,500	−2,000	−30[b]	—	—	0.52
Wolgemuth *et al.*, 1982	2,000	500	12.5	—	0.50	—
Strauss, 1986	3,000	−1,500	−40	—	0.66	—
	3,000	1,500	17	—	0.34	—
	3,750	750	—	—	0.12	—
Viteri *et al.*, 1975	2,800	350	0.2[c]	—	—	—
Deolalikar, 1988						
Calorie	—	—	—	0.2	—	—
Weight/height	—	—	—	—	—	2.0
Sahn and Alderman, 1988	—	—	—	0.2	—	—
Satyanarayana *et al.*, 1977	45	10	—	—	0.58	—
	45	15	—	—	0.81	—
Belavady, 1966	2,400	600	0	—	0	—

Source: Compiled by the authors
(a) Except for 'Satyanarayana *et al.*, 1977', which is in kilograms
(b) Refers to muscle strength, not to labour productivity
(c) Tonnes of additional sugarcane cut

● Body-mass is also significantly related to labour productivity among agricultural, construction and other manual workers in several developed and developing countries.[28]
● The relation between nutrition and productivity is more pronounced for workers at low levels of intake.[29]
● Changes in nutritional status has lesser effects on productivity in the short term.[30]

Assuming that the yearly productivity of low-income workers in poor, developing countries is in the $300–500 per capita bracket, the gains associated with an increase in calorie intake could be roughly assessed to be in the range of $60–200 per capita per year. This figure compares favourably with the cost of a food subsidy programme (or of similar child feeding or school lunches programmes) which is currently estimated at around $30 per year per 1,000 calories effectively transferred per day.[31]

Malnutrition, growth retardation at an early age and labour productivity in adulthood

Malnutrition at an early age leads to severe impairment of cognitive capacity and to stunting. There are essentially three mechanisms through which different forms of malnutrition in infancy and childhood affect labour productivity in adulthood: first, persistent protein energy malnutrition (PEM) in infancy and childhood leads to long-term stunting with effects discussed above; secondly, severe malnutrition before the age of five affects IQ, later learning ability (both directly and through the amount of schooling, which also depends on IQ), skill acquisition and future productivity; third under-nourishment in school children affects attention span, learning ability and school achievement.

A number of empirical studies provide evidence on the strength of these relationships: for example, ten out of the thirteen studies surveyed by Pollitt (1984) showed that severe PEM in infancy and early childhood affects intelligence tests and school performance negatively. The extent of the cognitive deficit among school-age children has been shown to be associated with the severity and duration of the nutritional deficit at an early age.[32]

In the absence of longitudinal studies, the loss of future income due to malnutrition in childhood can best be estimated by combining the evidence on the relation between child malnutrition, learning ability and amount of schooling completed with that on the relation between levels of schooling and earnings. A well-known study of Chilean children showed that providing nutritional supplements during the first two years of life to the children becoming malnourished would generate benefits equal to *six times* the cost of the intervention.[33] Similarly, a health and nutrition programme in Cali, Colombia, was estimated to increase the total value of the lifetime earnings of children previously malnourished from 2.5 and 8.9 times the yearly wage of an illiterate worker[34] (depending on the years of schooling completed and the increase in IQ).[35]

Inter-generational effects: malnutrition among mothers and reproductive efficiency

Perhaps the worst and most neglected effect of maternal malnutrition on female infants is that on their *reproductive efficiency* during adult life. Recent studies have shown that maternal malnutrition has a high probability of being passed on to at least the two successive generations, and thus, of affecting physical growth, learning ability and the expected earnings of future generations.[36] This influence can be reduced by nutritional supplements during pregnancy. Estimating the value of forgone income due to this inter-generational transmission of malnutrition is, however, highly conjectural and will not be pursued here.

Adding up the costs of F-mistakes and weighing them with the E-mistakes

While some of the evidence presented here has methodological problems which may bias the estimated coefficients, the findings still provide the basis of a tentative valuation of F-mistakes. On the basis of the preceding discussion one can assess the value of the E + F-mistake as:

$$E + F\text{-mistake} = L + Y^* + W$$

where

$$Y^* = \alpha \pi w P^{nc} + \beta \pi c P^{nc}$$

and where

$L =$ monetary value of the nutritional programme's leakage;

$W =$ immediate welfare cost;

$\pi =$ yearly productivity of a low-income manual worker;

$w =$ share of adult manual workers in P^{nc};

$c =$ proportion of P^{nc} accounted for by children under five;

$\alpha =$ percentage average loss of productivity of malnourished manual workers who are not reached by the nutritional programme;

$\beta =$ multiple of present value of future forgone income of malnourished children who are not reached by the nutritional programme, expressed in terms of the current productivity of low-income manual workers.

With α and β estimated to range respectively between 0.3–0.4 and 2.5 and 4.6, π at \$300–500, and w and c likely to range respectively between 0.2–0.3 to 0.4–0.5, it appears that the weights of F-mistakes can be extremely large even before estimating welfare costs. Food interventions which reduce E-mistakes but increase F-mistakes would therefore tend to raise the total value of the targeting error substantially. Although lack of information prevents an estimate of the values of Y^* and W for any of the programmes reviewed earlier on the basis of a broad survey of the literature the value of forgone income appears significant in relation to the average value of leakage of food interventions.[37]

CONCLUSIONS

This chapter has indicated that the design of targeted food interventions in adjustment programmes has focused almost exclusively on the E-mistake – that of 'wasting' resources by covering some or all of non-target groups. In so doing, it has neglected the F-mistake – that of failing to reach the whole target population.

Empirical studies show that in general as E-mistakes are reduced through targeting, F-mistakes are increased. While E-mistakes involve additional expenditure, F-mistakes have a different kind of cost which encompasses both the immediate welfare loss and the forgone future income as a result of malnutrition among the 'missed' target group. Both types of mistakes (i.e. the total mistargeting error) should be considered in designing good schemes.

In general, evidence summarised above, shows that the 'targeted' subsidies which replace universal subsidies in adjustment programmes involve reduced E-errors but typically increase F-errors seriously. This was most clearly illustrated by the examples of Jamaica and Sri Lanka. Since the real value of the subsidy per recipient is not normally increased, there is in most cases a net worsening of poverty as a consequence of replacing universal by targeted subsidies.[38]

Policy conclusions, based on the review of evidence in this chapter, about how to avoid excessive F- and E-mistakes are:

- Subsidies or other interventions must reach the rural areas. If they do not, as is quite common, then high F-mistakes are unavoidable.

- Universal subsidies on staple commodities are most effective in reaching the whole target population in very low-income countries and/or areas where the majority of the population are poor and malnourished. The exception is where there is a high degree of malnutrition among a subsistence population.[39] Other mechanisms – e.g. child-feeding programmes – will be needed to reach the subsistence population, which is among the most difficult to reach.

- Targeting food interventions will 'save' more resources than general food subsidies in middle-income countries, where malnutrition is fairly low. But in these contexts, targeting by commodity/geography can often (as in Tunisia) greatly reduce E-mistakes, without increasing F-mistakes, whereas targeting by income tends to involve high F-mistakes with little reduction in E-mistakes.

- Even where universal food subsidies are apparently regressive, with the well-off receiving a higher share of the subsidies than their share of the population warrants, they are usually progressive compared with the distribution of original income, and also confer real benefits on the poor in absolute terms. Consequently, policy-makers who wish to improve income distribution and reduce poverty should not abolish food subsidies without providing substitute interventions which are at least as effective in conferring benefits on the poor (taking into account potential F-mistakes).

- The objective of covering the highest possible number of the poor while minimising leakage may best be achieved by 'clawing back' some or all of the leakage from well-designed universal subsidies through a variety of direct and indirect tax measures – e.g. by increasing value-added tax on items other than food and shelter.

NOTES

1 This chapter is based on a paper presented to a World Bank Conference on 'Public Expenditures and the Poor: Incidence and Targeting', 17–19 June 1992. We are grateful to participants at the seminar and to Steven Coate for useful comments on an earlier draft.
2 Pinstrup-Andersen *et al.*, 1987; Grosh, 1990b, 1992a and b.
3 See, for example, Mateus, 1983; Grosh, 1992b.
4 In selecting interventions, general equilibrium effects should also be considered. General food subsidies are more likely to have significant general equilibrium effects than narrowly targeted schemes. If the subsidies come from depressing prices received by farmers they may reduce medium-term food availability and food prices or increase imports. But if they are paid by the exchequer, they need not affect food availability, although they may have other general equilibrium effects. This chapter does not explore such general equilibrium effects.
5 Mateus, 1983; Pinstrup-Andersen, 1991.
6 See Sukhatme, 1977; Dasgupta and Ray, 1987.
7 Mahendra Dev and Suryanarayana, 1991.
8 Grosh, 1992a, p. 39.
9 Edirisinghe, 1987, 1988.
10 Yusuf, 1989.
11 Yusuf, 1989.
12 World Bank, 1991.
13 See Babu and Arne Hallam, 1989.
14 Kesselman, 1982.
15 See Becker, 1981; Rosenzweig, 1986.
16 Manser and Brown, 1980; McElroy and Horney, 1981; Folbre, 1984, 1986; McElroy, 1990.
17 Rosenzweig, 1986, p. 235.
18 Folbre, 1986.
19 Results quoted in Haaga and Mason, 1987; Folbre, 1986; Chen *et al.*, 1981.
20 Deaton, 1987; Svedberg, 1990.
21 See, e.g., Guyer, 1980; Miller, 1981; Tripp, 1981; Sahn, 1990; Hoddinott and Haddad, 1991.
22 Hoddinott and Haddad, 1991.
23 Villasenor, 1982.
24 Villasenor, 1982.
25 Harriss, 1992.
26 See, e.g., Villasenor, 1982.
27 According to the Atkinson utility index, the income of a particular group is valued as

$$W(y) = \frac{1}{1-e} \, y^{1-e}$$

28 McGuire and Austin, 1987.
29 Strauss, 1986; Basta *et al.*, 1979.
30 Belavady, 1966. Limited and gradual declines/increases in intake might be accommodated by an adaptation of the basal metabolic rate (Scrimshaw, 1986).
31 World Bank, 1989a; Kennedy and Alderman, 1987.
32 See, e.g., Galler *et al.*, 1983; Winnick *et al.*, 1979.
33 Selowsky and Taylor, 1973.
34 Selowsky notes that in the early to mid-1970s, the wage of an illiterate worker in six developing countries varied between 40 per cent and 95 per cent of the GDP per capita. Only in one case was it above it.

35 Selowsky, 1981.
36 Hackman *et al.*, 1983; Martorell and Gonzalez-Cossio, 1987.
37 The average annual cost per beneficiary of food interventions was found to vary, for instance, between $7 and $40 for supplementary feeding programmes between $20 and $40 for integrated health care-based schemes and between $10 and $40 for food subsidies (see World Bank, 1989f, Tables 8 and 9; and Kennedy and Alderman, 1987, Table 9).
38 In the unusual case, where targeted subsidies are introduced in a situation where previously there had been no subsidies, then they have additional benefits for the poor even though their coverage is not comprehensive.
39 As in Peru – see Harrell *et al.*, 1989.

Chapter 5

Adjustment and social funds: political panacea or effective poverty reduction?

Frances Stewart and Willem van der Geest

INTRODUCTION

In the latter part of the 1980s, a number of countries introduced schemes, with donor support, aimed at offsetting the rising poverty which had accompanied their adjustment programmes. These took a variety of forms and have variously been referred to as 'emergency social funds' or 'social investment funds', respectively in Bolivia and Honduras and as a 'social recovery fund' (in Zambia). This chapter will review these initiatives in selected countries, referring to them generically as social funds (SFs).

The World Bank's *Poverty Reduction Handbook* characterises social funds as wholesale financing mechanisms designed to accompany adjustment programmes; Bolivia's Emergency Social Fund was a pioneering attempt. Another early example was Ghana's PAMSCAD (Programme of Action to Mitigate the Social Costs of Adjustment). Other social funds supported by the World Bank include Guinea's Socioeconomic Development Support Project, São Tomé and Principe's Multisector Project, Tunisia's Employment and Training Fund, and Social Investment Fund Projects in Haiti and Honduras. Social funds typically consist of a specified sum of money to be devoted to activities which will ease the pains of adjustment, including financing small-scale projects, training and infrastructural projects. They are intended to be quick disbursing and are often located outside the normal government machinery.

Some countries had designed their own schemes in the 1970s without reference to external agencies and without external finance. One example is Chile's emergency employment schemes initiated in the mid-1970s. Elsewhere schemes were introduced to protect people during periodic drought – for example, in Botswana and Maharashtra State in India. In Costa Rica a variety of social programmes were developed designed to reduce poverty – not specifically related to adjustment. These 'own- designed' schemes differ in significant respects from the externally supported social funds. They are included here to see whether some lessons might be learnt for the operation of social support schemes during adjustment.

This chapter does not provide a comprehensive review of SFs, but sets out to evaluate experience of SFs in selected countries, by comparing programmes across a range of countries, noting the different political and economic contexts in which they were implemented. The next section briefly discusses the context in which the schemes were initiated, the motives for their introduction and major characteristics of the schemes to be reviewed. The third and fourth sections describe and evaluate particular features of the schemes, including targeting aspects, institutional features and financial sustainability. The final section comes to some conclusions.

OBJECTIVES, CONTEXT AND MOTIVATION FOR SOCIAL FUNDS

The economic context of social funds

In general SFs were adopted in a context of extraordinary economic crisis and increasing incidence of poverty. Table 5.1 summarises the data for the selected case-study countries regarding the changing incidence of urban and rural poverty during adjustment, while Table 5.2 reveals the decline in average per capita income that occurred in many of these countries.

Bolivia's Emergency Social Fund (ESF) was initiated in 1987 after the country's economic performance had declined dramatically from 1980. Net foreign transfers had become strongly negative, GDP was falling, capital flight accelerating, economic policies were erratic, hyperinflation measured 24,000 per cent over the year up to September 1985 and public sector deficits had spiralled.[1] In August 1985, a new government launched a programme of orthodox economic reform to control inflation and re-establish internal and external equilibria. Inflation levels were curtailed, the exchange rate unified and the public deficit brought under control. The immediate social costs of the stabilisation programme were large and included laying off 23,000 of the 30,000 public sector miners. The programme did not succeed in restoring economic growth. Per capita incomes fell by 0.7 per cent per annum from 1986 to 1990, and the extremely high level of rural poverty recorded at the beginning of the decade showed a further increase to 97 per cent of the rural population by 1988.

Chile's employment schemes were also introduced during a period of economic stagnation and rising unemployment and poverty. Macro developments in Chile after the Pinochet coup included steep declines of GDP (minus 13 per cent in 1975), followed by a five-year period of growth. A second crisis developed in 1982–5, precipitated by appreciation of the real exchange rate. Investment declined partly due to capital outflows. Inflation was controlled at the cost of soaring unemployment. The average rate of unemployment between 1974 and 1982 stood at 18 per cent, rising to 22 per cent in 1982.[2] The 1981 per capita GDP level was only attained again in 1989. Poverty increased sharply to 48 per cent in 1983 and was still 40 per cent in 1990, double the 1970 rate.[3] The Minimum Employment Programme (PEM), introduced in 1975, and the Occupational Programme for Heads of Households (POJH), initiated in 1982,

Table 5.1 Incidence of poverty and change during adjustment (selected case-study countries)

Sub-Saharan Africa

Botswana					
1985/6[h]	55	64	30	small increase?[a]	
1991[p]	57	60	46		
Ghana					
1981[h]	44	59	44	undetermined	change of definition of poverty line ^
1985[p]	60/42				
1986		54[p]			
1987/8[p]	36	44	27		^
Madagascar					
1980[h]	34	37	21		2,200 kcalb
Senegal					
1988		70[p]			
Zambia					
1980[p]	60	80	25	sharp increase urban	$79.6c
1991[p]	71	92	47	as well as rural	$9.3d
Zimbabwe					
1988		60[p]			

Central and South America

Bolivia					
1980		86[p]		sharp increase (rural data	
1988		97[p]		only)	
Chile					
1970[h]	17	25	12	sharp increase nation-wide $168e	
1980		56			
1990[p]	40				
Costa Rica					
1981[h]	22.2	28.4	16.1	increase followed by decrease for rural; urban depends on measure	separate rural and urban poverty linesf
1988[h]	24.5	27.6	20.6	adopted	^
1981[p]	23.6	28.4	18.2		^
1988[p]	27.2	35.8	14.5		^
1990[p]	23.4	32.7	11.6		^
Honduras					
1980		80		small increase	
1990[h]	77.5	80.2	73.9		

Table 5.2 Changes in GNP per capita during adjustment
(constant prices)

Country	Annual growth of GNP (constant 1987 dollars per capita)	
	1981–5	*1985–90*
Bolivia	−7.2	−2.0[a]
Costa Rica	−0.4	1.8
Chile	−5.4	5.5
Honduras	−11.0	2.6[b]
Botswana	3.3	18.2[a]
Ghana	−3.2	1.8[a]
Madagascar	−2.0	−1.1[a]
Senegal	0.4	0.6
Zambia	−4.9	−2.3
Zimbabwe	−2.5	0.0

Sources: *World Tables 1991* and *World Development Report 1993*
(a) 1985–9
(b) 1985–8

became major instruments for preventing destitution for a great number of households, including many who previously had considered themselves better-off.

The Honduran economy is a traditional primary-product exporter (bananas and coffee), with agriculture providing 70 per cent of exports throughout the 1970s. The 1980s witnessed a decrease in GDP per capita of 1.6 per cent annually and a real-wage decrease of 30 per cent between 1980 and 1989. The fiscal deficit increased to more than 10 per cent of GDP, inflation was high and external debt doubled during the decade.[4] The poverty incidence in Honduras remained at a high level throughout the 1980s for both rural and urban households. The Callejas government inherited a fiscal deficit of 10.5 per cent of GDP in 1990, but nevertheless felt compelled to adopt the *Sistema de Compensación Social* (SCS) and within it the *Fondo Hondureno de Inversión Social* (Honduran Investment Social Fund – FHIS). By that time more than three-quarters of the households had fallen below the poverty line.

Costa Rica's social programmes were mostly introduced in the 1970s before the onset of the economic crisis. At the beginning of the 1980s, Costa Rica suffered from a sharp worsening in the terms of trade which, together with a heavy debt-servicing burden, led to recession. Devaluation and rising consumer prices pushed down real earnings. Formal sector wages took six years to regain their 1980 level; unemployment and under-employment levels jumped by nearly 9 per cent to a peak of 31.2 per cent of the labour force in 1982.[5] Poverty rose over these years, but fell again later in the decade. In contrast to most other countries reviewed here, by 1990 the incidence of poverty in Costa Rica had fallen back to the level of the early 1980s. One out of eight urban residents fell below the poverty line in 1990 compared with more than one out of six in 1981, but the incidence of rural poverty was above the level recorded in 1981. The social programmes in Costa Rica included the Fund for Social Development and Family Allowances *(Fondo de Desarrollo Social y Asignaciones Familiares –* FODESAF) introduced in 1975.

The macro-economic predicament of Latin American countries had clear parallels in sub-Saharan Africa: here too real per capita income fell in the first half of the 1980s and growth remained very weak or absent in the second half of the decade.

Ghana's economic recovery programme, initiated in 1983, came after over a decade of economic mismanagement and stagnation. Per capita growth turned from negative during the first half of the 1980s to positive in the second half; budget deficits were brought under control, inflation was checked and the cocoa sector started to recover. Ghana received exceptionally favourable external financing over the adjustment period, partly accounting for its positive economic achievements.[6] Ghana's poverty incidence appears to have increased in the early phase of adjustment, and may have declined during the latter half of the 1980s, though rural poverty incidence appeared to remain above that of the early 1980s. A relative measure of poverty for 1987–8 showed incidence of 36 per cent, based on a poverty line of two-thirds of mean per capita household expenditure. 'Hard-core' poverty, defined as below one-third of average income, stood at 7 per cent of the total population. Ghana's poverty is overwhelmingly rural and the poverty incidence in the north of Ghana is much greater than in the south.[7] It was in this context that the government, with donor funding, initiated the PAMSCAD initiative – a Programme of Action to Mitigate the Social Costs of Adjustment.

Adjustment measures were initiated in Madagascar in 1983, after a prolonged economic crisis involving worsening macro-balances and economic stagnation with falling incomes throughout the 1970s. Output and consumption per capita fell sharply during the first half of the 1980s; despite some recovery in later years, per capita income had not recovered to its 1980 level by the end of the decade. In 1986, per capita incomes were just 68 per cent of their 1972 level. Although there are no reliable measures of changing poverty, a World Bank study concludes that 'Most indicators point to a significant increase in the incidence of poverty in Madagascar since the mid-1970s'.[8] Rising poverty was indicated by falling levels of real wages, per capita consumption, food availability per capita and social expenditure and worsening social indicators. During the first half of the 1980s there was a rise in malnutrition among children and infants, and maternal mortality rates appear to have risen. The incidence of malaria spiralled, while the shortage of drugs contributed to a major epidemic in 1988 in which an estimated 100,000 persons died, nearly 1 per cent of the population.[9] The increase in poverty in the 1980s hit the urban population hardest – real urban expenditures are estimated to have declined by 14 per cent from 1982 to 1986, while real rural expenditures increased, but, despite this, rural incomes remained below urban incomes.[10] The government introduced an Economic Management and Social Action Programme (PASAGE) in 1989 to 'address some poverty issues and aid several vulnerable groups'.[11]

Senegal had among the worst growth performances in Africa although it received substantial foreign aid per capita, at four times the African average. Economic decline began in the late 1960s: per capita incomes fell quite sharply from 1969 to 1979, when the structural adjustment programmes were initiated. Sharp cuts in government expenditure led to an improvement in the budget, while inflation was brought under control. There was some recovery in the first half of the 1980s but per capita incomes again fell in the latter part of the decade. Urban workers in the formal sector were worst affected, suffering both a fall in real wages and a cutback in employment. Unemployment rates rose from 17 per cent in 1985 to 20 per cent in 1990 (30 per cent according to some estimates). The rural sector was more protected as its terms of trade improved and production expanded, but it is estimated that 70 per cent of the rural population had fallen below the poverty line in 1988. There are no estimates of changes in poverty incidence, but it is clear that urban poverty increased over these years, while rural poverty remained at very high levels.[12] The *Délégaçion à l'Insertion, à la Réinsertion et à l'Emploi* (DIRE) and the *Agence d'Exécution des Travaux d'Intérêt Public contre le sous-Emploi* (AGETIP) were created to reduce unemployment and under-employment among urban groups.

Zambia's macro-economic fate led it from being one of the richer African countries at independence in the early 1960s, to become one of the poorest, in large part due to a catastrophic fall in the price of copper which accounted for nearly 90 per cent of its exports. GNP fell by 50 per cent in the 1980s. Efforts at diversification failed. Formal sector employment fell sharply: during the period 1975 to 1979, some 22 per cent of jobs were lost. The nation-wide poverty incidence for 1980 was estimated to be 60 per cent, with urban poverty relatively low at 25 per cent and a very high level of rural poverty affecting 80 per cent of the population.[13] A survey in 1991 recorded that more than 90 per cent of the rural population and nearly half of the urban population had insufficient cash income to purchase the nutritionally minimal food basket and other essentials, indicating a further increase in the incidence of poverty during adjustment. After repeated breakdowns in negotiations on account of the food subsidy issue,[14] Zambia's structural adjustment programme was sustained in the early 1990s. It included programmes to address the social cost of adjustment, in particular the *Microproject Unit (MPU)*; the *Social Recovery Project (SRP)*; and the *Programme for Urban Self-Help (PUSH)*.

In Zimbabwe, low-income groups suffered as a result of the initial effects of the adjustment programmes introduced in 1991, although precise magnitudes cannot be established as the adjustment programme coincided with the severe 1992 drought.[15] The *Economic and Social Action Plan (ESAP)* involved a sharp decline in real wages and a retrenchment of 1.5 per cent of formal sector employment, in addition to job losses by workers on short-term contracts.

Reduced subsidies on basic commodities (e.g. on milk and maize) as well as a reduction of public expenditure for health and education adversely affected the conditions of much of the population. Key measures affecting-low income groups included a 10 per cent fall in the number of nurses employed in the public sector; a substantial decline in public funding of drugs; cost recovery measures in health; fewer teachers in primary and secondary schools; and the introduction of fees for urban primary schools and secondary schools country-wide. Some surveys, with limited coverage, indicate adverse effects on human well-being, including a decline of real household income from both regular and irregular sources in a low-income urban area, with a rise in the incidence of poverty from 23 to 43 per cent. Other adverse effects include a 40 per cent increase in numbers qualifying for public assistance; an increased number of births before admission at Harare Central Hospital and an increase in the proportion who subsequently died; declines in the use of clinics and hospitals; rising school drop-out rates and falling school attendance in 1992, especially in low-density rural areas.[16] Zimbabwe's *Programme of Action to Mitigate the Social Costs of Adjustment* was launched in 1991 in conjunction with the ESAP.

In contrast to the schemes noted above, the employment schemes in Botswana and Maharashtra – both areas subject to severe drought – were a response to the need to sustain incomes and employment during drought rather than problems arising during adjustment. Maharashtra State introduced the *Maharashtra Employment Guarantee Scheme (MEGS)* in 1972 at a time of severe drought. Botswana developed compensatory programmes to provide food and employment during drought after independence, altogether encompassing six different programmes.[17]

The motivation and characteristics of social funds programmes

Any evaluation depends in part on the objectives of the initiatives being considered. In the case of SFs a variety of objectives, not always clearly differentiated, complicates evaluation. These include: poverty reduction; compensation of those directly adversely affected by adjustment programmes; gaining political support for adjustment programmes; raising additional external finance. These objectives may conflict and often there is a mixture of motives. Whichever the main objective, there is the additional objective of achieving it (or them) in a least cost manner and/or using the funds in a way that maximises their contribution to the growth of domestic production (described below as 'output efficiency'). Our own view is that poverty reduction should be the overriding objective, and this is the way that social funds are normally presented by outside observers. But examination of the statements of those introducing the SFs and their operations suggest this was often not the overriding objective.

All the adjustment-related schemes were introduced to ease the costs of adjustment while leaving the macro characteristics of the adjustment programmes unchanged. In most cases, it would appear there was a mixture of motives, with the weight of motivation being a combination of securing political support and providing compensation to those directly hurt by the adjustment programmes. Reaching the poor in general, as against the 'new poor' whose poverty was created by the programmes, usually played a lesser role. But some schemes were more poverty-oriented – e.g. Chile and Honduras – and others more oriented towards political sustainability and direct compensation of those hurt by adjustment (e.g. Senegal and Zimbabwe). This conclusion is derived from examining the stated objectives of the schemes and reviewing their main characteristics.

Bolivia's ESF was a multi-sectoral programme which financed projects in four areas: economic and social infrastructure, social assistance and credit schemes. It was designed as a grant-giving institution to provide funding for locally generated labour-intensive projects. Initially it focused mainly on low-cost activities with high employment spin-offs, but it then shifted towards social assistance and the creation of infrastructure. The funds were obtained from a wide range of international organisations, including the World Bank, bilateral donors and non-govermental organisations (NGOs); and some 96 per cent was funded externally. Observers note that a prime objective of the Bolivian scheme was to contribute to the political sustainability of the adjustment process.[18]

The emergency employment programmes in Chile were intended to provide 'temporary compensation for laid off workers'.[19] The public works of the Minimum Employment Programme (PEM) included creating public parks, street cleaning, painting public buildings, and building sanitation facilities in poor areas. Employment was provided at very low wages, the equivalent of one-quarter of the minimum wage in a context of sharply declining real wages.[20] The occupational programme of heads of household (POJH) was created in 1982 to provide additional employment relief during the second crisis: it was intended specifically for heads of households who had had a stable job before. POJH workers were paid about 40 per cent of the minimum wage.[21] The labour-intensive programme (PIMO), initiated at the end of 1983, was intended to encourage private sector involvement in labour-intensive projects, by providing subsidies for jobs created in selected projects.

The main objective of the Honduras SCS/FHIS was to help those in poverty by financing social and economic development projects which would increase their productivity and employment opportunities and satisfy basic needs. It included finance of micro-enterprises, cooperatives, etc.; labour-intensive projects; projects which generated temporary and seasonal employment for poor groups; and projects in poor areas. Project activities focused on the creation of social infrastructure (for example, schools, health centres, roads, sewers, irrigation, markets in small towns), as well as feeding, nutrition, basic health and educational activities targeting under-nourished children under five years old, pregnant and nursing mothers and ethnic minorities.

Costa Rica's FODESAF aimed to develop schemes 'to benefit exclusively the poorer segments of the population' to complement existing social programmes.[22]

Its funding was through a regular 5 per cent charge on the wage bill of both the public and the private sector as well as a sales tax on consumer goods, excluding most basic goods. The expenditures under FODESAF ranged from 5.0 to 7.8 per cent of total government expenditure during the 1980s, with a peak in 1988. This level of expenditure, if well targeted, would have permitted an annual income supplement of $80 for each individual below the poverty line per year. The FODESAF was designed as a redistributive system of taxes and subsidies. Some key features of schemes reviewed in Latin America are presented in Table 5.3.

Table 5.3 Key features of social funds in Latin America

| | Bolivia | Costa Rica | Chile | | Honduras |
			Until 1990	*As of 1990*	
Overall objective:	Employment creation	Additional programmes for poorest	Employment safety net	Financing programmes for poorest	Financing programmes for poorest
Design:	Foreign (mainly)	Local	Local	Combination	Mainly foreign
Operation planned:	3–4 years	Permanent since 1975	Long-term 1975–89	Permanent as of 1990	Temporary
External funding:	96 per cent	0 per cent	0 per cent	49 per cent	88 per cent
Local sources:		Wage/sales taxes	Ordinary revenue		
Demand/ supply driven:	DD	SD	SD	DD	DD

The African schemes were also the outcome of a mixture of motives. In Ghana's PAMSCAD this was reflected in the criteria used to select projects for inclusion in the programme, which included targeting and output efficiency, and also overt political objectives such as 'visibility'. The programme covered a variety of activities including urban public works, rural income-generating projects, school feeding and nutrition education. A major element (around one-fifth of the funds) was allocated to the 'new poor' for compensation and training. Two-thirds of the planned projects were urban.[23]

The objectives of Madagascar's PASAGE were to activate programmes for groups adversely affected during adjustment; reinforce government capacity to deliver social programmes; and facilitate the implementation of the adjustment programme. Activities included labour-intensive rehabilitation, construction and maintenance of rural roads in the southern drought-prone parts of Madagascar, and also support for the development of small and medium-size enterprises through training and grants for the creation of economic and social infrastructure.

Senegal's DIRE explicitly targeted funds to laid-off public sector workers, usually civil servants, as well as university graduates who previously would have found jobs in the civil service.[24] The AGETIP programme was designed after the disturbances of February 1988 to fund labour-intensive public works executed by the private sector. It aimed to generate a substantial number of temporary jobs, to improve skills and to improve the competitiveness of the firms involved, and to generate economically and socially useful projects. Its political function was primarily to employ a potentially destabilising group, unemployed youth, and to restore civic pride in poor urban areas through rapid and visible activities. Given these political objectives targeting the poorest was not considered AGETIP's mandate.[25]

Zambia's Social Recovery Programme was intended both to make the adjustment programme politically acceptable and to reduce poverty. The social recovery programme was used comprehensively for purposes of political proselytisation during the 1992 election.[26] The three components of the programme had different characteristics: the Social Recovery Programme financed labour-intensive projects in urban areas, designed to reach the poor. The MPU, financed by the European Community, aimed to stimulate community participation in improving and maintaining social welfare infrastructure; it responded to requests from the community, and was not aimed exclusively at the poor; it required a 25 per cent community contribution. PUSH provided food for work and gave technological assistance for labour-intensive projects to improve sanitation in poor urban areas; the community provided free labour during the weekends.

In Zimbabwe, the Programme of Action to Mitigate the Social Costs of Adjustment consisted of a two-pronged strategy: to assist in the provision of training and employment 'so as to ensure that the population can adjust and take full advantage of a changed economic environment'; and 'to cushion the effect of increases in prices and the effects of cost recovery on vulnerable groups over the reform period'.[27] The Social Development Fund (SDF) was launched to achieve both objectives. Redeployment of the retrenched was viewed as 'an immediate and urgent social imperative', but the government also recognised that 'there still remains the larger unemployment problem'.[28] 'An overriding objective . . . is to fine tune the intervention to make sure that it is only the disadvantaged groups who are targeted'.[29] The SDF included an employment and training programme; provision of funds for projects initiated by ex-civil servants; targeted food subsidies; and refunds of cost-recovery measures for vulnerable groups. Key features of some African schemes are summarised in Table 5.4.

Drought-related schemes

The schemes in Botswana and Maharashtra were intended to help avoid extreme hardship during drought. In the case of Botswana, this was achieved by a variety of mechanisms including both employment schemes and food rations. The Maharashtra scheme provided employment at low wages.

Botswana's employment schemes aimed to address the problems of limited employment opportunities in the rural areas and to ensure 'entitlement sustenance during periods of severe drought'.[30] The main schemes for poor and vulnerable groups in Botswana were direct feeding programmes; agricultural assistance programmes for arable land development and rain-fed agriculture;[31] public works programmes; and job creation schemes. The feeding programmes were targeted to nursing mothers and children, school feeding programmes and 'destitutes'. The various public works schemes focused on employment creation, while the agricultural programmes extended subsidies to farming activities and land development. The programmes were largely internally financed, though with some support from donors. Execution was primarily by government with the assistance of NGOs.

The Maharashtra Employment Guarantee Scheme (MEGS) in India is perhaps 'the first programme which guarantees the right to work as a basic right in a developing country'.[32] The MEGS originated during the crop failure of 1972–3. In 1979 it was made a statutory programme, through a State Assembly Act, providing work on demand. Any rural resident applying for work who has not been granted employment within fifteen days gained an entitlement to unemployment compensation (at about a quarter of the MEGS wage). Employment generated under the scheme was of the order of 80 to 120 million days during 1988–93.

The motivation of the MEGS was thus to prevent entitlement collapse and to help reduce structural rural poverty; it preceded India's adjustment programmes, which only gained momentum in the early 1990s. Echeverri-Gent (1988) notes that politicians hoped that the scheme would stem the flow of rural migrants into Bombay; while within the rural economy, the MEGS helped affluent cultivators, freeing them from traditional obligations to maintain workers in the slack season as well as providing improved agricultural infrastructure and land development. While the rural poor got jobs, the 'politicians benefit from a progressive image not to mention an abundant source of patronage'.[33]

TARGETING EFFICIENCY OF SOCIAL FUNDS

This section focuses on the efficiency of SFs in reaching the poor, looking at some characteristics of the SFs related to targeting efficiency. Data are inadequate for estimating and valuing the output created by the schemes so it is not possible to conduct a cost–benefit analysis of the SFs. As 'targeting' is a key criterion for evaluating social funds some relevant issues are outlined here. These relate to the distinction between direct and indirect beneficiaries; the extent and implication of 'errors' of targeting; and the selection of which group(s) to target.

Direct and indirect beneficiaries

Direct beneficiaries enhance their income (in cash or kind) as a result of employment on the schemes or on projects they finance. Indirect beneficiaries

Table 5.4 Key features of social funds in sub-Saharan Africa and Maharashtra

	Botswana	Ghana	Senegal	Madagascar	Zambia	Zimbabwe	Maharashtra
Overall objective:	Employment creation	Employment creation and service provision for old and new poor	Social programmes for new poor	Financing programmes for poor and employment creation	Employment creation and safety net	Financing programmes for new poor	Seasonal employment guarantee for poor
Design:	Mainly local	Mainly foreign	Local	Foreign	Foreign	Combination	Local
Operation planned:	Permanent since 1975	Temporary	Temporary	Temporary	Temporary	Temporary	Permanent
External funding:	Mainly internal	90 per cent	Mainly external	100 per cent	88 per cent	60 per cent	0 per cent
Demand/supply driven:	SD and DD	SD and DD	DD	DD	DD and SD	DD	SD

are those who gain from the schemes in other ways. For example, a construction worker in a project funded by a social fund is evidently a direct beneficiary, whereas members of his household may be considered indirect beneficiaries, as are consumers of the services created by the construction. The SFs yield a variety of benefits indirectly: through gains to other members of the prime earner's household; from the services provided; from the infrastructure created; from any general rise in wage rates which may result from the scheme; and from multiplier or linked activities that result. The indirect benefits are typically difficult to measure.[34] They often appear to be given exaggerated emphasis by politicians defending the schemes. Both distributional and targeting implications of the schemes may be quite different as between direct and indirect benefits.

Types of targeting error

The previous chapter emphasised the importance of distinguishing two types of targeting errors in evaluating public expenditures for poverty reduction. First, targeting errors arise where benefits reach beneficiaries who are not in need and hence not part of the 'target' group, i.e. E-errors. The second type of error occurs where schemes fail to reach the target group, i.e. F-errors. Below a 'strongly' targeted programme (F-error) is defined as one which covers more than 50 per cent of the target population. A strongly targeted programme (E-error) is defined as one where more than half the beneficiaries come from households falling in the bottom quarter of the population.

The target group

Targeting efficiency of any scheme, with respect to either error, will depend on who the target group is. As noted above, the target group for SFs may be defined as the poor, or as the direct losers from the adjustment programme. In some contexts, schemes are targeted at particular sub-groups – e.g. poor women or the rural poor. Even where the aim is poverty reduction in general, gender and location targeting may be useful proxy indicators when there is a high correlation between these characteristics and the incidence of poverty. In looking at targeting efficiencies of the various SFs, we have had to use rather rough and ready proxy indicators because of the lack of data.

The targeting efficiency of social funds

Bolivia

Most of Bolivia's ESF employment was generated in the construction sector (an average of approximately 11,000 person-years during the programme) and, given the depressed state of the economy, this had only a small impact on overall wages in the sector. ESF workers were prime-age (twenty to sixty-five years), married (71 per cent), male and mostly (62 per cent) they were the only income earners. Ninety-three per cent of a sample of project workers reported themselves as the head of the household and 90 per cent of their income came from the ESF wage. Only 1 per cent of the ESF workers were female, often among the poorest women. The wages of ESF project employees were somewhat below the average for the sector, and the hours worked greater.[35] The ESF workers were not mainly among the poorest two deciles of the population, but one study concluded that 77 per cent of ESF workers would have been in the poorest 40 per cent of the income distribution.[36] Further analysis showed 32 per cent would have been in the lowest two income deciles in the absence of the programme.[37] But analysis of total family income, rather than wage earnings of the main earner alone, showed that only 13.5 per cent of the ESF families was drawn from the lowest two family income deciles, which indicates non-targeting from an E-perspective. The F-error was high as only a small per- centage of the unemployed – estimated at one-tenth – gained employment through the ESF, indicating a 90 per cent F-error if we take the unemployed as the target group. Moreover, given the estimate that 97 per cent of the rural inhabitants were below the poverty line in 1988,[38] and considering that only some 20 per cent of the ESF projects were rural, one may conclude that the F-error for exclusion of the rural poor may have been as high as 95 per cent.[39] However, these estimates do not include indirect beneficiaries.

Chile

The number of people in the Chilean employment schemes was exceptionally large. The programmes for head of households (POJH) enrolled 102,800 workers in 1982 which rose to 222,900 at the height of the second economic crisis in 1983; in the same year the enrolment through the PEM stood at 280,000 and together the schemes accounted for some 12.6 per cent of the labour force.[40] Enrolment decreased sharply later and by 1988 it stood at only 5,300. Over its life-time, 1982–8, nearly three-quarters of the direct beneficiaries of the POJH were male, most of them with a family and nearly half in the prime age range of twenty-six to forty-four years. Slightly more than half (56 per cent) had previously been blue-collar workers. Workers in the PIMO programme tended to be more skilled than those in PEM and POJH and hence were less likely to belong to poor groups. Less than a quarter of the direct beneficiaries of the schemes were female.[41] The very large size of the schemes indicates that F-errors may have been comparatively low (particularly if indirect beneficiaries are included) – this was partly because anyone who wanted could get a job in the schemes. The estimated proportion of households in the population falling below an 'indigence' income in 1983 was 30 per cent (i.e. over twice the proportion of the workforce covered by the schemes).[42] Assuming there were three indirect beneficiaries for every direct beneficiary and all the benefits went to families below the indigence level, approximately 57 per cent of the country's poor benefited from the employment schemes, while 43 per cent were not included. Chile had a number of other interventions (e.g. nutrition support), also targeted to poor people and if included this would suggest more comprehensive coverage.[43] In 1983 the E-errors may be assumed to have been relatively low: to qualify for the scheme people had to work for very low wages – approximately 25 per cent of the minimum wage in the PEM and 40 per cent for the POJH.

Costa Rica

Costa Rica's FODESAF is executed by eighteen different institutions, supporting a range of approximately forty programmes. The programmes are diverse. Some programmes report many beneficiaries with low expenditure on each, whereas others have few beneficiaries receiving high expenditures. For example, in 1992 some 473,000 primary school pupils benefited from small food rations, while 59,000 households had received mortgage subsidies over the five-year period up to 1992, with an annual expenditure of more than three times that of the food rations.[44] The evidence on targeting is incomplete, but it has been noted that the programmes which have expanded most since the late 1980s 'have been less clearly targeting the poorest groups'.[45] E-errors for the mortgage subsidy, which by law comprises one-third of all FODESAF expenditure, exceeded 40 per cent.[46] Though the F-errors of various programme components seem to be low in comparison with other countries, nevertheless failures to reach poor households have been reported for particular FODESAF activities. For example, the construction of water supply systems in rural areas has insufficiently covered isolated areas with a higher poverty incidence and the same has been observed for the school feeding scheme. This is important in view of the higher incidence of rural poverty at 33 per cent of the rural population in 1990, compared to an urban poverty incidence of 12 per cent.

Honduras

The FHIS has allocated the major share of funds to economic and social infrastructure. The evidence of targeting by the FHIS, though incomplete, suggests a bias in favour of municipalities with a lower incidence of poverty, reflecting the fact that such municipalities were better able to formulate projects to take advantage of the opportunities offered by the FHIS. Municipalities with a higher incidence of poverty obtained on average $5.4 per inhabitant during the first two years of the Fund, while the municipalities with the lowest poverty incidence obtained $6.5 per inhabitant.[47] Estimates of targeting errors could not be undertaken because of lack of data.

A major feature differentiating the targeting efficiency of the African schemes was the extent to which they reached the rural areas, where the majority of the poor are located.

Botswana

Botswana's job creation schemes had various components. with different targeting efficiencies. Those directed at developing skills and trade opportunities for school leavers and providing financial assistance to reduce enterprise risks are likely to have had high E- and F-errors. In contrast, the labour-intensive programmes and the labour-based relief public works programmes, which were targeted at rural households, probably had low errors of both types. Although no detailed data are available to support these suppositions, Botswana's success in containing the rise in malnutrition during severe drought suggests low F-errors.[48] The rural population participated on a large scale in the labour-based relief programme, with an average of 70,000 participants in the second half of the 1980s, engaged for an average of seventy-six days per annum, though participation varied among districts.[49] Given a rural poverty incidence of 64 per cent in 1985–6, more than one out of every six poor rural persons may have benefited from the schemes in that year, permitting a preliminary estimate of the F-error of the order of 50 per cent including indirect beneficiaries.[50]

Ghana

The activities proposed for PAMSCAD were wide ranging and ambitious. The manifold projects planned attempted to target the poor through a multi-sector approach including employment-generating projects (41 per cent of planned expenditure); compensation for public service employees made redundant under adjustment including training and technical advice with the objective of encouraging them to enter into small-scale business (21 per cent of planned expenditure); basic needs projects (18 per cent); strengthening education (12.5 per cent); and community initiative projects (7.5 per cent).

Notwithstanding the emphasis on this at the design stage, the effectiveness of the targeting of PAMSCAD was low. A UNICEF review observed that the redeployed and retrenched public sector employees benefited most from the PAMSCAD,[51] although the groups most in need were the low-income households in the Northern and Upper regions as well as poor urban households, with low-income retrenched public employees in third position.[52] One can thus point to considerable E-errors with too many resources directed to the redeployees; as well as considerable F-errors, with a programme small relative to the extent and incidence of poverty especially in the Northern and Upper regions.

The number of participants in the food-for-work schemes in the North was nearly 11,000 by the end of 1992. Using PAMSCAD's own estimate of four indirect beneficiaries for each participant, this would indicate some 55,000 direct and indirect beneficiaries[53] or only 6 per cent of those facing hard-core poverty, which stood at 9.5 per cent of the rural population, or just below 1 million persons, (i.e. an F-error exceeding 94 per cent). This assumes that all participants and indirect beneficiaries are drawn from the target groups, i.e. E-errors were zero.

By December 1992 nearly 61,000 civil servants had been redeployed. These were provided compensation and training by PAMSCAD. An assessment of the impact on a small sample of public employees found that that nearly all the redeployed had found some work, only half had recovered their previous employment status, i.e. 'fully' employed with comparable earnings. Overall earnings of the redeployed workers had fallen sharply (by approximately half); however, difficulties in measuring income from self-employment and informal activities may have led to under-estimation. Poverty among the redeployee households increased significantly – before redeployment, some 4 per cent were below the poverty line, whereas afterwards it had increased to 22 per cent.[54] From the point of view of targeting the poor, the compensation schemes were not efficient – public employees even in low grades were typically better-off than various other social groups, especially those in the rural North.

Madagascar

The direct beneficiaries of Madagascar's labour-intensive projects included the unskilled unemployed or under-employed who gained temporary employment and qualified workers who obtained regular employment through the micro-projects. Indirect benefits were intended to accrue to the inhabitants of the disadvantaged areas where micro-projects were started.[55] However, as the implementation of the various activities of PASAGE proved slow, evaluations of targeting efficiency are not possible.

Senegal

Senegal's DIRE and AGETIP are primarily urban-oriented, with nearly two-thirds of the investment of AGETIP concentrated in the capital city and the highly urbanised district Ziguinchor. This urban focus offers a striking example of weak targeting as the incidence of urban poverty is estimated at 24.5 per cent of the labour force, whereas the rural poverty incidence was estimated at 70 per cent in 1988.[56] The Senegalese experience presents high E-errors as well as high F-errors of targeting, reflecting the predominance of political objectives over those of poverty reduction.[57]

Zambia

By 1991 Zambia's Programme for Urban Self-Help (PUSH) had financed 150,000 work days and given food to 1,500 persons over two years. It succeeded in reaching poor urban women and through them delivered food to their children. In 1992, some 3,000 Lusaka-based families were engaged, of which 95 per cent were headed by females.[58] Hence, PUSH was well-targeted in terms of negligible E-errors, but F-errors were very large. As the overall urban poverty incidence stands at 47 per cent (or 1.6 million persons) the F-error for PUSH may well be as high as 98 per cent just for the urban poor for whom the scheme was intended.[59] The Social Recovery Fund, with a more rural orientation, had a more comprehensive coverage, with 131 projects initiated, and an estimated 400,000 beneficiaries (or nearly 5 per cent of the population). This estimate includes both direct and indirect beneficiaries – the latter being very widely defined to cover whole communities – an example of the possible exaggeration of numbers of indirect beneficiaries noted above. Even so, 90 per cent of the rural poor were not covered. Almost half the beneficiaries were female.

Zimbabwe

Both the social welfare and the employment/training components of Zimbabwe's programme covered only a small fraction of those adversely affected by the adjustment programme. By February 1993, around 8,000 people had received assistance with meeting the additional costs of food – compared with an estimated population in poverty of 1 million. The Ministry of Labour had expected 300,000 beneficiaries. School fee refunds covered approximately 3 per cent of the secondary school population or one-eighth to one-tenth of the probable total size of the 'target' population. The employment/retraining component of the scheme was also minuscule in relation to need, in part because it was confined to those directly 'retrenched' as a result of the programme, and in part because of very partial coverage of this group. At the end of February 1993 (after eighteen months of the programme), 1,055 had gone through the business training courses (6 per cent of the retrenchees) and by end of March 1993, 577 projects had been submitted, of which twenty-three had been approved for 'possible funding'. In mid-January only fourteen projects had received actual approval – i.e. just 0.13 per cent of the retrenchees (or 0.001 per cent of the unemployed). All successful applicants were male.

The Zimbabwean programme to date has shown very high F-errors. Careful means-testing in the administration of refunds for school fees and food payments probably led to quite low E-errors. If we take those below the poverty line as the target group, the E-errors of the employment component were high. In a sample of thirty applicants for funding from the SDF which had passed preliminary weeding-out and were at near-funding stage, just over half came from people who had completed secondary school and achieved GCE, and one applicant had a master's degree. Thus this group by no means represented the poorest in the community and within this group better-off people were more successful in securing projects (partly because some 'own' financing was required).

In marked contrast, Zimbabwe's drought relief operations during 1992/3 were comprehensive in coverage, including all children under five in areas with a high incidence of malnutrition, school meals in selected schools and adult feeding through rural food for work and/or free ration distribution. At the worst point requests for assistance were made by up to 5.6 million adults and 5.1 million requests were granted, amounting to over 75 per cent of the rural population (November 1992). The number of persons receiving assistance in the drought relief operation was more than 600 times higher than the number of beneficiaries of the food subsidy component of the SDF. Compared to the SDF performance, the drought relief's F-error seems to have been very low as it covered most of the rural population and specific vulnerable groups. There are no estimates of E-errors; screening occurred but most people could get access to the food being distributed; however, the near universality of need set a limit to the number of 'undeserving' recipients.

Maharashtra

As a result of paying very low wages, the MEGS is self-targeting while work is provided as a statutory right leading to wide coverage.[60] In principle, this should mean low targeting errors of both types. Estimates suggest a relatively low E-error, with one survey showing that 90 per cent of workers were living below the poverty line, and another 62 per cent.[61] Dandekar and Seth (1980) estimated that the scheme had eliminated three-quarters of unemployment and under- employment among landless or near-landless households in 1977–8, suggesting a low F-error. but others believe this to be an exaggerated estimate.[62] As with any employment scheme, errors of exclusion were unavoidable for some of the poorest, especially people with disabilities and those who are too old to work. Although the E-error is low, the F-error may remain significant.[63]

Conclusions on targeting errors

The evidence from these schemes is that the SFs introduced in the context of adjustment reached only a small fraction of the poor (Table 5.5). This arose in part from the limited total coverage of the schemes, so that even if they had only benefited the poor there would still have been high F-errors, and partly from their failure to target most of their benefits to the poorest. This double failure was even true of the 'star' performer, Bolivia, which had substantially more resources devoted to it than later schemes such as those of Honduras or Senegal.

Table 5.5 Indicators of errors of targeting

Country and name of scheme[a]	E-error (benefits to persons above poverty line)	F-error (failing to reach persons below poverty line)
Bolivia Emergency Social Fund	High with two-thirds of direct beneficiaries above two lowest income deciles	95 per cent of rural population 99 per cent of female poor 90 per cent of unemployed
Costa Rica FODESAF	High for some programme components, e.g. mortgages	High for rural water supply scheme and school feeding programmes, for example
Chile PEM and POJH	Low because of effective self-targeting	57 per cent of rural poor
Honduras FHIS	High with higher allocations to better resourced municipalities	Not available
Botswana LBRP	Low	50 per cent of rural poor
Ghana PAMSCAD	78 per cent of redeployed above poverty line	94 per cent of hard-core rural poor excluded
Madagascar PASAGE	Not available	Not available
Senegal DIRE and AGETIP	High	High (100 per cent for rural poor)
Zambia PUSH only	Low with targeting of female-headed households (FHH)	98 per cent of FHH
Zimbabwe SDF	High	High
Maharashtra EGS	10 per cent only	Moderate to high

Sources: See text
(a) For full name see text

In contrast, the own-designed schemes, initiated earlier in Chile, Costa Rica, Botswana and Maharashtra, had much more extensive coverage of the poor, although even in these some of the poor were not covered. Costa Rica had quite high E-errors, but the others had relatively low excess coverage, mainly because they were self-targeted, through offering work at low wages. Costa Rica's programmes are not strictly comparable with the other schemes since they include a large number of social programmes which extend well beyond the normal concerns of social funds. Other countries also have some such programmes which we have not reviewed. The Botswana and Maharashtra schemes were drought-related, rather than adjustment-related, which may explain their political support – it is noteworthy that in Zimbabwe drought relief was comprehensive, while the adjustment scheme was paltry in effects. However, Chile's employment schemes, which were adjustment-related, reached 13 per cent of the workforce at one point, a very significant contribution, although still less than half the estimated households in poverty but roughly as many as the additional poverty associated with the prolonged adjustment process. Moreover, one should not expect any single scheme to reach everyone, since different poor households have different needs. An employment-based scheme, for example, can reach only the able-bodied. The targeting performance of the various schemes is summarised in Table 5.5.

Supply- and demand-driven approaches and targeting

The different impact on target groups between schemes appears to be related to whether they are demand- or supply-driven. 'Demand-driven' describes a scheme where project activities are proposed by the potential beneficiaries, sometimes through intermediate organisations such as municipalities or non-governmental organisations (NGOs). In supply-driven schemes, the government (or its agencies) determines the projects together with general criteria for participation.

Demand-driven schemes

Bolivia's ESF responded to proposals for projects from local and municipal governments, NGOs and grassroots groups. Since poor communities are less organised, fewer project proposals were forthcoming from them.[64] Project selection depended mainly on geographic location of expenditure, rather than the characteristics of the beneficiaries. The same limitations occurred in Honduras, where expenditure allocations were made among those who put in requests.[65] In Madagascar, selection was made among those small and medium-size enterprises putting forward proposals, while in Senegal and Zimbabwe project selection was confined to proposals put forward by civil servants who had been made redundant.

Inevitably, the demand-driven approach made it difficult to ensure that particular groups (e.g. those falling below the poverty line) received most of the benefits. However, some schemes imposed prior restrictions on the category of eligible applicants which improved targeting. For example, Zambia's PUSH was restricted to poor households. The Grameen Bank in Bangladesh achieves very good targeting (low E-errors) using a demand-driven approach but restricting applicants to the landless or near-landless.

Supply-driven schemes

Botswana's labour-intensive employment schemes – Chile's PEM, Costa Rica's DESAF, Maharashtra's EGS and major parts of Ghana's PAMSCAD – were supply-driven schemes in which the government determined the projects to be financed, and potential beneficiaries applied for jobs in the programmes. As indicated above, the targeting performance of this group of schemes was generally better in terms of both types of errors of targeting. The supply-driven schemes were either targeted via employment (generally at low wages and for unskilled work, and therefore well 'self-targeted') or through some screening system which tended to reduce E-errors. Lower F-errors among supply-driven schemes arose from two features; first, the uptake was generally higher because the coverage of demand-driven schemes was limited by the number of satisfactory applicants – for example, in Zimbabwe after eighteen months only a fraction of the available resources had been allocated; and secondly, the supply-driven schemes were also mostly relatively open-ended, providing help (food or work) to almost anyone who came along. This open-ended charac-teristic, which is very important in reducing F-errors, need not be associated with the demand/supply-driven nature of the scheme, but also depends on the availability of finance. The social funds typically were allocated a certain amount of finance which limited the size of their operations and therefore prevented them being open-ended. In contrast, the employment schemes were not financially restrained in this way.

Higher E-errors among demand-driven schemes arose because they require initiative, well-defined plans, etc., which are more likely to occur among better-off and better-educated groups, or emanate from better-resourced mu-nicipalities (Honduras). In some cases, for example Ghana, Zambia and Zimbabwe, the schemes also required some financial contributions from the individual or community. The demand-driven approach of some schemes is more participatory and less state-oriented than the supply-driven schemes, but these characteristics are achieved at the cost of less effective targeting towards the poor. Further targeting improvements in supply-driven schemes are feasible with more information, better design and administration, whereas this seems less likely with the demand-driven approach as these activities are more decentralised. But improvements in targeting of the demand-driven schemes could be achieved by imposing restrictions on the category of beneficiaries that would be eligible, as suggested above.

There appears to be a difference between the supply-driven and the demand-driven schemes in the nature of the output generated. The supply-driven schemes mainly concentrated on economic infrastructure (e.g. rural roads and infrastructure in Maharashtra and Botswana), while the more recent demand-driven SFs have financed a combination of small-scale projects (Zimbabwe) and economic and social infrastructure (Bolivia's ESF and Honduras's FHIS), some focusing almost exclusively on social infrastructure (e.g. Zambia's SRF). These choices affect the distribution of indirect benefits. For Maharashtra's employ-ment schemes, it appears that the economic infrastructure primarily benefited the non-poor. Indeed, the assets that were created that benefited the non-poor appear to have been an important part of the political equation which sustained the implementation of the schemes.[66] Works executed under Chile's PEM and POJH included creating public parks, street cleaning, painting public buildings

Table 5.6 Social and economic infrastructural accomplishments (Bolivia, Honduras and Ghana)

Country	Social	Economic
Bolivia[a]	181km of water/sewerage systems 7,084 low-income houses 259 health centres 224 schools	2,760 blocks of urban street paved 6,368 km road improvement 30.7 km of irrigation works
Honduras[b]	1.6 km of water reservoirs 4.5 km of sewers 83 km of gutters 30,000 latrines 68 health centres 1,270 classrooms	800 km of urban road repair 890 bridges reinforced 34.2 ha of urban pavements 4,850 micro-farms 20 km of earth-walls (confining a bank of earth)
Ghana[c]	Community initiative projects: 606 schools/health centres improved Wells and sanitation programme: 612 hand-dug wells 462 latrines Rehabilitation low-income houses: 1,227 houses completed (27 per cent of target) Food-for-work (North): 52 schools improved 10 clinics built Formal and non-formal education and training Essential drugs supply	Priority works programme: 71.7 km road improvement 499 culverts constructed Food-for-work (North): 2,358 acres of agroforestry other infrastructure

Sources: Jorgensen et al., 1991; Gaude, 1993; Egger et al., 1993; PAMSCAD Secretariat, 1990 and 1992
(a) Bolivia: For three-year period 1987–90; expenditure of $100.5 million for completed projects and $69.8 million under implementation
(b) Honduras: For two years 1990 to June 1992; expenditure approximately $31 million, which is 60 per cent of total FHIS fund of $50.8 million received up to June 1992
(c) Ghana: For a two-and-half-year period 1989–92; expenditure approximately $50 million

and building sanitation facilities in poor areas; however, building projects for the military (an air force aerodrome) and for the wealthy in the northern suburbs of Santiago (an access road to the airport) were also included.[67] In contrast, some of the recent SFs have created economic and social infrastructure largely benefiting poorer households, as shown for Bolivia, Honduras and Ghana in Table 5.6.

FINANCING OF THE SCHEMES

Magnitude of the schemes

Estimates of the finances of SFs sometimes pose problems: in many cases, notwithstanding firm commitments, disbursement was delayed and the real value of resources reduced. For example, the IDA credit for Madagascar's PASAGE amounted to $22 million and was approved in 1989; but by July 1992 only 17 per cent had been spent, while Ghana's PAMSCAD was scheduled to spend $84 million in two years starting from 1988, but eventually spent just half the amount in more than double the scheduled time (1989–92). The real value of commitments may be eroded in the context of devaluation and inflation. Nonetheless, financial estimates are shown in Table 5.7, as they give some broad indication of relative magnitude of the schemes. This varied considerably. Bolivia's scheme amounted to 1.6 per cent of GDP and 35 per cent of public expenditure on health and education, compared with 0.05 and 0.3 per cent respectively in Zimbabwe. There was a similar variation in employment. Chile's scheme created roughly as many jobs as the redundancy associated with adjustment; Bolivia's was approximately the same as the redundancy in the tin industry; Ghana's PAMSCAD created about 7,000 person-years of employment, only a fraction of the 61,000 redundancies in the civil service and education service, although this does not include the jobs provided indirectly through provision of training and credit.

The magnitude of the expenditures devoted to the schemes limited their potential to reduce poverty. Even if there had been *no* targeting errors and *no* administrative costs, the maximum the poor could have received per head was very small in all cases shown in Table 5.7, with the exception of Bolivia and Costa Rica. Of course, targeting errors discussed earlier mean that the actual receipts by many of the poor were much smaller than the figures shown, and often zero.

Financial sustainability of social funds

A key question is whether the SFs are financially sustainable, which appears to be related to the balance of internal and external finance. The financial and administrative sustainability of the older internally initiated schemes is evident through their resilience; it is too early to determine to what extent the temporary 'new generation' SFs will succeed in consolidating themselves.

Externally funded schemes

Most of the social funds initiated in the 1980s were largely externally financed. Bolivia's ESF was almost entirely externally financed; domestic resources were only used for the initial set-up and some limited counterpart financing from grassroots organisations and cooperatives. The ESF was planned as a temporary

Table 5.7 Comparative indicators of expenditure of social funds

Country (name of scheme)[a]	Average annual expenditure (current $m)	Maximum possible average expenditure per poor ($ per person below poverty line)[b]	GNP per capita during scheme in 1989 unless otherwise indicated (current dollars)	Public expenditure on health and education (% of GNP 1988–90)	SF as percentage of GNP in 1989, unless otherwise indicated	SF as percentage of public expenditure on health and education
Bolivia (ESF)	68.4[c]	15	620	4.6	1.59	35
Costa Rica (FODESAF)	60.0[d]	80	1,780	10.2	1.13	11
Chile (FOSIS)	7.5[e]	1.4	2,160[f]	4.7[g]	0.03[f]	0.6
Honduras (FHIS)	21.5[g]	5.3	580[f]	4.6[h]	0.70[f]	15
Ghana (PAMSCAD)	19.5[i]	3.5	390	4.6[j]	0.35	7.6
Madagascar (PASAGE)	7.5[k]	1.8	230	2.8	0.30	10.7
Senegal (AGETIP)	15.0[l]	3.5	650	3.2	0.32[f]	10
Zambia (PUSH, MPU and SRF)	5.0[m]	less than 1.0	412[f]	8.0	0.15[f]	1.8
Zimbabwe (SDF)	3.3[n]	less than 1.0	650[f]	13.7	0.05[f]	0.3

Source: IMF, Government Finance Statistics Yearbook 1992, International Finance Statistics Yearbook 1992 and International Financial Statistics, various issues; UNDP, Human Development Report, various issues; World Bank, World Development Report 1993

(a) For full name see text
(b) average annual expenditure divided by the number of persons below the poverty line (see Table 5.1 above); it presupposes that E- and F-errors of targeting would be zero and incur no administrative costs
(c) See Jorgensen et al., 1991
(d) See ILO, 1992a
(e) See Wurgraft, 1993
(f) 1991 data used because SF scheme started in the 1990s
(g) Excludes social security expenditures at 9.9 per cent of GNP
(h) Education expenditure only
(i) See PAMSCAD Secretariat, 1990 and 1992
(j) Health and social security expenditures only
(k) See Egger et al., 1993
(l) See Egger et al., 1993
(m) See Seshamani et al., 1993
(n) See Stewart, 1993

institution and was wound up in 1991, though experience was retained in the follow-up social investment fund. Heavy reliance on external funds is also a feature of SFs in Honduras, Ghana, Madagascar, Senegal, Zambia and Zimbabwe, which may create problems of sustainability.

PAMSCAD experience illustrates some problems of external funding. The scope of PAMSCAD was reduced to less than half of the planned expenditure because of limited external commitments.[68] By early 1993 PAMSCAD had finished, though it had not managed to use all the funds allocated to it. Yet quite a number of the projects remained incomplete as these had run out of funds because donors were unwilling to reallocate across components. One informal estimate puts the number of incomplete projects at approximately 400 out of 1,100.[69]

Internally funded schemes

An important factor contributing to their established sustainability is the wide sourcing of their revenues. Specifically allocated taxes financed the programmes in Costa Rica and Maharashtra. Additional wage and sales taxes were the main source of revenue for Costa Rica's DESAF; in Maharashtra, as well as extra wage and sales tax, special taxes on irrigated agricultural land, land revenues and non-residential urban lands were allocated to finance the MEGS.

CONCLUSION

This chapter has contrasted the experiences of social funds and special employment schemes across developing countries. The general context in which these SFs were developed was one of economic crisis followed by adjustment measures which have tended to increase the incidence of poverty generally, as well as create 'new' poverty. The key criterion for any evaluation of SFs relates to their ability to transfer incomes to the poor, thereby helping to offset the rising hardship. A secondary objective is that the schemes should contribute to the creation of economic and social assets which assist economic development in general and improve the human development and the productive capability of poor households in particular.

The evidence reviewed in this chapter shows that the 'new' SF programmes have in general reached only a small fraction of the poor, partly because their total size is limited and partly because of poor targeting. Schemes designed, initiated and financed by the country itself in order to assist the poor during crisis have been more effective in achieving that objective, being much more extensive and better targeted.

Most of the 'new generation' SF schemes, following in the footsteps of Bolivia's ESF, are mainly foreign designed and financed. Foreign design does appear to succeed in attracting external funding, ranging from 49 to 96 per cent for this sample. Undoubtedly some part of this external funding is additional to finance which these countries would have been able to obtain without the SF programmes. Most of the schemes are intended to be temporary, with the expected lifetime ranging from two to four years, with options for renewal subject to evaluation. Some candidly focus on compensating the politically powerful losers of the first rounds of the adjustment programmes, but awareness has grown that wider coalitions are imperative for sustaining inherently unpopular adjustment programmes.

These 'new generation' SF programmes can be contrasted with the primarily internally funded, largely locally designed programmes, many of which were initiated during the 1970s: Maharashtra's EGS, Costa Rica's DESAF, Chile's PEM and Botswana's employment schemes were reviewed above. These programmes have become institutionalised and remained active, though changes in their objectives have taken place over time.[70] The schemes are generally supply-driven and utilise self-targeting, in particular through low wage payments for unskilled work. These schemes appear to have been more effective in targeting the poor, primarily as a result of self-selection mechanisms.

In summary, this review has shown that the 'add-on' temporary institutions, depending heavily on external funds, have been poorly targeted and have not been able to provide for effective poverty reduction during adjustment – i.e. they represent very inadequate safety nets. They seem often to constitute political panacea during unpopular adjustment programmes. Their main strength appears to have been their ability to create useful economic and social infrastructure, on a small scale, relatively rapidly. In this area they may offer some lessons for the 'older' generation of internally financed and administered schemes. The latter employed more of the 'right' target groups to create assets, but these typically had fewer indirect benefits for the target groups, whereas the 'newer' generation of SFs were not well targeted in terms of direct beneficiaries but in some cases focused more on the creation of economic and social assets likely to benefit the poor.

NOTES

1 Jorgensen *et al.*, 1991, p. 13.
2 Ffrench-Davis and Raczynski, 1990.
3 Infante and Klein, 1992.
4 Moreno, 1993a, pp. 2–3.
5 Gindling and Berry, 1992, pp. 1601–2.
6 Toye, 1991.
7 Boateng *et al.*, 1992.
8 World Bank, 1989b.
9 Dorosh *et al.*, 1990.
10 World Bank, 1989b, p. 60.
11 World Bank, 1989b, p. iv.
12 Lee *et al.*, 1992.
13 Tabatabai and Fouad, 1993; Lyngstad, 1993; Siegel and Alwang, 1993.

14 See Jones and Pearce, both in van der Geest, 1994.

15 Zimbabwe's 1992 maize production declined by 67 per cent among commercial farmers and by over 90 per cent in the communal and resettlement areas, compared with its 1990 level.

16 Chisvo, 1993; Illif, 1992; Kanji and Jazdowska, 1993; Lowenson, 1993; Ministry of Labour; UNICEF and Sentinel SDA Monitoring Survey, second round, 1993; all quoted in Stewart, 1993.

17 Quinn *et al.*, 1987, Table 1.6.

18 Graham, 1994, Chapter 3; ADB *et al.*, 1991, p. 43.

19 Graham, 1994, Chapter 2.

20 Real wages in 1975–6 fell below two-thirds of their value of 1970; the extent of this reduction was not repeated subsequently even during the high unemployment period of 1982–6.

21 In contrast, other schemes (e.g. Maharashtra's EGS) have paid official minimum wages as part of a strategy to ensure subsistence wages.

22 ILO, 1992a, p. 27.

23 Jolly, 1988.

24 The Senegal government made loans to those who volunteered to start a business. According to one report the loans averaged $7,500 and the repayment rate was only 10 per cent (Egger *et al.*, 1993). But Kingsbury reports that the 1987 Civil Servant Redeployment Programme provided much higher interest-free loans of between $10,000 and $50,000 for the creation of small enterprises in Senegal. In Mali volunteers for retrenchment received $4,000 on average, in Guinea it was $900 and in Ghana $350 to $750 (Kingsbury, 1992).

25 Graham, 1994, Chapter 5.

26 Graham, 1994, Chapter 6.

27 GOZ, 1991, p. 2.

28 GOZ, 1991, p. 3.

29 GOZ, 1991, p. 4.

30 Andrews, 1993, p. 16.

31 Botswana's percentage of arable land and land under pemanent crops stands at 2.4 and compares to Sahelian countries like Chad (2.5) or Niger (2.8), see UNCTAD, 1992, Table A-77.

32 Acharya, 1990, p. i.

33 Echeverri-Gent, 1988, p. 1300.

34 Whereas direct benefits may be measured through an analysis of the project expenditure, the measurement of indirect benefits requires partial, multi-sectoral and/or general equilibrium analysis.

35 Newman *et al.*, 1990, p. 29.

36 Jorgensen *et al.*, 1991, p. 48 and Chapter 6.

37 Newman *et al.*, 1990, p. 32.

38 Based on Tabatabai and Fouad, 1993, p. 42; and UNDP, 1993, p 141.

39 The estimate assumes that the total number of direct and indirect rural beneficiaries did not exceed 150,000 persons. This is based on a very high ratio of indirect to direct beneficiaries i.e. that for every person-year of employment in rural project some sevety-five persons had indirect benefits. If this assumption is not valid, the F-error would be even higher.

40 Ffrench-Davis and Raczynski, 1990, p. 27; see also Graham, 1994, Chapter 2, for a critical account of Chile's special employment schemes.

41 Graham, 1994, Chapter 2.

42 In 1983 the estimated monthly subsidy per person through PEM was $25, while for POJH it stood at $51. The 'indigence' line of family income was $17 per month for 1985. Families with one member in any of the programmes would cross the

'indigence' line, but one person in PEM was not enough to cross the poverty line of $33 which was required to meet minimal housing and clothing expenses as well. For a further discussion see Meller, 1992, pp. 21–5 and 66.

43 See Raczynski, 1987; Raczynski and Romaguera, 1992.

44 Moreno de Padilla, 1993b.

45 ILO, 1992a, p. 31.

46 Families in the fifth or higher income decile received 40 per cent of the subsidy, worth approximately $4,000 per beneficiary; the national poverty line estimated that about one-quarter of the households were below the poverty line and hence the E-error certainly exceeds 40 per cent (ILO, 1993, p. 30; and Moreno de Padilla 1993b).

47 Moreno de Padilla, 1993; see also Gaude, 1993, p. 30.

48 Andrews, 1993. The number of persons involved in the Labour Based Relief Programme ranged between 70,000 to 90,000 (approximately 10 per cent of the total rural population) during the five-year drought period 1984/5 to 1988/9, on average for seventy-six days of employment; the Labour Intensive Road Improvement and Maintenance Programme created much less employment involving up to 3,277 persons during its peak in 1988/9.

49 Valentine, 1993, p. 120.

50 The reported number of participants was 84,000 in 1985–6 when approximately 484,000 persons faced rural poverty in Botswana. The average disbursement in cash per participant stood at 97.28 pula, while the median household cash income per month stood at 53 pula (Valentine, 1993, pp. 113–20). The preliminary F-error estimate assumes that there were two indirect beneficiaries for every participant and zero E-error.

51 UNICEF, 1990.

52 Klugman, 1990, p. 22.

53 PAMSCAD Secretariat, 1992, p. 13.

54 Younger et al., 1994, p. 18.

55 Egger et al., 1993.

56 Egger, 1993, pp. 20 and 35; and Table 5.1 above.

57 See Graham, 1994, Chapter 5.

58 Seshamani et al., 1993, p. 7.

59 The F-error estimate assumes ten indirect beneficiaries per family directly involved in the programme.

60 Ravallion, 1991.

61 Dandekar and Seth, 1980; Acharya, 1990.

62 Osmani, 1988; Ravallion, 1991.

63 The coverage of the MEGS in 1991 was approximately 91 million person-days of employment generated; estimates of the number of days worked vary, but a study for 1987–8 puts this at 102 days for male and 104 for female. This would suggest that nearly 0.9 million persons derived direct income benefits. Dhatt and Ravallion, 1994, show that participants obtained a significant increase in income, after allowing for opportunities forgone as a result of participating.

64 Jorgensen et al., 1991, p. 26.

65 Some of the smaller sub-programmes in Honduras are supply-driven and targeted at pre-specified social groups, such as mothers of infants and female-headed households; these accounted for 25 per cent of the total expenditures.

66 Echeverri-Gent, 1988, and Ravallion, 1991, on Maharashtra.

67 Graham, 1994, Chapter 2.

68 The original planned expenditure was $89.8 million, of which $5.8 million was to be met through local cost recovery and $11.2 million was to create a revolving fund. Hence, the revised planned project expenditure of $42.6 million replaced the original planned project expenditure of $72.8 million.

69 Personal communication from donor official.
70 Maharashtra's EGS has in recent years focused on improving the efficiency of providing productive assets; Costa Rica's DESAF has lessened its targeting of only the ultra-poor, Botswana's drought relief employment programmes have sought continuity by improving their output efficiency, while Chile's PEM was replaced by a demand-driven social investment fund.

Chapter 6

Structural adjustment policies and the poor in Africa: an analysis of the 1980s

Anuradha Basu and Frances Stewart

INTRODUCTION

The two regions most affected by adjustment during the 1980s were sub-Saharan Africa (SSA)[1] and Latin America and the Caribbean (LA). While the earlier parts of this book discussed adjustment policies as they affected developing countries generally, this chapter focuses especially on developments in sub- Saharan Africa; the next chapter provides an overview of Latin America and the Caribbean.

Most countries in SSA faced an acute economic crisis in the 1980s, characterised by worsening living standards, and high and often rising levels of poverty and malnutrition. The deepening crisis in these countries is indicated by declining growth rates in per capita incomes (Table 6.1). In human terms, the crisis has meant worsening poverty, declining social sector expenditures per head, falling school enrolment ratios, worsening nutrition in some cases and the persistence of a high rate of infant and maternal mortality.

Both the IMF and the World Bank played an increasingly prominent role in policy-making in African economies undergoing adjustment. During the 1980s, thirty-four developing countries in sub-Saharan Africa negotiated adjustment loans from either the World Bank or the International Monetary Fund or both (Table 6.2).

The aim of this chapter is to evaluate the changing conditions of the poor in SSA during the 1980s, and the way in which they were affected by the economic crisis, stabilisation and adjustment policies, examining the impact on the poor of policies at macro-, structural and meso-levels.

MACRO-ECONOMIC TRENDS

The widespread decline in per capita incomes over the decade, extending to both adjusting and non-adjusting countries, was a strong adverse influence on conditions of the poor. Between 1981 and 1989, SSA witnessed a cumulative decline of over 21 per cent in real GNP per capita. Of the thirty-five SSA countries for which data are available, GNP per capita fell in twenty-seven

Table 6.1 Annual growth rates of real gross national income per capita (per cent)

Country	1981–5	1985–90	1981–90
IALs			
Côte d'Ivoire	−2.7	−8.3	−5.8
Ghana	−3.2	1.8[a]	−1.1[b]
Guinea Bissau	3.0	1.4[c]	2.2[d]
Kenya	−2.8	2.2[c]	−0.3[d]
Madagascar	−2.0	−1.1[c]	−1.5[d]
Malawi	0.0	−2.5	−1.4
Mauritania	−2.5	0.5[c]	−1.0[d]
Mauritius	2.5	8.1	5.6
Nigeria	−9.1	−5.2	−7.0
Senegal	0.4	0.6	0.5
Tanzania	−1.7	−3.0	−2.4
Togo	−3.6	0.7[c]	−1.5[d]
Zambia	−4.9	−2.3	−3.5
Average IALs	**−2.0 (3+/13)**	**−0.6 (7+/13)**	**−0.9 (3+/13)**
OALs			
Benin	0.6	−2.4[c]	−0.9[d]
Burkina Faso	1.8	1.7[c]	1.7[d]
Burundi	1.1	0.0[a]	0.6[b]
Cameroon	3.6	−5.2	−1.4
Central African Republic	0.6	−2.5[c]	−1.0[d]
Congo	6.0	−9.5	−2.9
Gabon	−6.3	−18.4[a]	−11.7[b]
Gambia	−3.4	1.2[c]	−1.1[d]
Mali	−1.2	4.5[c]	1.6[d]
Niger	−6.9	−2.6[c]	−4.8[d]
Sierra Leone	−5.1	0.0[c]	−2.6[d]
Somalia	−2.7	−1.5[c]	−2.1[d]
Sudan	−3.0	1.3[c]	−0.9[d]
Zaire	−4.3	−3.0[c]	−3.7[d]
Zimbabwe	−2.5	0.3	−1.1
Average OALs	**−1.4 (6+/15)**	**−2.4 (5+/15)**	**−2.0 (3+/15)**
NALs			
Botswana	3.3	18.2[c]	10.5[d]
Lesotho	0.0	−0.5	−0.3
Rwanda	−0.7	−4.6[c]	−2.7[d]
Average NALs	**0.9 (1+/3)**	**4.4 (1+/3)**	**2.5 (1+/3)**
Others			
Cape Verde	3.2	3.2[c]	3.2[d]
Chad	6.9	0.0	3.0
Comoros	−1.9[e]	−1.3[f]	−2.5[g]
Mozambique	−8.8	0.0	−4.0
Average others	**−0.2 (2+/4)**	**0.5 (1+/4)**	**−0.1 (2+/4)**

Source: World Bank, 1991, *World Tables 1991*
Note: Growth rates are calculated using GNP per capita figures in 1987 US dollars
(a) 1985–8
(b) 1981–8
(c) 1985–9
(d) 1981–9
(e) 1983–5
(f) 1985–7
(g) 1983–7

Table 6.2 African countries with stabilisation/adjustment loans, 1980s

Country	World Bank	IMF
Benin	1989	1989
Burkina Faso	1985	
Burundi	1986, 1988, 1989	1986
Cameroon ·	1989	1988
Central African Republic	1987, 1988	1985, 1987
Chad	1988, 1989	1987
Congo	1987	1986
Côte d'Ivoire	1982, 1984, 1986	1981, 1984, 1985, 1986, 1988
Equatorial Guinea		1988[a]
Gabon	1988	1986
Gambia	1987, 1989	1986, 1988
Ghana	1983, 1984, 1985, 1986, 1987, 1988, 1989	1983, 1984, 1986, 1987, 1988
Guinea	1986, 1988	1986, 1987
Guinea Bissau	1985, 1987, 1989	1987
Kenya	1980, 1983, 1986, 1988, 1989	1980, 1982, 1983, 1985, 1988, 1989
Madagascar	1985, 1986, 1987, 1988	1985, 1986, 1987, 1988, 1989
Malawi	1981, 1983, 1984, 1986, 1988	1982, 1983, 1988
Mali	1988, 1989	1983, 1988
Mauritania	1985, 1986, 1987	1985, 1986, 1987, 1989
Mauritius	1981, 1984, 1987	1980, 1981, 1983, 1985
Morocco	1984, 1985, 1986, 1987, 1988, 1989	1983, 1985, 1986, 1988
Mozambique	1988, 1989	1987
Niger	1986	1985, 1986, 1988
Nigeria	1984, 1987, 1989	1987, 1989
São Tomé	1987	1989
Senegal	1981, 1986, 1987	1980, 1981, 1982, 1985, 1986, 1987, 1988
Sierra Leone	1984	1984, 1986
Somalia	1986, 1989	1987
Sudan	1980, 1983	1982, 1983, 1984
Tanzania	1981, 1987, 1989	1980, 1986, 1987
Togo	1983, 1985, 1988	1983, 1984, 1985, 1986, 1988, 1989
Tunisia	1987, 1988, 1989	1986, 1988
Uganda	1983, 1988	1982, 1983, 1987, 1989
Zaire	1986, 1987	1986, 1987, 1989
Zambia	1984, 1985, 1986	1981, 1983, 1984, 1986
Zimbabwe	1983	1983

Sources: World Bank, 1990a, pp. 74–80; except (a): UNCTAD, 1992, pp. 24–5

countries during the decade of the 1980s. The most severe reductions were in Gabon (58 per cent between 1981 and 1988), Nigeria (almost 50 per cent), Côte d'Ivoire (41.8 per cent), Mozambique and Niger (over 30 per cent), Zaire (over 25 per cent), Congo and Zambia (over 20 per cent).

Comparing the first with the second half of the decade, eight countries showed some signs of recovery, indicated by a shift from negative to positive growth rates; but economic performance worsened in eleven countries which experienced either an opposite shift or a worsening in already negative growth rates. For 1981-5, the IALs, on average, recorded a steeper decline in GNP per capita than the other SSA countries. The average GNP per capita growth rate in IALs continued to be negative between 1985 and 1989/90. But seven out of thirteen IALs recorded positive growth rates in GNP per capita during this period, compared with six out of fifteen OALs and two out of seven other countries. From these data, it seems that countries with adjustment programmes were more successful in macro-terms than those without towards the end of the decade, after making greater income sacrifices in the early years. Nonetheless, eleven adjusting countries had falling per capita incomes, 1985–90, and the average was also negative. The intensive adjusting countries also received more import-finance from external sources, partly accounting for their improved performance.[2]

More general analyses of the effects of SALs on economic growth show that in SSA, SALs had relatively disappointing results:

> Although overall performance of the 'adjustment lending' countries was better on all the indicators selected (except investment) than that of 'non-adjusting' countries, within the low income and sub-Saharan groups the growth and export performance of non-adjusting countries was superior to that of the countries which received adjustment loans.
>
> (Mosley, 1994, p. 71).

Elbadawi concludes that in SSA 'World Bank adjustment lending has not significantly affected economic growth and has contributed to a statistically significant drop in the investment ratio.'[3] A World Bank review of Africa adjustment, focusing on a comparison between 1981–6 and 1987–91, broadly agrees with these findings.[4] The report differentiates countries according to the extent of macro-economic reforms and finds that growth in per capita incomes for the groups of adjusting countries as a whole was negative for the entire period, falling by 0.7 per cent per annum in the first period and rising by 0.1 per cent per annum in the later years. But six countries defined as having had the biggest turnround in macro-policies had a better performance in the second period, with a rise in income per capita on average of 1.1 per cent per annum. The World Bank's third report on adjustment lending notes that low-income countries (which covers most SSA countries) did less well than middle-income, and that there are no 'star performers' among African countries, with even the more successful showing signs of fragility.[5]

There is debate about the reasons for this generally weak growth performance. First, there is the question of the extent of responsibility of exogenous as against domestic policy influences; secondly, there is debate about the effectiveness of the macro-policy adjustment package introduced under the auspices of the IFIs. Both issues are difficult to evaluate.

During the 1980s, the external conditions facing SSA deteriorated markedly as evidenced by the steep fall in prices of primary commodities. From 1980 to 1990 the average deterioration in Africa's terms of trade was about 40 per cent, amounting to as much as 12.8 per cent of 1990 GDP in Ghana, 29.1 per cent in Nigeria, 16.9 per cent in Congo and 16.1 per cent in Côte d'Ivoire.[6] In eight out of thirteen non-oil-producing countries, the terms of trade loss more than exceeded any increases in official development assistance over the period.[7] Moreover, rising debt service obligations pre-empted resources that might have been used for imports. Debt servicing as a proportion of exports rose from 11 per cent of exports in 1980 to 27 per cent in 1985, then gradually fell to 19 per cent in 1992. The deterioration in external conditions was undoubtedly one factor behind the weak performance of African economies. Because of financial constraints, imports fell by 4.2 per cent per annum from 1980–90; this in turn severely constrained output.

Statistical analysis for the late 1970s suggests that exogenous shocks (including rainfall as well as external conditions) were the main factor behind the deteriorating performance, not domestic policies,[8] while some more recent evaluations of African performance in the 1980s also attribute disappointing results from policy reform to the deteriorating external environment.[9] But others claim 'The evidence shows that poor policies clearly hurt Africa's long term growth far more than a hostile external environment did'.[10] Countries elsewhere also suffered adverse external shocks, while their aggregate performance was much stronger – e.g. Malaysia, which suffered a terms of trade worsening greater than SSA, and still enjoyed a high growth rate over the period.

Irrespective of the cause, countries in difficulties have to adjust to the new situation if it is irreversible. Nonetheless, the cause can be relevant to determining the type of adjustment which is appropriate. The focus on macro-policy reforms associated with adjustment lending stemmed from the belief that wrong policies were at the heart of Africa's problems.[11] To the extent that these were not the fundamental (or only) problem, it becomes less surprising that the policy changes were not very effective in turning the economies around.

Recent evaluations by the World Bank attribute the relative lack of success to 'long-term conditions: a weaker human resource base, inadequate and sometimes declining economic infrastructure, less diversified economic structures, and poorly functioning institutions'.[12] Jaycox, vice-president of the WB for Africa has 'acknowledge[d] that the World Bank has been unable to devise solutions to Africa's economic problems'.[13]

To some extent, the adjustment measures themselves contributed to the very problems identified as fundamental by the Bank. First, restraints on government expenditure were associated with a curtailment of public investment expenditure and therefore deteriorating infrastructure. Secondly, tight monetary policy, foreign exchange shortages, depressed expectations and deficient infrastructure led to reduced private investment. Real gross domestic investment per capita declined in twenty-two out of thirty-five SSA countries and in nine of the thirteen IALs between 1981 and 1990.[14] As the WB RAL III report states, private investment in SSA 'remains generally at inadequate levels'. Thirdly, cuts

Table 6.3   Budgetary and external imbalances, 1990

IAl s			
Côte d'Ivoire	n.a.	−12.2	18.0
Ghana	0.4	−7.1	3.5
Guinea Bissau	n.a.	−44.4	0.6[c]
Kenya	−6.8	−7.8	6.8
Madagascar	−4.2[a]	−10.5	3.9
Malawi	−1.9	−8.7	1.5
Mauritania	−4.2	−18.9	2.2
Mauritius	−0.5	−5.2	0.9
Nigeria	−10.5	6.3	36.1
Senegal	n.a.	−8.2	3.7
Tanzania	n.a.	−39.9	5.9
Togo	−2.6	−12.8	1.3
Zambia	−5.0	−15.7	7.2
Average IALs	**−3.9**	**−14.2**	**7.1**
OALs			
Benin	n.a.	−6.2[b]	1.4
Burkina Faso	0.3	−12.1	0.8
Burundi	n.a.	−18.5	0.9
Cameroon	−3.2	−2.5	6.0
Central African Republic	n.a.	−19.0	0.9
Congo	n.a.	−6.8	5.1
Gabon	n.a.	4.7	3.6
Gambia	n.a.	−3.5	0.3[c]
Mali	−4.6	−14.9	2.4
Niger	n.a.	−9.8	1.8
Sierra Leone	−1.4	−15.1	1.2
Somalia	n.a.	−37.1	2.4
Sudan	n.a.	−14.3	15.4
Zaire	1.9	−11.4	10.1
Zimbabwe	−7.9	−4.3	3.2
Average OALs	**−2.5**	**−11.4**	**3.7**
NALs			
Botswana	12.6	−6.6	0.5
Lesotho	−2.8	−26.4	0.4
Rwanda	n.a.	−10.5	0.7
Average NALs	**4.9**	**−14.5**	**0.5**
Others			
Cape Verde	n.a.	−5.4	0.1[c]
Chad	n.a.	−27.0	0.5
Comoros	n.a.	−19.6	0.2[c]
Mozambique	n.a.	−54.4	4.7
Uganda	n.a.	−14.4	2.7
Average others	**n.a.**	**−24.2**	**1.6**

Sources: World Bank, 1991 and 1992, *World Development Report*, Washington DC; World Bank, 1992 *World Tables 1992*

(a) Figures for 1987 from Dorosh *et al.*, 1990

(b) Figures for 1989

(c) Estimates for 1990 from World Bank, *World Tables 1992*. All other figures in this column are form World Bank, *World Development Report* 1991 or 1992

in public expenditure per capita on education (see below) further weakened the human resource base.

In addition to the poor achievements with respect to economic growth, the persistence of macro-economic imbalances until the end of the 1980s – reflected in continued budgetary and current account deficits and rising external debt in a number of adjusting and non-adjusting countries – is another indicator of deficient achievement of the macro-policy package (Table 6.3). These imbalances imply that adjustment is likely to be a continuing issue throughout the next decade.

In summary, for the majority of SSA countries, macro-economic performance was poor, generating a generally adverse influence on the conditions of the poor. The poor performance was shared by adjusting as well as non-adjusting countries, and indeed was worse among adjusting countries in the first half of the decade. There was some evidence of turnround in the later years among some countries (proportionately more among adjusting countries), but not enough to reverse the general conclusion that, for the most part, macro-performance had negative effects on the poor over the decade as a whole, including both adjusting and non-adjusting countries.

STRUCTURAL CHANGES

In theory, successful structural adjustment would be accompanied by significant changes in the structure of an economy, leading to more efficient resource allocation. Some of the structural changes expected to follow successful adjustment would be likely to lead to a more equitable distribution of income and reduced poverty. These include: an expansion of labour-intensive manufacturing; development of the small-scale sector; growth in exports, trade diversification and more favourable rural/urban terms of trade.

Sectoral shifts

There is little indication of any shift in the sectoral employment structure in SSA during the 1980s. If we regard textiles and clothing as an indicator of the extent of labour-intensive manufacturing sector, we find that the increase in the share of exports from this sector was insignificant (i.e., less than 5 per cent) in all SSA countries (Table 6.4), while the share declined in three IALs – Malawi,

Table 6.4 Share of industry in total exports

Country	Textiles and clothing as percentage of total exports			Manufacturing as percentage of total exports		
	1980	1990	Change	1980	1990	Change
IALs						
Côte d'Ivoire	3	2	–	8	10	+
Ghana	0[a]	0	=	2[a]	1	–
Kenya	1	1	=	16	11	–
Madagascar	2	3	+	7	8	+
Malawi	5	3	–	10	5	–
Mauritania	n.a.	n.a.	n.a.	2[a]	6	+
Mauritius	19[a]	21	+	29[a]	30	+
Nigeria	0	0	=	1	0	–
Senegal	1	1	=	15	22	+
Tanzania	8	3	–	16	11	–
Togo	4	0	–	10	8	–
Zambia	n.a.	n.a.	n.a.	1[a]	2[a] (1987)	+
OALs						
Benin	0[a]	2	+	4[a]	131 (1991)	+
Burkina Faso	2	2	=	11	10	–
Burundi	0	1	+	1	1	=
Cameroon	1	2	+	3	16	+
Central African Republic	0	0	=	26	26	=
Congo	0	0	=	7	3	–
Gabon	n.a.	n.a.	n.a.	1[a]	8[a] (1987)	+
Gambia	n.a.	n.a.	n.a.	4[a]	7[a] (1987)	+
Mali	1[a]	2	+	16[a]	29[a] (1987)	+
Niger	1[a]	1	=	3[a]	3	=
Sierra Leone	n.a.	n.a.	n.a.	56[a]	31	–
Somalia	0	0	=	1	4	+
Sudan	1	1	=	3[a]	1[a]	–
Zaire	n.a.	n.a.	n.a.	7[a]	7	=
Zimbabwe	0[a]	3 (1989)	+	28[a]	37[a] (1987)	+
NALs						
Botswana	n.a.	n.a.	n.a.	70[a]	61[a] (1987)	–
Ethiopia	0	1	+	0	3	+
Lesotho	n.a.	n.a.	n.a.	24[a]	36[a] (1987)	+
Liberia	0	0 (1989)	=	3	1	–
Others						
Seychelles	n.a.	n.a.	n.a.	4	5	+

Source: World Bank, *World Development Report* (various) except (a) where source is World Bank, 1989c
Notes: +, increase; –, decrease; =, no change in share

Tanzania and Togo. In all the other countries (except for Mauritius), the share remained between 0 and 3 per cent. The share of the manufacturing sector as a whole in total exports increased significantly (by 5 per cent or more) in only seven out of thirty-three countries. Among the twelve IALs, half witnessed an increase in the share of manufacturing exports, but the increase was significant (exceeding 5 per cent) only in the case of Senegal. The share increased in half the OALs and rose by more than 5 per cent in four. An analysis of fourteen African countries indicates that industrial wage employment rose by less than 0.1 per cent per annum between 1980 and 1985, while the share of industrial wage employment in total wage employment declined marginally from 25.6 to 24.4 per cent, indicating no structural change over these years.[15] Agricultural activity continued to be the primary source of employment and exports in most African countries.

Reduced urban bias

Adjustment policies typically aim to raise rural incomes and reduce urban bias which is regarded as a characteristic distortion of most African economies.[16] The policy measures commonly used are those of devaluation and price liberalisation.

Net changes in agriculture/industry terms of trade depend on many factors, including movements in prices of non-food agricultural commodities and the impact of devaluation and elimination of input subsidies on agricultural input prices. World prices of primary products which form important export earners in most African countries followed a declining trend during the 1980s, placing downward pressure on the rural/urban terms of trade, but this was often offset by devaluation and domestic price policies.[17]

The exchange rate was devalued in twenty-five out of twenty-eight SSA countries during the 1980s. Real exchange rates declined in all the IALs and in eleven out of fifteen OALs (Table 6.5). Devaluation appears to have succeeded in shifting the terms of trade in favour of agriculture, increasing the real income of farmers producing export crops in the majority of cases, but some of the improvement in terms of trade was offset by reductions in sectoral expenditure (e.g. fertiliser subsidies).

Trends in agriculture-industry terms of trade are difficult to gauge owing to the paucity of relevant and comparable data. Figures on movements in real cereal prices are available for a few countries. Although these estimates may be compared with those of changes in real wages, the computation of the terms of trade ratio using these two independent sets of estimates with different bases is hazardous, while it includes only cereal prices and does not take into account prices of other non-food agricultural commodities. Moreover, the direction and steepness of the price trends differ depending on the particular cereal considered and on whether we look at free market or administered prices. Nevertheless, we have attempted a rough estimate of the terms of trade for thirteen countries. In addition, Jamal and Weeks (1993) estimate the agriculture-industry terms of trade ratio for six African countries.

Table 6.5 Domestic terms of trade

Country	Real exchange rate 1980 = 100; figures for 1988	Share of agricultural exports in total (%); figures for 1989	Agriculture/industry terms of trade 1980 = 100; 1989
IALs			
Côte d'Ivoire	91.1	91	100.1
Ghana	22.4	63	59.5
Guinea Bissau	n.a.	n.a.	83.3
Kenya	72.7	85	100.7
Madagascar	51.3	85	100.8
Malawi	85.6	94	100.0
Mauritania	87.0	54	164.3
Mauritius	79.5	38	125.3
Nigeria	28.6	5	122.4
Senegal	99.8	72	142.5
Tanzania	54.7	84	123.9
Togo	81.6	38	83.1
Zambia	66.3	3	78.1
OALs			
Benin	n.a.	71	102.8
Burkina Faso	80.0[a]	88	115.9
Burundi	97.4[a]	93	84.1
Cameroon	112.5[a]	49	134.2
Central African Republic	98.8[a]	47	138.1
Congo	99.3[a]	15	163.9
Gabon	80.7[a]	21	169.3
Gambia	80.0[a]	n.a.	97.5
Mali	77.4[a]	90	93.6
Niger	64.3[a]	n.a.	61.8
Sierra Leone	121.8[a]	21	114.5
Somalia	65.1[a]	96	56.9
Sudan	119.7[a]	95	100.0
Zaire	30.3[a]	6	106.8
Zimbabwe	72.7	40	81.8
NALs			
Botswana	84.0[a]	n.a.	75.4
Lesotho	93.2[a]	n.a.	110.7
Liberia	n.a.	n.a.	69.9
Rwanda	n.a.	98	103.2
Others			
Chad	n.a.	90	100.0
Mozambique	n.a.	43	138.0
Uganda	n.a.	n.a.	76.7

Sources: World Bank, 1990a; World Bank, 1991, *World Development Report 1991*; World Bank, 1992, *World Tables 1992*; Sahn, 1990.
(a) 1978–80 = 100, index for 1988–9.

Of the nineteen countries for which comparisons are possible, twelve witnessed an upward trend in the domestic agriculture/industry terms of trade ratio[18] during the 1980s. In the remaining seven, the ratio declined, albeit only marginally in some of them, like Liberia and Uganda. Of the nine IALs for which there are estimates, the ratio appears to have increased in all but one, namely, Ghana. However, rising domestic prices of agricultural inputs partially offset the effects of improved terms of trade on farmer incomes. Fertiliser prices increased in several countries as a result of devaluation and the withdrawal of input subsidies. For instance, in Malawi, the weighted average price of the three main types of fertiliser used by smallholders increased by 87 per cent between 1983/4 and 1987/8.[19]

Small-scale sector

An important structural change that adjustment policies intend to bring about is the promotion of the small-scale sector, through reduced financial repression and more competitive allocation of foreign exchange. Figures on the share of the small-scale sector in credit allocation, employment and output are not available on a systematic base.

The few case studies show mixed effects, with some negative effects on the small-scale sector arising from import liberalisation in Tanzania and from depressed markets in Zimbabwe and Nigeria, but also improved access to inputs and sometimes credit.[20] In Zambia, the foreign exchange auction had a more severe adverse effect on small firms than on large ones.[21] In Nigeria, a 1992 survey of developments among urban small-scale enterprises from 1985 showed that the small-scale sector's access to inputs was little changed by import liberalisation, while it suffered from depressed demand in the economy as a whole and greater competition from large-scale enterprises.[22] A detailed study of changes in the small-scale sector in Ghana during the 1980s showed that employment in small-scale firms grew significantly from 1983–9 (compared with zero growth, 1975–83), whereas employment fell in large-scale firms, but output growth was less favourable with the majority of small firms showing a fall in production, indicating that to a significant extent the sector was acting as a support for the under-employed rather than a source of economic growth.[23] In contrast, the output performance of the large-scale sector was more favourable. Nearly all firms of all sizes reported that credit was harder to get.

Surveys in Niger in 1982 and 1987 suggested more buoyancy of output in the informal sector than evidence elsewhere, with rising levels of activity and wage-rates.[24] Comprehensive data from seven countries in eastern and southern Africa also show rapid growth in employment in micro-enterprises during the 1980s, far higher than growth of formal sector employment. Several of the countries fall into the 'adjusting' category, but no systematic differences are to be detected as between the adjusting and non-adjusting. No output data was collected, so it is not possible to infer that output and income share of the sector was growing.[25] The aggregate data for the employment structure in Africa over the 1980s also indicates a rapid rise in the informal sector,[26] but this is more likely to have been a response to limited opportunities in the formal sector than to a change in credit or foreign exchange allocations, since the informal sector has almost no access to formal sector credit.

In summary, of the predicted structural changes that might have been expected to improve income distribution and reduce poverty, there is evidence of improved rural/urban terms of trade, but very little diversification into labour-intensive industrial products, and only partial evidence on the effects on the small-scale sector's role, with some evidence of a rising share of employment, but almost no evidence of positive effects on the share of credit, foreign exchange or output.

PRIMARY INCOMES OF THE POOR

Given that per capita incomes declined over the 1980s in a majority of African countries, without a marked improvement in income distribution it is probable that poverty rose on average in SSA, both in terms of the number of poor and in percentage terms.

Trends in consumption are an indicator of immediate hardship (Table 6.1). Real per capita consumption declined in a majority (twenty-seven out of forty-one) of SSA countries during 1980–5, and in sixteen out of thirty countries during 1985–7. Private consumption per capita declined in eight out of thirteen IALs during 1981–5. In the years 1986 to 1990, average private per capita consumption fell in four out of thirteen IALs and in eight out of fifteen OALs.

The available estimates of income distribution for SSA (Table 6.6) show high levels of inequality in the mid-1970s, not significantly less than those observed in Latin America, often pointed to as the most unequal region in the world. There is very little direct evidence on changing income distribution in Africa, with some (unreliable) data only for three countries for more than one point in time.[27] One shows an improving distribution – Côte d'Ivoire – one little change (Kenya) and one a distinct worsening (Tanzania). Evidence also suggests a worsening of distribution in Botswana, where rising per capita income was accompanied by rising poverty incidence. For a more general picture it is necessary to turn to other relevant indicators.

The number of people in poverty in the rural areas hugely exceed those of the urban areas (Table 6.7), with rural poverty typically accounting for 80 per cent or more of total poverty, in part because, in most countries, the incidence of poverty is higher in the rural areas, and also because the majority of people live in the rural areas. Consequently, the evidence of generally improved rural/urban terms just noted might indicate an improvement in aggregate income distribution.[28] But as noted in Chapter 2, this also depends on what happens to intra-sectoral income distribution within the urban and rural sectors.

Table 6.6 Income distribution estimates in sub-Saharan Africa

Country	Year	Bottom 40%	Top 20%	Top 10%	Gini index
Botswana	1985–6	9.0	59.0	42.8	—
Burkina Faso	1980	16.0	50.0	—	0.372
Côte d'Ivoire*	1970	10.8	57.1	—	0.456
	1986–7[a]	13.0	52.7	36.3	0.540[b]
	1988[a]	19.2	42.2	26.9	—́
Ethiopia	1981–2[c]	21.3	41.3	27.5	
Gabon	1980	10.2	57.3	—	0.462
Ghana*	1988–9[a]	18.3	44.1	29.0	—
Kenya*	1976	9.0	60.3	45.8	0.490
	1981–3[d]	9.1	60.9	45.4	
Lesotho	1986–7[e]	11.0	61.3	45.0	—
Madagascar*	1962	—	—	—	0.391[f]
	1980	—	—	—	0.447[f]
Malawi*	1967–8	21.5	50.6	40.1	—
Mauritius*	1980	11.5	60.5	—	0.471
Rwanda	1983–5[a]	22.8	38.9	24.6	—
Sierra Leone	1968	15.2	52.5	37.8	0.393
Sudan	1979	12.4	53.3	—	0.421
Tanzania*	1969	16.0	50.4	35.6	0.374
	1991[a]	8.1	62.7	46.5	—
Uganda	1989–90[a]	20.6	41.9	27.5	—
Zambia*	1976	10.8	61.1	46.3	0.480

Sources: ILO, *African Employment Report 1988*; World Bank, *World Development Report*, various years; sources mentioned in notes below
*IAL countries.
(a) Data refers to per capita expenditure
(b) Data from Kozel, 1990
(c) Data refers to household expenditure
(d) Data ranked by household income
(e) Data ranked by per capita income
(f) Data from Dorosh *et al.*, 1990

Table 6.7 Incidence of poverty in sub-Saharan Africa

Country		Percentage of population below poverty line			Percentage of poor in rural areas[a]
	Year	Total	Urban	Rural	
Benin†	1978	—	—	65	—
Botswana	1979	51	40	55	83
	1985/6	55 (h)	30 (h)	64 (h)	88
Burkina Faso†	1988	—	—	90	—
Burundi†	1978	83	55	85	95
Cameroon†	1978	30	15	40	75
Chad	1978	48	30	56	81
Côte d'Ivoire*	1980–6	28	30	26	51
	1986	31	—	—	—
Ethiopia	1976	64	60	65	89
	1988	—	—	43	—

Table 6.7 (Contd.)

Country	Year	Percentage of population below poverty line			Percentage of poor in rural areas[a]
		Total	Urban	Rural	
Gabon†	1975	15	—	25	—
	1988	—	—	41	—
Gambia†	1977	—	—	40	—
	1988	—	—	85	—
	1989	—	64	58	—
Ghana*	1981	44	59	37	57
	1985	59.5/41.8[b]	—	—	—
	1986	—	—	54	—
	1987–8	36	29	44	80
Kenya*	1978	44	10	55	95
Lesotho	1979	54	50	55	83
Madagascar*	1980	34 (h)	21 (h)	37 (h)	83
Malawi*	1977	78	25	85	94
	1988	—	—	90	—
Mali†	1975	44	27	48	88
	1988	—	—	60	—
Mauritius*	1979	12	12	12	58
Mozambique	1980–9	55	40	70	97
Nigeria*	1978	38 (h)	33 (h)	40 (h)	69
Senegal*	1988	—	—	70	—
Sierra Leone†	1977	40	50	45	—
Somalia†	1978	59	40	70	77
Swaziland	1980	49	45	50	—
Tanzania*	1980	30	15	27	—
Togo*	1988	—	—	30	—
Uganda	1989/90	32	25	33	93
Zambia*	1980	60	26	80	63
	1989[c]	70	42	—	—
Zimbabwe†	1988	—	—	60	—

Source (in addition to (a) and (c) below): Tabatabai and Fouad, 1993
* IAL countries
† OAL countries
— Figures not available
(h) Households
(a) Based on UNDP data for 1988 for proportion of total population in rural areas
(b) According to poverty line adopted
(c) Graham, 1994

There is evidence of relative and absolute deterioration in the position of formal sector urban workers. Since 1980, the position of wage earners in the non-agricultural sector, and especially in the public sector, has worsened compared to other socio-economic groups. As Table 6.8 indicates, an average wage earner in the non-agricultural sector earned three times the country's average per capita income in the mid-1980s compared to more than four times the average in 1975. During the 1980s, average real wages declined in twenty-six out of twenty-eight African countries (Table 6.9). Similarly, the real minimum wage fell in twenty-two out of the twenty-nine countries for which figures are available.[29] In some cases, the fall was very large. For example, in Tanzania the real minimum wage in 1987 was only 36 per cent of its 1980 value. In general, the decline in real urban wages was greater than the improvement in the rural/urban terms of trade, indicating a relative worsening of the share of urban formal sector workers in urban incomes. The decline in wages was largely due to the policies of wage and employment restraint, together with liberalisation of food prices adopted in the adjusting countries. The steep decline in public sector wages relative to those in the private sector suggests that the decline was policy-induced rather than being a product of market forces.[30]

Table 6.8 Ratio of non-agricultural wages to per capita income

Country	1975	1980	Mid 1980s
Burundi	6.81	5.67	4.96 (1987)
Ghana	2.30	1.50	1.53 (1984)
Kenya	5.71	5.10	5.01 (1987)
Madagascar	2.29	1.66	1.73 (1985)
Malawi	4.96	5.55	3.99 (1986)
Mauritius	0.68	0.80	0.58 (1987)
Sierra Leone	2.86	2.36	2.05 (1986)
Swaziland	4.62	3.85	4.04 (1986)
Tanzania	6.86	5.26	2.55 (1986)
Zambia	4.76	4.67	1.68 (1984)
Zimbabwe	4.37	5.28	5.07 (1984)
Average	4.20	3.79	3.02
Change (%)	−9.76	−20.3	

Sources: ILO, *Yearbook of Labour Statistics* (various years), JASPA country studies, IMF International Financial Statistics. Table adapted from Vandemoortele, 1991

Table 6.9 Real wages in sub-Saharan Africa

Country	Real average wage (1980 = 100)			Real minimum wage (1980 = 100) 1986
	Coverage	Year	Index	
Botswana	Public sector	1984	85.3	94 (1989)
Burkina Faso	—	—	—	100 (1988)
Burundi	Nonagrl sector	1986	111.6	115 (1985)
Cameroon	—	—	—	108
Cape Verde	Public sector	1984	71.4	—
Central African Republic	Public sector	1985	52.8	59 (1985)
Congo	—	—	—	61
Côte d'Ivoire	—	—	—	79
Ethiopia	Civil service	1984	84.1	77
Gabon	—	—	—	96
Gambia	Modern sector	1984	80.5	65 (1985)
Ghana	Modern sector	1985	79.8	110 (1988)[a]

Table 6.9 (Contd.)

Country	Real average wage (1980 = 100)			Real minimum wage (1980 = 100) 1986
	Coverage	Year	Index	
Guinea	—	—	—	64 (1985)
Kenya	Nonagrl sector	1988	193.4	60 (1987)
Lesotho	Civil service	1988	66.8	—
Liberia	—	—	—	83
Madagascar	Public sector	1987	48.3	64
Malawi	Nonagrl sector	1986	67.1	121 (1989)
Mali	Public sector	1985	70.0	108
Mauritania	Civil service	1984	76.4	86 (1984)
Mauritius.	Nonagrl sector	1988	124.6	76
Niger	Modern sector	1988	78.2	77
Nigeria	Unskilled	1985	73.1[b]	79 (1985)
Rwanda	—	—	—	73 (1985)
Senegal	Civil service	1985	70.0	73 (1987)
Seychelles	Nonagrl sector	1988	104.7	—
Sierra Leone	Nonagrl sector	1986	25.5	—
Somalia	Nonagrl sector	1986	39.0	16
Sudan	Civil service	1985	52.2	45 (1985)
Swaziland	Nonagrl sector	1986	83.2	—
Tanzania	Nonagrl sector	1987	26.1	29 (1989)[b]
Togo	—	—	—	77
Uganda	—	—	—	166 (1990)
Zambia	Nonagrl sector	1987	97.1	75 (1985)
Zimbabwe	Nonagrl sector	1987	90.0	123

Sources (except for (a) and (b)): ILO, 1988, 1992, African Employment Report.
Vandemoortele, 1991
(a) Alderman, 1991. With 1985 = 100, the real minimum wage in Ghana fell to 76
    in 1988.
(b) Jamal and Weeks, 1993

The 1980s saw increasing informalisation of the labour market. Between 1980 and 1985, urban informal sector employment increased by 6.7 per cent per annum, while industrial wage employment increased by only 0.1 per cent per annum (Table 6.10) – a considerable slow-down compared with 1975–80 when industrial wage employment grew at 2.6 per cent per annum. The rate of growth of public sector employment fell particularly sharply in the 1980s. Estimates of urban unemployment suggest an increase from 2.8 million in 1980 to 4.5 million in 1985, an annual increase of 10 per cent per annum.[31]

The rising proportion of employment in the urban informal sector, together with the decline in real average and minimum wages in the formal sector, depressed real incomes in the urban areas – often severely – leading to a rising incidence and intensity of urban poverty. This is indicated by the rather piecemeal evidence available. For example, there is evidence of increased incidence of urban poverty for some years in the 1980s in Zambia, Tanzania, Ghana, Senegal, Côte d'Ivoire, Nigeria and Zimbabwe from individual case studies,[32] while Jamal and Weeks provide evidence for seven more countries as

Table 6.10 Changes in employment structure, 1980s

	Employment index,[a] 1985 (1980 = 100)	Rate of growth[a] (% per annum)	
		1975–80	1980–5
Total wage employment (urban and rural)	105.3	2.9	1.0
Industrial wage employment	100.5	2.6	0.1
Urban wage employment	105.2	—	1.0
Urban informal sector employment	138.2	—	6.7
Urban unemployment	160.7	—	10.0
Importance of wage employment in total labour force[b]	85.1	—	−14.9

Source: ILO, 1988, *African Employment Report*
Note: —, not available
(a) Based on data for fourteen SSA countries
(b) Based on data for thirty-six SSA countries

well as three of those just mentioned. Jamal and Weeks summarise their findings as follows:

> Real wages have fallen sharply, employment in the formal sector has declined, living standards of urban workers and peasants have drawn closer together, and in some countries urban poverty now rivals rural poverty in intensity and extent.[33]

Evidence of reverse migration (urban–rural) in Ghana, Tanzania, Zaire, Côte d'Ivoire and Nigeria[34] also suggests rising urban impoverishment.

While the rural sector benefited from improved terms of trade, the improvement was greater for cash crop (and especially export crop) producers. Three categories of rural dweller were less favourably (or unfavourably) affected: subsistence farmers; those with little or no land who are net food purchasers; and food producers. Each of these groups contains a particularly high concentration of those below the poverty line. Subsistence producers were broadly unaffected by the adjustment programmes; net food purchasers, who often account for some of the poorest households,[35] faced rising prices of purchases. Food producers, who are also among the poorest rural dwellers according to the detailed data available for Ghana and Côte d'Ivoire, benefited less from the policy changes or experienced a loss in income.[36] In Madagascar, the roughly one-third of farmers who fell below the poverty line suffered negative effects from the rise in rice prices, while only a small minority of more affluent farmers gained.[37]

On the basis of computable general equilibrium models and simulation analysis, Sahn and Sarris concluded that 'The results indicate that there is no unequivocal pattern of increase or decline in the real welfare of the rural poor but that there are marked differences in and among countries and regions.'[38] Their approach is to assume a 'typical' poor rural household and analyse the impact of policies on such a household.[39] This does not allow for differentiation within the rural small-scale sector, apart from some geographic differences. But evidence suggests marked differences within the rural small-holder sector, with the very poor households being less involved in cash crops and more in subsistence and food production for local markets in Ghana and Côte D'Ivoire, for example.[40]

Estimated aggregate changes in poverty

There are very few countries in SSA for which there are comprehensive estimates of poverty incidence for more than one year during the 1980s, so that trends over time have to be inferred. The limited evidence over time for this period (Table 6.7) shows increasing poverty in almost every case: of the four national estimates, poverty rates increased in three while the change was ambiguous in Ghana, according to the poverty line selected; of the seven estimates of rural poverty incidence, poverty rose in six and declined in one; however, in the three countries for which comprehensive urban poverty estimates are available, the results conflict – poverty declined in Botswana (which grew rapidly over this period) and rose in Zambia, while the case of Ghana is again ambiguous because of lack of consistent data. Problems of comparability between any of these estimates over time must be stressed; poverty estimates can vary enormously depending on the selection of a poverty line, as indicated in Chapter 1. Some estimates use a poverty line based on estimates of incomes and costs of a minimum consumption bundle,[41] but others simply define all those below some fraction of average income to be below the poverty line.[42] In the latter case, absolute standards might deteriorate without any change in measured poverty incidence so long as the distribution of income remained unchanged.

The evidence remains shockingly incomplete – in view of the importance of the subject – making it possible to draw different inferences about changes in poverty over these years.[43] Nonetheless, our interpretation of the evidence presented above suggests that the overall impact of changes over these years was to increase the aggregate incidence of poverty in many adjusting and non-adjusting countries over the decade. The evidence is stronger with respect to rising urban poverty; but we have not been able to find evidence to support the hypothesis that rural poverty declined – in fact there are bits of evidence suggesting rising rural poverty as well, in some countries.

MESO-POLICY TRENDS IN THE 1980s

The impact of meso-policies on public expenditure allocations towards the poor will be analysed in terms of the ratios discussed in Chapter 3.

Trends in the expenditure and revenue ratios

During the 1980s (1981–90), the expenditure ratio declined in the majority of countries, adjusting and non-adjusting, for which data are available (Table 6.11), with little difference between the two. The revenue ratio also fell. But the fall in the revenue ratio was less than the fall in the expenditure ratio and the budget deficit improved in eleven adjusting and two other countries. The adjustment policies in Africa, thus, succeeded in improving the budgetary position, but at the cost of declining expenditure. One reason for the declining revenue ratio was that many adjustment packages included reduced taxation of export crops and of imports.

Table 6.11 Fiscal changes in African countries 1981–90

	Expenditure ratio			Revenue ratio			Budget deficit		
	1981	1990	Change	1981	1990	Change	1981	1990	Change
Adjusting countries[a]									
Ghana†	10.10	14.00	3.90	4.20	13.90	9.70	−5.90	0.40	6.30
Kenya†	28.40	31.40	3.00	23.10	22.60	−0.50	−5.30	−6.80	−1.50
Malawi†	35.30	29.20	−6.10	19.50	23.70	4.20	−15.80	−1.90	13.90
Mauritania†	40.10[b]	33.50	−6.60	34.80[b]	21.80	−13.00	−5.30[b]	4.20	9.50
Mauritius†	27.40[b]	24.20	−3.20	17.00[b]	24.20	7.20	−10.40[b]	−0.50	9.90
Nigeria†	13.10[b]	27.70	14.60	11.50[b]	15.70	4.20	−1.60[b]	−10.50[d]	−8.90
Tanzania†	33.00	20.90[c]	−12.10	19.60	16.00[c]	−3.60	−13.40	−4.90[c]	8.50
Togo†	35.30	32.50	−2.80	34.80	30.20	−4.60	−0.50	−2.60	−2.10
Zambia†	39.80	21.90	−17.90	25.10	11.10	−14.00	−14.00	−5.00	+9.00
Burkina Faso	14.5[b]	16.3[c]	+1.8	14.00[b]	15.3[c]	+1.3	−0.3[b]	1.6[c]	1.3
Gabon*	41.10[b]	45.90[c]	4.80	48.00[b]	46.00[c]	−2.00	6.90	0.10[c]	−6.80
Mali*	25.90	28.90	3.00	14.40	18.90	4.50	−5.60[e]	−4.60	1.00
Sierra Leone*	27.20	11.10	−16.10	16.80	8.80	−8.00	−9.20	−1.40	7.80
Zaire*	33.80	13.00	−20.80	21.50	12.00	−9.50	−5.90	1.90	7.80
Zimbabwe*	31.30	40.50	9.20	26.30	35.60	9.30	−7.30	−7.10	0.20
Other countries									
Botswana	40.00[b]	42.20	2.20	40.00[b]	60.90	20.90	0.00[b]	18.70	18.70
Cameroon	21.6	22.3	0.7	18.30	17.70	−0.60	−3.40	−3.50	−0.10
Liberia	33.70	25.70[c]	−8.00	22.70	17.80	−4.90	−11.50	−7.90[c]	3.60
Swaziland	28.20[b]	24.90[c]	−3.30	34.80[b]	26.70[c]	−8.10	6.60[b]	1.80[c]	−4.80
Average, adjusting	29.20	25.73	−3.47	22.04	20.79	−1.25	−6.37	−2.56	3.81
Average, intensive-adjusting	32.81	29.41	−3.40	23.70	22.40	−1.30	−9.11	−3.45	5.66
Average, other adjusting	29.25	25.10	−4.15	23.50	22.12	−1.38	−3.78	−1.80	1.98
Average, other	33.90	29.63	−4.28	28.95	30.78	1.83	−2.08	2.35	4.43
Average, all	30.19	26.55	−3.64	23.49	22.89	−0.60	−5.47	−1.53	3.94

Sources: World Bank, *World Debt Tables 1991*; World Bank, *Sub Saharan Africa: From Crisis to Sustainable Growth*, 1989; UNDP, *Human Development Report 1992*; World Bank, *World Development Reports* (various)
* Other adjustment lending countries, according to World Bank, 1992c
†Intensively adjusting as defined by World Bank, 1992c – see text
(a) Some countries omitted because of lack of data – including Madagascar, Benin, Burundi, Guinea, Guinea-Bissau and Côte d'Ivoire
(b) Data for 1980
(c) 1987
(d) 1989
(e) Data from World Bank: not consistent with revenue and expenditure data

The effect of a declining expenditure ratio, combined with falling GNP per capita, was severe cuts in total government expenditure per head, which fell in nine adjusting and three other countries. The worst cuts among adjusting countries were in Tanzania (nearly 50 per cent), Zambia (60 per cent), Sierra Leone and Zaire (around 70 per cent). From 1981 to 1990, government expenditure per capita fell by over 1 per cent per annum in all adjusting countries, falling particularly sharply among intensive-adjusters (by 1.5 per cent per annum – Table 6.11). The main fall, taking SSA as a whole, occurred from 1980 to 1986, with a recovery thereafter. The decline in government expenditure, however, followed a rise in the late 1970s, so the average 1990 level was above that of the mid-1970s.[44]

Countries which managed significant *increases* in per capita government expenditure over this period were Ghana (with big rises in expenditure and especially revenue ratios), Mauritius (a falling expenditure ratio, but high growth in incomes), Nigeria (a large rise in the expenditure ratio, partly financed by a big increase in the budget deficit), Mali and Zimbabwe (a rise in expenditure and revenue ratios), and Botswana (mainly through economic growth). The experiences of Ghana and Mali are particularly exceptional from the perspective of meso-policies because they succeeded in combining improved budget deficits with increases in government expenditure through strong performance on revenue raising, despite falling incomes per capita. Ghana's improvement started from a virtual collapse of revenue-raising in the early 1980s. Revenue collections subsequently grew following inflows of foreign funds, tax reforms and improvements in economic and weather conditions leading to higher revenues from cocoa duties.[45] Of course, good macro-performance is to be preferred, such as in the cases of Mauritius and Botswana, permitting a rise in government expenditure without additional revenue-raising efforts.

'Classic' weak performance on the fiscal side is shown by Tanzania and Zambia with large falls in expenditure ratios and revenue ratios, compounded by falling per capita incomes. However, Tanzanian revenue collection improved after 1989 and was estimated to amount to 23.5 per cent of GDP in 1992.[46]

Social allocation ratio

In general, there was a negative trend in the social allocation ratio. Between 1981 and 1990, the social allocation ratio (for education and health) fell in ten out of thirteen adjusting countries for which data are available, and in two out of four other SSA countries (Table 6.12). Significant exceptions were Ghana, Zimbabwe, Sierra Leone and Lesotho. Lesotho showed a significant rise in the social allocation ratio, with the share of health and welfare rising from 6 to 10 per cent of government expenditure, and education from 15 to 20 per cent between 1982 and 1983 and the early 1990s, while the allocation to the military was halved from 24 per cent in 1982/3 to around 12 per cent. Ethiopia has shown similar restructuring in the latter part of the decade and the early 1990s.[47]

In most countries, there was also a fall in the allocation to defence and to economic expenditure, but it was not so pervasive (seven out of thirteen adjusting countries in each case, in contrast to ten out of thirteen experiencing falls in social allocation). The fall in defence and in economic share was greater among adjusters than others, but the greatest fall was borne by the social sectors for both adjusters and others. The sector which gained share was the 'other' category which includes interest payments. This rose in nine out of thirteen

Table 6.12 Changes in social sector expenditure and social allocation ratio, 1981–90

Adjusting countries	Health and education as percentage of GNP			Social expenditure		Index of expenditure per capita (1981 = 1)	
	1981	1990	Change	1981	1990	Change	1990
Ghana*†	2.90	4.86	1.96	29.00	34.70	5.70	1.29
Kenya*	8.10	7.91	−0.19	28.40	25.20	−3.20	1.07
Malawi*	5.80	4.73	−1.07	16.30	16.20	−0.10	0.73
Mauritius	5.00	5.59	0.59	25.10	23.00	−2.10	1.44
Nigeria*†	1.60	1.00	−0.60	7.00	3.60	−3.40	1.12
Tanzania*	5.90	2.93	−2.97	25.90	14.00	−11.90	0.53
Togo*	9.50	8.16	−1.34	29.00	25.10	−3.90	0.80
Zambia*	7.20	3.50	−3.70	18.00	16.00	−2.00	0.40
Burkina Faso	3.60	2.15	−1.45	22.30	19.20	−3.10	0.80
Mali‡	4.90	3.21	−1.69	18.80	11.10	−7.70	1.28
Sierra Leone	5.80	1.55	−4.25	13.70	14.00	0.30	0.32
Zaire†	6.59	0.27	−6.32	19.50	2.10	−17.40	0.27
Zimbabwe	7.70	12.56	4.86	26.40	31.00	4.60	1.18
Other countries							
Botswana	11.04	10.55	−0.49	27.60	25.00	−2.60	2.59
Cameroon	3.44	3.96	0.52	10.20	15.40	5.20	0.85
Liberia	7.95	4.37	−3.58	23.60	17.00	−6.60	0.52
Swaziland	8.97	8.52	−0.45	31.80	34.20	2.40	0.93
Average, adjusting	5.74	4.49	−1.24	21.49	17.00	−4.49	0.86
Average, intensive adjusting	5.75	4.83	−0.92	22.34	19.73	−2.61	0.92
Average, other adjusting	5.72	3.95	−1.77	20.14	15.48	−4.66	0.77
Average, other	7.85	6.85	−1.00	23.30	17.73	−5.57	1.22
Average, all	6.23	5.05	−1.19	21.92	17.01	−4.91	0.90

Source: World Bank, *World Development Report* (various)
*Intensive adjusters according to World Bank, 1992c
†1982 values, not 1981
‡1980 values, not 1981

adjusters and three out of four others, with a greater average rise among adjusters than non-adjusters (Table 6.12). Among the adjusting countries, there was a greater fall in education than health. On average adjusters' expenditure on education fell from 15.4 per cent to 12.8 per cent, while that on health fell only slightly from 5.5 per cent to 5.3 per cent.

As a proportion of GNP, public expenditure on education and health declined in most countries, including ten of the thirteen adjusting countries, during the decade of the 1980s (Table 6.12). Only three adjusting countries – Ghana, Mauritius and Zimbabwe – experienced an increase in health and education expenditure as a share of GNP, owing to increases in their expenditure and social allocation ratios. In the case of Ghana, the increase in health and education expenditure was partly a matter of restoring previous expenditure levels reached in 1977–8 which preceded a sharp deterioration;[48] external donors (led by the World Bank) put especial emphasis on social sector recovery. This was less often the case in other countries.[49] In Mauritius, there was a decline in the share of education expenditure but the share of health increased. In Zimbabwe, the share of each sector gained over the period.

Per capita expenditure on health and education declined in all countries for which data were available other than the three discussed above (Table 6.13). The largest falls were in Tanzania, Zambia, Sierra Leone and Zaire. On average, expenditure per head fell by 25 per cent among adjusting countries, but, in contrast, it rose by a similar proportion among the other categories. Detailed analysis of the education sector suggests much of the fall in expenditure was accounted for by severe cuts in teachers' salaries.[50]

Table 6.13 Educational changes in the 1980s

	1981–5	1985–latest date
Gross primary enrolment		
No. countries decreasing	4 (3)	2 (1)
No. increasing < presumed cohort expansion	9 (3)	12 (3)
No. increasing > presumed cohort expansion	20 (5)	15 (4)
New entrants		
No. countries decreasing	7 (2)	5 (1)
No. increasing < presumed cohort expansion	11 (4)	3 (0)
No. increasing > presumed cohort expansion	8 (1)	15 (4)
Average length of study		
No. increasing	9 (2)	11 (3)
No. decreasing	7 (2)	5 (2)
Survival to grade 5		
No. decreasing	10 (5)	6 (0)
No. increasing	8 (0)	11 (4)
Secondary enrolment ratio		
No. decreasing	6 (2)	5 (0)
No. increasing	21 (5)	16 (7)
No. unchanged	4 (3)	5 (3)

Source: R. Carr-Hill, 1991, 'Educational indicators during the 1980s', paper prepared for Commonwealth Secretariat; World Bank, 1992, *World Development Report 1992*; World Bank, 1989, *Sub-Saharan Africa: From Crisis to Sustainable Growth*.
Note: Numbers in parentheses are for IAL countries.

There is evidence of quite sharply divergent experience among countries with respect to health expenditure in the 1980s. Comparing a date in the latter half of the 1980s with a base of 1980–5, five relatively high-spending countries increased their per capita health expenditures, on average, by over a third – Botswana, Mauritius, Swaziland, Lesotho and Zimbabwe – while a further twenty medium- or low-spending countries decreased their per capita expenditures on average by nearly 10 per cent. The countries with the increase in expenditure together had a population of 21.4 million while the declining expenditure countries had a population of 313 million. On average, countries spent less on health during adjustment years than non-adjustment years, but no statistically significant relationships between health expenditure and adjustment were identified.[51]

Priority ratios

Taking the share of education expenditure going to primary schooling as an indicator, an increase in the priority ratio for education occurred in about half the SSA countries during the 1980s. A similar trend emerges if expenditure on secondary education is included. Among the eleven IALs, the ratio for primary education increased in only four countries. Data on recurrent expenditure per pupil at the primary school level for 1980–5 indicate a declining trend in seventeen of the twenty-four countries for which there is evidence, including most IALs. A number of World Bank sectoral loans included provisions for reducing the share of university education in total expenditure, but these met substantial political resistance and were almost never successful.[52]

Data are lacking on trends in priority ratios in the health sector, although there is evidence of attempts to shift expenditure towards primary health care in at least nine countries.[53] Cuts fell disproportionately on investment, maintenance and non-wage recurrent expenditure, with a rise in the share of wages in total expenditure. Expenditure on drugs was especially hard hit.[54] Internationally supported immunisation efforts permitted a big improvement in coverage; for example, regional coverage of measles vaccination increased from 29 to 61 per cent, between 1981 and 1989.[55]

User charges

User charges for social services form part of many adjustment packages as noted in Chapter 3. Charges for social services were introduced and/or increased in countries including Ghana, Guinea-Bissau, Niger, Nigeria, Swaziland, Tanzania, Zaire, Zambia, Zimbabwe. In principle, low-income users are often intended to be exempt, or eligible to receive refunds. But in practice the exemption system appears to work haphazardly, as in Niger, requiring complex procedures, while refunds covered only a proportion of those who should qualify.[56] In Zimbabwe only about 10 per cent of the school children who should have qualified for refunds in fact received them.[57]

OUTCOMES

The combination of economic decline, macro- and meso-adjustment policies had a definite negative impact on some human indicators – especially health and food availability – and surprisingly little apparent effect on others, notably health indicators.

Education

The crisis and the subsequent policies undoubtedly had a negative impact on educational access (Table 6.13).[58] In the previous decades (1960–80) there had been an increase in enrolment rates at both primary and secondary levels in nearly every country. But in the first half of the 1980s, over a third of SSA countries showed expansion of numbers in primary school smaller than the rate of increase of the school-age children, implying falling school enrolment rates, while in the latter years of the decade this fall had spread to almost half the countries. Intensive adjusters showed a lower rate of improvement in primary enrolment (38 per cent) from 1980–9 than all SSA (49 per cent). The number of new entrants grew at a rate below the expansion of the cohort in three-quarters of the countries from 1981–5, but in only a third in the later years. Secondary enrolment rates stayed the same or fell in 31 per cent of countries, 1980–6 and 38 per cent from 1986–9. Again it seems that intensively-adjusting countries suffered more than others.

Negative influences on school attendance included falling parental incomes which meant that children's labour became more important for family survival and the ability to finance costs of school attendance fell; this was compounded by rising fees and 'voluntary' contributions, as well as the deterioration in resource availability in education. School fees appear to have had a direct effect in reducing attendance in Tanzania, where attendance at primary school fell from near universal levels in the 1970s to 66 per cent in 1987, at a time when 'voluntary' school fees were introduced. Negative effects of declining incomes and fees on attendance and other educational expenditure were observed in Zimbabwe, as noted earlier. The proportion of children remaining at school to the end of primary school fell in the majority of countries, 1981–5, and in a third of the cases, 1986–90; the average time taken to complete primary education increased in the majority of countries throughout the decade, indicating rising repetition rates.

For Côte d'Ivoire there is information about enrolment rates by income group for 1985–8. This shows reduced enrolment rates among the extreme and moderately poor, with the sharpest fall among the poorest, while the overall primary enrolment rate rose as a result of rising enrolment among the non-poor. Similar trends occurred at the secondary level, with enrolment rates falling among the poor and rising among the non-poor, but in this case, the aggregate rate fell (see Table 6.13). At each level the worst falls occurred among girls.[59] Côte d'Ivoire is unique in having the data broken down by income group. It is likely that similar differential trends occurred elsewhere, where falling incomes among the poor led them to keep their children away from school to help in sustaining family livelihoods and to avoid the costs of attending school.

Health services

Estimates of the share of population with access to health services during 1985–7 indicate that thirteen countries had less than 50 per cent coverage in the rural areas. There are very little data on change in access. However, evidence from UNICEF Annual Reports notes that over the 1980s access fell in three countries and rose in four.[60] The number of people per physician worsened in over half the countries for which data are available and the ratio of nurses to population in one-third between 1980 and 1990. Deterioration was worst among the IALs, where the population per physician ratio deteriorated in three-quarters of the countries.

Use of health services was adversely affected by the combined effect of reduced resources (including drugs), reduced incomes and rising charges. Rising charges appeared to have negative effects on use in Zaire where pre-natal contacts fell from 95 per cent to 84 per cent, with greater falls among the low-income.[61] In Ghana, there was a big increase in fees in 1985. Sharp drops in use of clinics followed; among the urban clinics attendance gradually got back to the pre-1985 level, but the drop in rural utilisation rates remained.[62] In Swaziland, there was a large increase in charges for government health facilities. The result was a big shift towards mission facilities and an overall drop of 17 per cent in use of modern health facilities. There appeared to be a disproportionate drop in the use of modern services among low-income households and particular decline in treatment for sexually transmitted and respiratory diseases. In Lesotho, following an increase in fees, attendance at government clinics dropped – as in Ghana, the drop in attendance appeared to be long lasting in remote areas.[63] In Zimbabwe, attendance at clinics fell by a quarter, and the number of births before arrival at hospital (and mortality rates among those births) rose, as health charges were enforced and raised.[64]

An experiment in the Cameroon combined the introduction of charges with quality improvements in clinics, and found that there was a significant increase in the use of health facilities especially among the poor.[65] This contrasts with the more usual findings of a reduction in use by the poor when charges were introduced with no change in quality.

In Côte d'Ivoire, the proportion of people consulting a doctor fell sharply among the very poor, 1985–8; it also fell among the moderately poor, but rose among the non-poor. Overall consultations fell generally among rural groups. However, preventative consultations rose in every group, reflecting the success of the immunisation drive.[66]

Immunisation rates generally recorded a positive trend during the 1980s, nonetheless. Between 1981 and 1988–9, the proportion of one-year-olds immunised increased in most adjusting countries. Two IALs – Côte d'Ivoire and Mauritius – witnessed a small decline in their immunisation rates during the 1980s, but while immunisation was low in Côte d'Ivoire, it remained high in Mauritius.

Reliable data on infant mortality rates – based on direct evidence from censuses and other enquiries – for more than one date in the 1980s are only available for thirteen countries (Table 6.14). All show an improvement except for Ghana's under-five mortality rate, which rose; there was no change (on a very low IMR) in the Seychelles, and a very small improvement in Togo. More comprehensive, but less well based, data show the IMR declined in thirty-eight out of forty-one SSA countries. Two IALs – Madagascar and Senegal – showed a rise.

Table 6.14 Infant and under-fives mortality rates
(per 1,000 births)

Country		Infant mortality rate	Under-fives mortality rate
Botswana	1979	80	112
	1984	51	66
Burundi†	1976	130	219
	1984	113	188
Cape Verde	1976–80	85	—
	1983–5	68	—
Ghana*	1978–82	86	152
	1983–7	77	155
Kenya*	1975	93	151
	1984–9	60	89
Liberia	1976–80	164	243
	1981–6	144	220
Mauritius*	1984–6	25	—
	1987–8	23	—
São Tomé	1977	80	—
	1986–8	68	—
Senegal*	1976–80	90	236
	1981–5	86	191
Seychelles	1981–5	18	—
	1986–8	18	—
Togo*	1978–82	87	159
	1983–7	81	158
Uganda	1978–82	114	200
	1983–8	101	180
Zimbabwe†	1980	84	135
	1984	62	96

Source: Jespersen, 1992, pp. 44–5
*IAL countries
†OAL countries

Food and nutrition

Adjustment packages might be expected to raise the relative price of food, as a result of the abolition/reduction of food subsidies, devaluation and increases in agricultural producer prices. However, the evidence for twelve countries (1980–7) shows that this occurred in only three, while in nine, relative food prices declined, albeit marginally in three cases (Table 6.15).[67] In four cases the available price ratio pertains to a single town and may not reflect general conditions in the country.[68] However, although it appears that relative food prices did not change significantly, there was a steep fall in real average and minimum non-agricultural wages in many SSA countries, as shown earlier. For example, the real urban minimum wage in Madagascar fell by 75 per cent between 1980 and 1986 until it barely covered the rice needs of an average urban family.[69] With the abolition of maize-meal subsidy in Tanzania in 1984, prices of maize-meal escalated in the mid-1980s. As a result, the purchasing power of the minimum wage fell sharply between 1984 and 1991, to bare subsistence levels.[70] In Zambia, it is estimated that 40 per cent of urban households earned less than the minimum needs basket in 1984. The cost of a basic food basket (meeting minimum nutritional requirements) as a proportion of unskilled wages increased from 64 to 88 per cent between 1980 and 1988.[71]

Table 6.15 Changes in relative food prices, 1980s

		1987 (1980 = 100)
IALs		
Ghana	food : non-food price index	43.8
Madagascar	food : general price index	95.0
	farmgate rice: consumer price index	175.0 (1986)
Malawi (Lilongwe)	food : general price index	98.0 (1988)
Senegal (Dakar)	food : general price index	89.4
	official producer prices of millet, rice and maize: consumer price index	106.0
Tanzania	food : general price index	99.1 (1984 = 100)
	farmgate price of tea: consumer price index	102.7
Zambia	food : general price index	101.0
OALs		
Mali (Bamako)	food : non-food price index	101.0 (1986)
Niger	food : general price index	80.0 (1988)
Somalia (Mogadishu)	food : general price index	79.6 (1985)
Zimbabwe	food : general price index	107.3
	food : non-food prices[a]	91.3
NALs		
Rwanda	food : general price index	73.1 (1986)

Sources: Clark and Manuh, 1991, for Ghana; Sahn, 1990, for others; World Bank, 1989, *African Economic and Financial Data*, for ratios specifying farmgate/official producer prices for particular food items
Note: Ratios represent the national average, unless otherwise specified above
(a) Farmgate price ratio of maize + wheat to tobacco + cotton

Trends in food production per capita during 1980–9 show that twenty-nine out of forty countries experienced a decline in per capita production. Among the thirteen IALs, there was a decline in eight. The six countries identified by the World Bank as having shown the biggest improvement in macro-economic policies in the 1980s saw a *decline* in their agricultural growth on average, 1987–91 compared with 1981–6. Since export growth was shown to have accelerated this suggests the decline in growth of food production was particularly marked.[72] Many factors may have been responsible for the poor performance, including weather and shortages of inputs. But the data suggest that the adjustment policies were frequently not effective in boosting output. In part this was due to the fact that pricing policies often favoured export crops, not food.[73] For instance, in the case of Malawi, producer price incentives were focused on exportable cash crops rather than cereals (maize) which led to an initial decline in producer prices of maize. The latter, compounded by the rise in fertiliser prices, following the withdrawal of subsidies, discouraged small-holder farmers from growing maize beyond their own consumption require-ments. This resulted in a depletion of government food stocks and a sharp rise in maize prices by 1986/7, which adversely affected poorer households.[74]

The declining trend in per capita food production suggests that per capita food availability and average nutritional levels fell in the majority of countries during the 1980s; this is supported by the available evidence. Between 1980 and 1988–90, daily calorie supply per capita deteriorated in twenty-one out of forty-one countries (Table 6.16). Among adjusting countries half had lower nutritional levels by this measure at the end of the 1980s than the beginning.

Table 6.16 Changes in per capita food production and nutritional levels, 1980s

Country	Food production per capita (1987 = 100)			Daily calories supply per capita		
	1980	1989	Change	1980	1988–90	Change
IALs						
Côte d'Ivoire	103.6	96.1	–	2,546	2,570	+
Ghana	92.3	102.8	+	1,795	2,140	+
Guinea-Bissau	68.4	101.7	+	1,906	2,240	+
Kenya	100.6	104.4	+	2,225	2,060	–
Madagascar	108.0	97.8	–	2,491	2,160	–
Malawi	119.0	103.8	–	2,406	2,050	–
Mauritania	113.7	99.2	–	2,065	2,450	+
Mauritius	80.7	87.3	+	2,715	2,900	+
Nigeria	105.4	98.6	–	2,254	2,200	–
Senegal	71.4	88.5	+	2,401	2,320	–
Tanzania	109.0	99.7	–	2,310	2,200	–
Togo	116.4	108.9	–	2,178	2,270	+
Zambia	113.4	106.2	–	n.a.	2,020	
			5+/13			6+/12
OALs						
Benin	95.1	118.9	+	2,041	2,380	+
Burkina Faso	86.8	103.6	+	2,029	2,220	+
Burundi	95.8	86.1	–	2,304	1,950	–
Cameroon	101.8	98.8	–	2,130	2,210	+
Central African Republic	112.7	100.9	–	2,136	1,850	–
Congo	100.5	97.2	–	2,472	2,300	–
Gabon	124.3	95.8	–	2,274	2,440	–

Table 6.16 (Contd.)

Country	Food production per capita (1987 = 100)			Daily calories supply per capita		
	1980	1989	Change	1980	1988–90	Change
Gambia	100.2	102.7	+	2,154	2,290	+
Mali	104.9	108.2	+	1,720	2,260	+
Niger	133.4	109.8	–	2,362	2,240	–
Sierra Leone	108.6	94.1	–	2,034	1,900	–
Somalia	106.2	101.5	–	2,099	1,870	–
Sudan	124.9	104.5	–	2,417	2,040	–
Zaire	104.3	95.4	–	2,123	2,130	+
Zimbabwe	124.7	129.1	+	2,137	2,260	+
			5+/15			8+/15
NALs						
Botswana	146.6	113.6	–	2,152	2,260	+
Ethiopia	112.0	100.4	–	1,807	1,700	–
Lesotho	125.1	92.2	–	2,400	2,120	–
Liberia	100.7	94.4	–	2,375	2,260	–
Rwanda	122.1	89.6	–	2,007	1,910	–
			0+/5			2+/5
Others						
Cape Verde	85.3	73.8	–	2,567	2,780	+
Chad	104.0	100.3	–	1,799	1,740	–
Comoros	91.3	92.4	+	2,074	1,760	–
Guinea	n.a.	n.a.		1,806	2,240	+
Mozambique	119.9	98.5	–	1,810	1,810	+
São Tomé	136.7	98.7	–	2,297	2,150	–
Seychelles	n.a.	n.a.		2,306	2,360	+
Swaziland	103.7	93.1	–	2,483	2,630	+
Uganda	109.9	94.9	–	2,151	2,180	+
			1+/7			5+/9

Sources: World Bank, *World Tables 1991*; World Bank, 1989, *Sub-Saharan Africa: From Crisis to Sustainable Growth*; UNDP, *Human Development Report* 1994

The persistence of malnutrition in two-thirds of the countries of SSA is indicated by estimates for 1990 with malnutrition rates frequently above 30 per cent. Consistent data over time are rarely available, although there are indicators of rising rates of child malnutrition, on the basis of micro-studies including hospital data, during the 1980s in ten SSA countries – Benin, Botswana, Ghana, Kenya, Lesotho, Madagascar, Niger, Nigeria, Togo and Zambia – with the rise being temporary in Botswana, Ghana and Togo.[75] There was a slight improvement in child malnutrition during the 1980s in Sierra Leone and Zimbabwe.[76]

CONCLUSION

The evidence suggests that poverty was high and increasing in many countries of sub-Saharan Africa during the 1980s. Real per capita incomes and consumption fell in a majority of countries during the decade. This, together with the decline in public expenditure and investment per capita, and the fall in per capita food production in a number of countries, had an adverse effect on welfare generally, including on the poorest sections of society. These adverse changes occurred in both adjusting and non-adjusting countries. Although the situation does not appear to have been generally worse in adjusting countries, except for some specific changes such as the introduction or raising of user fees for social services, the adjustment policies were clearly not satisfactory from a poverty perspective. While it is often hypothesised that adjustment policies in Africa reduce poverty because they improve the rural/urban terms of trade and therefore reduce rural poverty, which is of far greater magnitude than urban, the rather limited evidence does not show a reduction in rural poverty – indeed it increased in most of the countries for which there is evidence.

The World Bank and IMF did not play explicit attention to problems of poverty and adjustment until around 1987. Since then, there have been attempts to redirect public expenditure and to develop funds to offset the social costs of adjustment. The evidence on government expenditure allocations among adjusting countries relative to others and on the impact of the social funds (see Chapter 5) suggests neither change has been effective on a significant scale. Considering the decade as a whole, the international financial institutions' response to the plight of the poor was therefore tardy and inadequate. Even in Ghana, which is commonly regarded as an example of a successful adjuster, malnutrition continued to afflict a sizeable share of the population until the end of the decade, there is no indication of reduced poverty and PAMSCAD was largely ineffective.

One factor undermining recovery at the macro-level was the continued fall in commodity prices which outweighed the additional aid received over this period in a number of countries.[77] The fall in commodity prices was greater for the adjusting group of countries than for others.[78] For some commodities this deterioration was the direct result of expansion in production due to the adjustment policies – a notable example is cocoa. Success at the macro-level is an essential precondition for sustained reduction of poverty. The present strategy of adjustment which relies heavily on expansion of commodity exports is not likely to succeed because of the implications for commodity prices. Tackling the commodity price problem, and diversification of production and exports is therefore central to success in adjustment and poverty reduction in the medium term.

In conclusion, our study indicates that the World Bank's view that 'adjustment is much better for the poor than non-adjustment'[79] is difficult to support based on the evidence available over this ten-year period for sub-Saharan Africa. The poor suffered in both adjusting and non-adjusting countries.

NOTES

1 All countries of Africa excluding South Africa, Namibia, Morocco, Algeria, Tunisia, Libya and Egypt.

2 According to World Bank, 1994, about one-third of the improvement in performance was due to extra finance.

3 Elbadawi, 1992, p. 5.

4 World Bank, 1994.

5 World Bank, 1992a.

6 Helleiner, 1993.

7 Ibid.

8 Wheeler, 1984.

9 World Bank, 1992a; Hussein, 1993.

10 World Bank, 1994; p. 31. See also Killick, 1992. Both support this view with cross-country regression analysis.

11 See Berg Report (World Bank, 1981).

12 World Bank, 1992a.

13 Quoted in *The Guardian*, 24 May 1993.

14 Based on data in World Bank, World Tables 1991.

15 ILO, 1988.

16 The existence of an urban bias in Africa has been emphasised since the 1960s by, for instance, Elliot Berg who was the main author of the World Bank (1981) report on sub-Saharan Africa which subscribed to this thesis.

17 For instance, between 1980 and 1989, world cocoa prices declined from $2.6 to $1.24 per kilogram (Alderman, 1991). Cocoa is a major primary export of several African economies, including Côte d'Ivoire and Ghana.

18 Measured here as the change in the ratio of agricultural to industrial prices. This is a gross measure and does not take into account the effects of changing prices of inputs.

19 It is sometimes argued that poor farmers do not use fertilisers so will not be adversely affected – but this does not seem to be the case in Ghana – see Jebuni and Seini, 1993.

20 See de Valk, 1993; Dawson, 1994.

21 Stein, 1992.

22 Dawson, 1994.

23 Steel and Webster, 1992.

24 Azam *et al.*, 1993.

25 Liedholm and Mead, 1993. The main body of data concerns existing enterprises, and does not allow for births and deaths of enterprises. However, their surveys suggest that there were net births over the period.

26 ILO, 1988; 1992b.

27 The data for Côte d'Ivoire are believed to exclude the white and immigrant population, while that for Tanzania is not on a consistent basis over time (personal communication from R. Green).

28 Hussein, 1993, argues that this was the case.

29 It should be noted that in a number of cases (eleven countries) wage data relate to the public sector alone.

30 For instance, data on Kenya show that between 1977 and 1987, wages fell by 25 per cent in the public sector compared to a 4 per cent decrease in tthe private sector. In Côte d'Ivoire, public sector wages dropped by 4.4 per cent beween 1979 and 1984, while private sector wages rose by 13.4 per cent (Vandemoortele, 1991).

31 ILO, 1988, estimates.

32 See Wagao, 1990, on Tanzania; Graham, 1994, Chapter 6, and Pearce, 1990, on Zambia; Graham, 1994, and Lee *et al.*, 1992, on Senegal; UNICEF, 1987, 1990, on Ghana; ILO, 1993, on Zimbabwe; Grootaert, 1993, on the Côte d'Ivoire; Roy, 1993, on Nigeria.

33 Jamal and Weeks, 1993, p. 5.

34 Horton *et al.*, 1994; Mustapha, 1990.

35 In Zambia, for example; see Graham, 1994, Chapter 6.

36 Data from Living Standard Surveys of Ghana and Côte d'Ivoire – see Kanbur, 1990, and Boateng *et al.*, 1992.

37 Barrett and Dorosh, 1994.

38 Sahn and Sarris, 1991, pp. 281–2.

39 This is also the method adopted by Dorosh and Sahn, 1992.

40 See, e.g., Boateng *et al.*, 1992.

41 E.g., Pearce, 1990, for Zambia.

42 E.g., Boateng *et al.*, 1992, for Ghana.

43 For example, the Cornell Food and Nutrition Policy Program broadly concludes that poverty in adjusting countries in Africa did not increase in the 1980s on the basis of computable general equilibrium models and analysis – see especially Dorosh and Sahn, 1992.

44 Younger, 1994.

45 Alderman, 1991.

46 Mans in Hussein and Faruquee, 1994.

47 Neither Ethiopia nor Lesotho is included in Table 6.12 because data were incomplete for the period shown. Data for Lesotho, above, come from World Bank, 1993b; information for Ethiopia from R. Jolly.

48 Per capita expenditure on education dropped from $20 in 1972 to $1 in 1983. Health care utilisation levels declined by more than 40 per cent bettween 1979 and 1984. See Alderman, 1991.

49 This is acknowledged by World Bank, 1992a. The report compares the case of Ghana with that of Kenya where WB loans did not typically focus on the composition of expenditures.

50 Stewart, 1994.

51 Evidence from World Bank, 1993b.

52 Stevenson, 1991.

53 Jespersen, 1992, p. 37.

54 Ibid. But there are very little data of changes over time to back up these assertions.

55 UNICEF, 1991.

56 See Tinguiri, 1992.

57 Evidence from Ministry of Labour, Harare.

58 The World Bank's own assessments show negative effects of adjustment policies on educational indicators (including expenditure per head and secondary enrolment rates) (World Bank, 1990a).

59 Evidence from Grootaert, 1993.

60 Jespersen, 1992.

61 Bethune *et al.*, 1989.

62 Waddington and Enyimayew, 1989.

63 Creese, 1990.

64 Chisvo, 1993; Illif, 1992.

65 Litvack, 1992.

66 Grootaert, 1993.

67 If this data are correct the finding is at variance with the evidence of improving agricultural/industrial terms of trade, shown earlier – Table 6.7 – unless the improvement in the agriculural/industrial terms of trade was due only to improved prices for export crops.

68 In the case of Côte d'Ivoire, for example, the government cut subsidies on rice, which is believed to have contributed to an increase in food prices relative to the price of non-agricultural products.

69 World Bank, 1989b.

70 Jamal and Weeks, 1993, pp. 85–6.
71 Estimates by Loxley, 1990, cited in Jamal and Weeks, 1993, p. 133.
72 World Bank, 1994.
73 As noted earlier, this is consistent with the finding that the agricultural/industrial terms of trade generally fell while food prices also fell.
74 UNCTAD, 1992; Harrigan, in Mosley *et al.*, Vol. 2, 1991.
75 UN ACC/SCN data; World Bank, 1989b; Ayako, 1990; Clark with Keen, 1988; Jesperson, 1992. A survey in one hospital in Madagascar revealed that the proportion of children suffering from malnutrition increased from 6 per cent in 1978 to 9.5 per cent in 1984 and close to 100 per cent for children under the age of six in 1985/6, with 15 per cent suffering from severe malnutrition. Another study of children attending health clinics showed that the proportion of children with signs of malnutrition increased from 48 per cent in 1982 to 56 per cent in 1987 (World Bank, 1989b).
76 Kamara *et al.*, 1990; Davies *et al.*, 1991.
77 Helleiner, 1993.
78 See Singer, 1991.
79 World Bank, 1992a, p. 19.

Chapter 7

The Latin American and Caribbean story[1]

INTRODUCTION

The 1980s were a bad decade for Latin America,[2] with falling per capita incomes in almost every country (Table 7.1). The number of people in poverty rose from 91 million in 1980 to 133 million in 1990 a rise from 26 per cent to 32 per cent of the population falling below the poverty line; the numbers and the incidence of poverty rose in *both* urban and rural areas.[3] Most countries in Latin America adopted adjustment measures during the decade for various lengths of time, generally in collaboration with the IFIs (see Table 7.2).

Table 7.1 GDP per capita, 1981–92

Country	Change p.a. (%)				Cumulative change (%)	
	1982–5	*1986–90*	*1991*	*1992*	*1981–9*	*1981–92*
Latin America and the Caribbean	−2.0	−0.5	+1.6	+0.5	−9.7	−7.3
IALs[a]						
Bolivia	−5.1	−0.8	+1.7	+1.3	−23.3	−21.1
Brazil	+0.4	0.0	−0.8	−3.1	−5.5	−9.3
Chile	−3.6	+4.1	+4.1	+7.8	+9.2	+25.4
Colombia	+0.5	+2.6	+0.5	+1.4	+16.2	+19.9
Costa Rica	−1.9	+1.5	−1.4	+1.5	−5.0	−5.7
Mexico	−2.0	−1.2	+1.4	+0.6	−8.4	−4.8
Jamaica	−2.6	+2.4	0.9	+0.5	+1.9	+6.6
Average[e]	−2.0	+1.2	−0.9	+1.4	−2.1	+1.5
OALs[b]						
Argentina	−2.7	−1.5	+6.0	+4.8	−24.3	−11.2
Ecuador	−0.4	−0.5	+1.7	+1.1	−4.6	−5.2
Guyana	−5.5	−1.8	+5.3	+2.1	−27.9	−23.4
Honduras	−2.9	−0.1	−0.9	+1.2	−14.2	−10.3
Panama	+0.1	−4.1	+7.0	+5.4	−18.3	−3.0
Uruguay[c]	−4.9	+2.6	+1.0	+6.4	−6.7	+2.6
Average[e]	−2.7	−0.9	+3.9	+3.5	−16.0	−8.4
Other						
Barbados	−0.3	+2.4	−3.6	−3.0	+8.0	−1.0

Table 7.1 (Contd.)

Country	Change p.a. (%)				Cumulative change (%)	
	1982–5	*1986–90*	*1991*	*1992*	*1981–9*	*1981–92*
Dominican Republic	−1.2	+0.3	−3.1	+5.5	−2.2	−1.4
El Salvador	−1.0	−0.3	+1.2	+2.4	−15.3	−10.4
Guatemala	−4.4	0.0	+0.3	+1.2	−18.0	−16.9
Haiti	−2.0	−2.6	−2.3	−6.9	−22.3	−27.8
Nicaragua	−3.7	−7.4	−4.0	−3.4	−40.8	−38.6
Paraguay	−2.3	+0.9	−0.5	−1.3	+0.4	−1.3
Peru	−30.2	−3.7	−0.1	−4.5	−3.9	−31.8
Trinidad and Tobago[d]	+2.6	−4.1	+0.6	−1.2	−13.8	−30.0
Venezuela[d]	−4.8	+0.4	+7.8	+5.0	−19.9	−8.3
Average[e]	−4.3	−1.4	+0.4	−0.6	−11.1	−16.8

Sources: ECLA, 1989; 1991; 1992
(a) Intensive adjustment lending countries, as defined by World Bank, 1990a, RAL II
(b) Other adjustment lending countries; as defined by World Bank 1990a
(c) Classified as intensive adjustment lending; RAL III, World Bank, 1992a
(d) Classified as adjustment lending; RAL III
(e) Averages are unweighted country averages

Table 7.2 Latin American and Caribbean countries with stabilisation/
adjustment loans, 1980s

Country	World Bank	IMF
Argentina†	1986, 1987, 1989	1983, 1984, 1985, 1986, 1987
Barbados		1982, 1983
Bolivia*†	1980, 1986, 1987, 1988	1980, 1986, 1987
Brazil*†	1984, 1986, 1988	1983, 1984, 1988
Chile*†	1985, 1986, 1987, 1988	1983, 1984, 1985, 1986
Colombia*	1985, 1986, 1988	
Costa Rica*†	1983, 1985, 1989	1980, 1981, 1982, 1985, 1987, 1988, 1989
Ecuador†	1986, 1988	1983, 1985, 1986, 1988
El Salvador		1982
Guatemala		1983, 1988
Guyana	1980, 1981	1980, 1981
Haiti	1987	1982, 1983
Honduras	1989	1980, 1981
Jamaica*†	1980, 1981, 1982, 1983, 1985, 1987	1981, 1982, 1983, 1984, 1985, 1986, 1987, 1988
Mexico*†	1983, 1986, 1987, 1988, 1989	1982, 1983, 1984, 1985, 1986, 1989
Panama†	1984, 1987	1980, 1981, 1982, 1983, 1984, 1985, 1986
Peru†		1980, 1982, 1983, 1984
São Tomé	1987	1989
Uruguay†	1984, 1987, 1989	1983, 1985, 1986
Venezuela	1989	1989

Source: World Bank, RAL II, 1990a; Khan, 1990; Noss, 1991
*Defined as 'early-intensive adjusters' by World Bank
†IMF-intensive (three or more years with programmes)

The general squeeze on incomes translated into worsening conditions for the poor, especially in the towns, through deteriorating employment opportunities (increased informalisation of employment and reduced real wages) and cuts in government expenditures on the social sectors. Despite some upturn in the last few years of the decade, taken as a whole these were years of regress for social welfare.

THE 1980S AND THE POOR IN LATIN AMERICA: MACRO-DEVELOPMENTS

Adverse macro-developments over these years were the prime cause of problems for the poor, affecting both primary and secondary incomes. GDP per capita fell over the decade by almost 10 per cent for the region as a whole, and in eighteen out of twenty-three countries. The severest falls were in Nicaragua (over 40 per cent, 1981–90), Bolivia, Guyana, Venezuela, Argentina and Haiti (20 per cent or more). There was some recovery in the last few years of the decade, with positive growth in per capita GDP in nine countries, 1986–90, and less severe falls in seven others, while five countries showed a worsening performance. For 1991 to 1993, most countries recorded positive growth with GDP rising by 4.3 per cent over the three years, mainly due to a large turnround in the capital account. The net transfer of resources to the region was negative in every year from 1982 to 1990, inclusive, with an outflow amounting to about one-fifth of the value of exports on average. From 1991 to 1993, the net transfer was positive, at around 17 per cent of the value of exports.

Major imbalances, especially in the budget, persisted throughout much of the 1980s, but by the early 1990s there had been considerable improvement, with much reduced budget and current account deficits among most adjusting countries. Throughout the 1980s the debt burden retained a stranglehold over developments, pre-empting resources that might have gone to investment and the social sectors, as well as making deflation a necessary policy tool in most countries in order to keep imports down. However, the Brady initiative, which began to bite in 1990, and the return of private capital inflows that followed, permitted more expansionary adjustment policies.

There has been much debate – as noted earlier in this book – on the question of responsibility for the adverse macro-developments during the decade of the 1980s, a decade at least as bad as any in recorded modern history. The accumulation of debt in the 1970s, high international interest rates and the cessation of voluntary lending in the 1980s and worsening terms of trade necessitated severe adjustments. In the Latin American and Caribbean sample, the countries most affected by World Bank adjustment policies (IALs) showed little difference in growth performance compared with other countries in the region in the years up to 1985, but in the 1986–90 period they performed better, with four of the seven having positive growth in per capita incomes, compared with one out of six in the 'other adjustment lending' countries, and four out of ten countries not receiving adjustment lending (see Table 7.1). The macro-record of the 'other adjustment lending' group was poor, for the most part showing negative per capita growth even in the latter part of the 1980s. (This was also the case for those countries most intensively assisted by the Fund which was heavily involved in the other adjustment lending group as well as lending to some of the countries which did not receive WB adjustment loans.) However, in the early 1990s this group of countries recovered. In each period, the non-adjusting group showed significant decline in per capita income. Chile, Colombia and Jamaica had the best macro-performance over the 1980s, with Costa Rica doing well in the latter part of the decade.

Despite some improvement in the later years, macro-developments for the decade as a whole, therefore, were adverse for the poor in most countries. Macro-policies can be faulted in particular on two levels:

(a) They were excessively deflationary – which can be attributed to a combination of unrealistic assumptions about flexibility and responses and a far too hesitant approach to the debt problem, so that debt-servicing obligations and the need to transfer massive resources abroad dogged these economies throughout the decade (Table 7.3).

(b) There were major cuts in investment thereby protecting short-run consumption relatively but offering dim prospects for future growth.[4]

Table 7.3 Net transfers abroad, Latin America and the Caribbean, 1980s

Year	Net transfer[a] ($bn)	(%) Exports
1980	+13.1	+12.5
1981	+11.3	+10.0
1982	−18.7	−18.2
1983	−31.6	−30.9
1984	−26.9	−23.6
1985	−32.3	−29.6
1986	−22.8	−24.1
1987	−16.3	−15.1
1988	−28.8	−23.5
1989	−27.3	−20.0
1990	−18.9	−12.8
1980–90 inclusive	−199.2	−15.9
1991–3 inclusive	+66.8	+13.7

Sources: ECLAC, 1991 and 1993
(a) Defined as gross inflow of capital less amortisation and interest payments

STRUCTURAL CHANGES

Egalitarian changes in structure of asset ownership, for example through land reform, were not introduced over this period except in revolutionary Nicaragua.

In contrast, a number of countries initiated privatisation programmes. These had not materialised on a sufficient scale to make much difference to income and asset distribution in the decade, but can be expected to have inegalitarian effects in the coming years.

There were changes in economic policies, however, associated with the adjustment package, which affected economic structure in ways that would be likely to change income distribution and the primary incomes of the poor. There were four relevant structural changes: in employment and wages; the composition of exports; the domestic terms of trade; and in the financial sector.

Employment and wages

The 1980s saw some important changes in the nature and status of employment. Devaluation and policies of wage and employment restraint led to a decline in the share of wage income in the formal sector (Table 7.4). As a consequence of the severe deflation of the early 1980s, urban unemployment in Latin America rose to unprecedented levels of over 10 per cent on average by the mid-1980s (Table 7.5). There was some recovery in the latter half of the decade, but unemployment remained significantly above its 1980 level in most countries.

Table 7.4 Wage share in Latin American countries[a] (per cent)

Country	1977–81	1982–6
Colombia	40.4	43.0
Costa Rica	49.5	45.3
Mexico	40.4	34.0
Peru	33.8	32.5
Venezuela	45.3	44.1

All Latin America[b]

1980	1983	1986	1989
44	41	40	38

Sources: Pastor, 1991; ILO, 1991
(a) Employee compensation as a share of net domestic product
(b) Shares as a percentage of gross national product

The general crisis and the adjustment policies adopted also affected wages. Several changes are noticeable: all wage indicators in 1990 were lower than at the beginning of the decade and furthermore declined faster than GDP per capita. Until the mid-1980s there was a decline of the same magnitude for the minimum wage, the construction workers' wage (often taken as a proxy for unskilled wages) and the agricultural wage, but the industrial wage, which reflects higher skills, had declined less than other wages. After 1985, the picture changes. The minimum wage declined much faster and so did the industrial wage, while the construction wage rose a little (Table 7.6).

Table 7.5 Unemployment rates (per cent)

Country	1980	1985	1990	1993
Argentina	2.6	6.1	8.6	9.5
Bolivia*	7.1	5.8	7.0	5.4
Brazil*	6.2	5.3	4.3	5.6
Chile*	11.7	17.0	6.6	4.7
Colombia*	9.7	14.0	10.2	8.5
Costa Rica*	6.0	6.7	5.4	4.3 (1992)
Ecuador	5.7	10.4	14.3 (1989)	4.7
Guatemala	2.2	12.0	14.0	5.5
Honduras	8.8	11.7	13.8	7.5
Mexico*	4.5	4.4	2.8	3.4
Panama	10.4	15.6	20.8	12.4
Peru	7.1	10.1	7.9 (1989)	9.4 (1992)
Uruguay	7.4	13.1	9.2	9.0
Venezuela	6.6	14.3	10.6	6.9

Sources: ECLAC, 1991 and 1993
* Early-intensively adjusting countries

Table 7.6 Real wages in Latin America

Country	Average real wages (1980 = 100)		Urban minimum wage (1980 = 100)	
	1990	1993	1990	1993
Argentina	78.7	81.0	40.2	49.13
Brazil: Rio de Janeiro	87.6	114.9	53.4	56.2
São Paulo	142.1	144.6		
Colombia	113.4	124.0	107.9	105.8
Costa Rica	87.2	88.5 (1992)	120.5	112.8
Chile	104.8	119.2	87.5	104.6
Ecuador	n.a.	n.a.	36.2	21.4
Mexico	77.9	92.1	45.5	41.6
Paraguay	n.a.	n.a.	131.6	115.5 (1992)
Uruguay	76.1	79.7	69.1	52.4
Venezuela	n.a.	59.3	60.7 (1992)	
All Latin America	*1980*	*1985*	*1990*	
Minimum wage	100	86.4	68.3	
Industry wage	100	93.1	85.3	
Agricultural wage	100	87.1	73.5	
Construction wage	100	85.3	88.7	

Sources: ILO, 1991; ECLAC, 1993

In all IALs except Colombia and Costa Rica, the minimum wage dropped considerably more than the industrial wage. In Costa Rica the minimum wage increased while the industrial wage fell, which was a major factor behind the decline in poverty there.[5] The OALs and the non-adjustment lending countries showed the same pattern of declining minimum wages, with the exception of Paraguay.

The major conclusion from the wage trends is that the recession and adjustment together drove minimum wages down quickly, with an adverse effect on urban poverty, except where special measures were taken, as in Colombia and Costa Rica, where the process was halted even in recessionary periods.

The employment structure also changed over this period, with a rapid increase in informal sector employment and employment in the small-scale sector relative to employment in large and medium-sized firms. This change in structure (Table 7.7) also depressed real average wages.

Table 7.7 Structure of employment (outside agriculture) in Latin America in the 1980s

	Total labour force (%)		
	1980	*1990*	*1992*
Formal sector of which:	59.8	47.3	45.7
public sector	15.7	15.6	14.9
large private enterprises	44.1	31.7	30.8
Informal sector of which:	40.2	52.7	54.4
self-employed	19.2	24.0	25.0
small enterprises	14.6	21.8	22.5
domestic service	6.4	6.9	6.9

Source: Information supplied by PREALC

Labour-intensive exports

Devaluation and trade liberalisation is expected to be associated with an expansion of labour-intensive manufactured exports, which may help to sustain employment, thereby reducing the adverse effects of cuts in employment elsewhere in the economy. Taking the share of textiles and clothing in total exports as an indicator of the magnitude of labour-intensive exports (Table 7.8), there appears to have been a significant expansion in the 1980s (an increase in 5 per cent or more in the share) in Costa Rica, Guatemala, Jamaica, Honduras and the Dominican Republic, but not elsewhere. Another indication of expanding labour-intensive exports is the increase in exports of footwear, where Latin America increased its share of world markets from 0.9 per cent in 1970 to 4.4 per cent in 1980 and 7.5 per cent in 1990.

Domestic terms of trade

The adjustment policies were intended to improve the terms of trade of the agricultural sector, thereby improving real rural incomes. Of the seven countries for which direct estimates of the agricultural/industrial terms of trade are available (Table 7.9), only three show a significant improvement over the years

Table 7.8 Textiles and clothing as a
              percentage of total exports

Country	1980	1989
Argentina	2	3
Bolivia	n.a.	1
Brazil	4	3
Chile	0	1
Colombia	6	6
Costa Rica	5	18
Dominican Republic	0	35
Ecuador	1	0
El Salvador	13	11
Guatemala	6	11
Honduras	2	7
Jamaica	1	13
Mexico	3	2
Panama	3	7
Paraguay	0	1
Peru	6	9
Trinidad and Tobago	0	0
Venezuela	0	0

Source: *World Development Report*, 1983, 1991

Table 7.9 Domestic terms of trade

Country	Real exchange rate (1980 = 100) 1988	Share of agricultural exports as % of total 1989	Terms of trade A/I* (1980 = 100) 1987
Argentina	232.6[a]	64	n.a.
Bolivia	75.1	15	111.8
Brazil	102.6	33	109.2[c]
Chile	50.5	33	n.a.
Colombia	58.5	49	85.1
Costa Rica	60.4	69	97.7
Dominican Republic	51.0[b]	28	100.6[c]
Ecuador	37.0[d]	48	n.a.
Jamaica	68.2	26	n.a.
Mexico	68.6	14	100.9
Paraguay	56.0[d]	92	n.a.
Uruguay	51.0[d]	61	99.4
Venezuela	50.0[b]	1	114.1

Sources: World Bank, 1992a; *World Development Report*, 1991; Berry, 1990; Byerlee
and Sain, 1991; Pastor, 1991
*Agricultural/industrial terms of trade
(a) 1980–7 (Berry, 1990)
(b) 1982 = 100
(c) 1986
(d) 1981 = 100

1980–7. A much higher proportion of countries experienced substantial real exchange rate devaluation – which would be expected to increase the real returns from agricultural exports unless this was offset by the worsening of world prices which occurred for many commodities over this period. Where there were improvements in agricultural prices, these were sometimes offset by reduced subsidisation of agricultural inputs.[6] Moreover, where there is considerable inequality in land distribution, as in many Latin American countries,[7] the extent to which an improvement in the rural/urban terms of trade filters down to the poor may be limited, especially if focused on export prices. Significant reductions in real agricultural wages (by more than a quarter over the decade) and very slow growth in agricultural employment (around 5 per cent for the whole decade) suggest that conditions for the poor in agriculture may have worsened over this period.

Reduced financial repression

A fourth change in economic structure which is claimed for adjustment policies is that reduced financial repression will be associated with a reorientation of credit away from favoured large-scale businesses and towards the small-scale sector. Often, however, lending to small-scale enterprises is restricted by various institutional barriers, so that simply letting the market work does not bring about a major redirection. Nonetheless, although there is no direct evidence on credit distribution, employment in the small-scale sector was generally buoyant in Latin America over the 1980s, in contrast to the slow growth in the large-scale sector. Expansion of formal sector small enterprises' employment (less than ten employees) was 7.5 per cent per annum 1980–9 compared with only 0.5 per cent per annum in medium and large enterprises, while informal sector employment grew more than twice as fast as the formal sector.[8] This served to mitigate the downward pressure on employment caused by contraction and then slow growth in the large-scale formal sector. The share of the labour force in the informal sector grew from 40 per cent in 1980 to 53 per cent in 1990, while there was a sharp fall in the share of large private enterprises (Table 7.7). But wage levels are generally much lower in small and informal sector firms, so the change in composition of employment implied reduced average earnings, while ILO estimates indicate a sharper fall in average earnings in the informal sector than in the formal sector over the decade.

Thus taken as a whole, we find that changes in economic structure over the 1980s, associated with the stabilisation and adjustment policies, worked in two directions – to increase urban poverty by depressing real wages and employment, partly offset by rising employment in labour-intensive manufactures and the small-scale sector; and to reduce rural poverty by some small improvement in the terms of trade, partly offset by reduced subsidies to the sector and, in places, increasing rural differentiation.

PRIMARY INCOMES OF THE POOR: THE EVIDENCE

The net effect of these macro- and structural changes on the incidence of poverty in the 1980s was negative. While the 1970s saw a reduced incidence of poverty in Latin America as a whole, from 40 per cent in 1970 to 35 per cent in the 1980s, this was reversed and poverty incidence rose again to 39 per cent by 1990 (CEPALC estimates), or from 27 per cent (1980, estimate of Psacharapoulos *et al.*) to 32 per cent by 1989.[9]

Poverty worsened in both rural and urban areas in sixteen out of twenty-five countries (Table 7.10). Among IALs for the period as a whole, both urban and rural poverty worsened in the two largest countries, improved in four countries and showed mixed performance (urban worsening, rural improvement

Table 7.10 Poverty in Latin America in the 1980s

Country	Below poverty line[a] (per cent)			
	1980		1989	
	Urban	Rural	Urban	Rural
Argentina	3.0 (7)	11.0 (16)	6.4 (12)	23.4 (17)
Barbados	4.9	10.5	2.3	21.1
Bolivia*	34.1	81.3	54.0	76.2
Brazil*	23.9 (30)	55.0 (62)	33.2 (39)	63.1 (56)
Chile*	15.9	34.0	9.9 (37[c])	10.4 (45[c])
Colombia*	13.0 (36)	58.4 (45)	8.0 (36[c])	40.6 (42[c])
Costa Rica*	9.9 (16)	16.7 (21)	3.5 (22[d])	3.2 (25[d])
Dominican Republic	19.7[b]	n.a.	24.1[b]	n.a.
Ecuador	19.2	41.2	24.2	47.4
El Salvador	23.6	50.6	41.5	51.4
Guatemala	35.7 (41)	52.7 (79)	50.9 (54[c])	76.5 (75[c])
Guyana	51.9	70.7	74.8	93.6
Haiti	72.2	91.0	79.7	98.5
Honduras	38.8	70.6	54.4 (65[d])	82.6 (84[d])
Jamaica*	25.0	53.5	4.4	18.3
Mexico*	9.4	19.7	14.1	27.9
Nicaragua	24.3	52.0	57.5	76.2
Panama	26.0 (31)	33.0 (45)	26.9 (34[d])	36.8 (48[d])
Paraguay	9.0	58.4	7.6 (37[d])	47.9
Peru	30.9 (35)	46.0 (65)	49.4 (45[c])	73.4 (64[c])
Trinidad and Tobago	1.6	3.4	2.3	21.1
Uruguay	6.2 (9)	13.5 (21)	5.3 (10)	31.3 (23)
Venezuela	2.5 (18)	9.0 (35)	10.8 (33[d])	23.5 (38[d])

Sources: Psacharopoulos *et al.*, 1993; ECLAC, 1990; 1992a
*IALs
(a) The data in parentheses comes from ECLAC, which adopts a higher poverty line than the World Bank data in Psacharapolous *et al.* the differences are large in some cases, but the changes over time are similar
(b) Total poverty
(c) Data for 1986
(d) Data for 1990

with aggregate worsening) in one. Poverty worsened in both sectors in six of the OALs, with a mixed performance (but net deterioration) in one. The data do not bear out the expectation that rural poverty would lessen during adjustment while urban poverty worsens. In most cases the two moved together, and where they did not, in two out of three cases rural poverty increased. For the few countries for which more detailed year-by-year data are available, it appears that poverty worsened sharply in the early years of the decade and has shown some improvement since then.[10]

In some countries, poverty rose to intolerably high levels – for example, in Brazil, in 1989, the overall incidence was 40 per cent, with an urban incidence of over 60 per cent; in Bolivia the overall incidence was 65 per cent; in Honduras over 70 per cent. In contrast, Costa Rica,[11] which was unique in achieving a poverty rate below 10 per cent, the rate was only 3.4 per cent. For the region as a whole (and in seven individual countries) by 1989, urban poverty exceeded rural poverty in numbers (an estimated 69 million urban against 64 million rural) though the proportion of the rural population in poverty was more than double urban incidence. This contrasts with 1980, when the numbers of rural poor were considerably above the numbers of urban poor for the region as a whole. Although both rural and urban poverty increased over the decade, the percentage increase in the numbers of urban poor was far greater at 81 per cent, compared with an increase of 20 per cent in the numbers of rural poor. In part this reflects increasing urbanisation of the population as a whole: urban population as a proportion of the total rose from 66 to 71 per cent over the decade.

The worsening poverty in most countries was due to *stagnation with inequity*. Average per capita incomes fell (as shown earlier), while income distribution worsened in the 1980s in nine out of fourteen countries, including all intensive adjusting lending countries except Colombia and Costa Rica, and all the other adjustment lending countries for which data are available apart from Uruguay (Table 7.11). This is in part due to the falling share of wages (noted above, Table 7.4), itself the combined effect of falling real wages, a worsening structure of employment, with a higher proportion of employment in low-wage sectors, including in the informal sector, and a rise in unemployment, as shown above. Only Colombia succeeded in combining growth with improved income distribution, and consequently saw a reduction of urban poverty from 13 to 8 per cent and of rural poverty from 58 to 41 per cent from 1980 to 1989.

MESO-PERFORMANCE IN THE 1980s

Meso-policies act as a filter between macro-developments and the poor. In Latin America, as elsewhere, there were considerable variations in meso-choices: in the majority of countries, the adverse effects of macro-developments were accentuated by meso-behaviour, but in a few, meso-policies acted to protect the poor during this period of extreme vulnerability.

Table 7.11 Income distribution in Latin America in
the 1980s (individuals)

Country	Gini coefficient	
	(around 1980)	*(around 1989)*
Argentina (M)	0.408	0.476
Bolivia* (urban)	0.516 (1986)	0.525
Brazil*	0.594	0.633
Chile* (M)	0.519	0.531
Colombia* (urban)	0.585	0.532
Costa Rica*	0.475	0.460
Guatemala	0.579 (1986–7)	0.595
Honduras	0.549 (1986)	0.591
Mexico*	0.506 (1984)	0.550
Panama	0.488	0.565
Paraguay (M)	0.450 (1983)	0.398
Peru (M)	0.428 (1985)	0.438
Uruguay	0.436	0.424
Venezuela	0.428	0.441

Source: Psacharapoulos *et al.*, 1993; Graham, 1994
*IALs
Note: M, Metropolitan area

Expenditure ratios improved notably among intensive-adjustment lending
countries, worsening elsewhere (Table 7.12). The improvement in the intensive-
adjustment lending countries reflected an improved revenue performance, as
budget deficits were simultaneously reduced in four out of the six IAL cases.

Table 7.12 Allocation ratios during the 1980s

	Education		Health		Economic		Defence		Other, including interest[a]	
	1981	1990	1981	1990	1981	1990	1981	1990	1981	1990
Adjusting countries										
Bolivia*	24.40	18.00	7.20	2.30	29.30	19.10	22.70	14.10	9.20	28.60
Brazil*	3.80	5.30	7.40	7.20	24.10	6.90	3.40	4.20	26.50	56.20
Chile*	14.40	10.10	6.40	5.90	11.40	8.80	12.00	8.40	13.30	33.00
Costa Rica*	23.70	17.00	29.70	27.20	15.20	11.40	2.60	1.70	16.20	25.90
Jamaica*‡	14.20	13.30	7.10	6.50	n.a.	n.a.	n.a.	n.a.	n.a.	n.a.
Mexico*	18.20	13.90	1.90	1.90	36.40	13.40	2.50	2.40	23.30	55.50
Uruguay*	7.70	7.40	3.80	4.50	13.30	8.70	12.90	9.20	10.70	20.00
Argentina	7.30	9.30	1.40	2.00	17.90	20.50	11.40	8.60	27.80	18.70
Ecuador	30.10	18.20	7.90	11.00	17.60	11.80	11.80	12.90	32.30	43.60
Panama	12.80	18.50	13.20	17.90	18.40	7.50	n.a.	7.90	42.80	31.80
Venezuela†	18.30	19.60	7.30	10.00	32.80	17.30	3.90	5.80	30.90	35.60
Other countries										
Dominican Republic	13.90	9.50	9.70	11.30	37.30	36.70	8.90	4.60	16.80	13.60
El Salvador	17.90	16.20	8.40	7.80	24.70	16.70	16.80	24.50	26.90	29.30

Table 7.12 (Contd.)

	Education		Health		Economic		Defence		Other, including interest[a]	
	1981	1990	1981	1990	1981	1990	1981	1990	1981	1990
Guatemala	n.a.	19.50	n.a.	9.90	n.a.	21.70	n.a.	13.30	n.a.	27.80
Nicaragua	11.60	12.00	14.60	12.29	20.60	n.a.	11.00	n.a.	34.90	n.a.
Paraguay	11.80	12.70	4.50	4.30	19.00	12.80	13.20	13.30	28.80	42.10
Peru	11.30	16.20	5.30	5.10	n.a.	n.a.	13.80	11.20	68.40	67.40
Trinidad and Tobago†	11.20	15.70	6.90	8.10	31.10	n.a.	2.00	2.70	32.40	n.a.
Average, all adjusting	15.90	13.69	8.48	8.76	19.67	11.40	7.56	6.84	21.18	31.72
Intensive-adjusting	15.20	12.14	9.07	7.93	18.53	9.76	8.01	5.71	14.17	31.31
Other adjusting	17.13	16.40	7.45	10.23	21.68	14.28	6.78	8.80	33.45	32.43
Average, all other	11.10	14.54	7.06	8.40	18.96	12.56	9.39	9.94	29.74	25.74

Source: World Bank, *World Development Reports*, various
*Intensively adjusting, according to World Bank, 1992c
†Data for 1989, not 1990
‡Data for 1988, not 1990
(a) Housing and social security are not included in this table. Averages are unweighted

However, the improvement in expenditure ratios among intensive-adjustment lending countries was more than offset by a worsening in social allocation ratios[12] (Table 7.13). The social allocation ratio fell in the IAL countries except for Brazil and Uruguay, falling particularly sharply in Bolivia, Mexico and Costa Rica. Economic expenditure and defence expenditure as a share of the total also fell in most IAL countries, with the chief 'gainer' being the 'other' category, consisting mainly of interest payments, which rose sharply in all IAL countries (Table 7.12). In contrast, among the other adjustment lending countries and the non-adjustment lending countries, the share of health and education in total expenditure rose and the share of interest payments fell.

It thus appears that the World Bank policies were effective in raising revenue and expenditure ratios, but the extra was more than spent on paying interest, not on raising social expenditures, and the social allocation ratio fell. The evidence bears out the view of the IFIs as efficient debt-collectors.

The combined effect of the changes in expenditure and allocation ratios was a fall in the share of GNP going to health and education in five out of seven of the IAL countries (Brazil and Uruguay being the exceptions), and in three out of four of the other adjustment lending countries. In the non-adjustment lending group the share of health and education fell in four countries and rose in two. The effect on per capita expenditure in health and education in absolute terms was compounded by the widespread fall in per capita GNP. There were sharp falls in expenditure per head on health and education over the decade (of over 20 per cent) in Bolivia, Mexico, Argentina, Ecuador and Venezuela among

Table 7.13 Expenditure on health and education in the 1980s (1980 = 100)

	Expenditure ratio		H + E as % expenditure		H + E as % GNP		Index of H + E expenditure per capita 1990 (1981 = 1)
	1981	1990	1981	1990	1981	1990	
Adjusting countries							
Bolivia*	12.70	18.80	31.60	20.30	4.01	3.82	0.78
Brazil*	19.50	36.00	11.20	12.50	2.18	2.44	2.09
Chile*	31.00	32.80	20.80	16.00	6.45	5.25	1.77
Costa Rica*	23.70	27.10	53.40	44.20	12.66	11.98	1.02
Jamaica*‡	48.50	42.10	21.30	19.80	10.33	8.34	0.83
Mexico*	20.80	18.40	20.10	15.80	4.18	2.91	0.61
Uruguay*	24.90	27.50	11.50	11.90	2.86	3.27	1.09
Argentina	23.60	15.50	8.70	11.30	2.05	1.75	0.71
Ecuador	17.10	15.60	38.00	29.20	6.50	4.56	0.67
Panama	36.10	31.80	26.00	36.40	9.39	11.58	1.40
Venezuela†	28.90	23.10	25.60	29.60	7.40	6.84	0.74
Other countries							
Dominican Republic	17.00	15.30	23.60	20.80	4.01	3.18	0.76
El Salvador	18.50	9.90	26.30	24.00	4.87	2.38	0.47
Guatemala	16.20	12.00	n.a.	29.40	n.a.	3.53	n.a.
Nicaragua	30.20	40.70	26.20	24.29	7.91	9.89	0.78
Paraguay	13.10	9.30	16.30	17.00	2.14	1.58	0.70
Peru	20.20	10.00	16.60	21.30	3.35	2.13	0.45
Trinidad and Tobago†	40.80	36.90	18.10	23.80	7.38	8.78	0.84
Average, all adjusting	26.07	26.25	24.38	22.45	6.18	5.70	1.06
Intensive-adjusting	25.87	28.96	24.27	20.07	6.10	5.43	1.17
Other adjusting	26.43	21.50	21.96	26.63	6.33	6.18	0.88
Average, all other	22.29	19.16	18.16	22.94	4.24	4.50	0.57

Source: World Bank, *World Development Reports*, various
Note: Averages are unweighted
*Intensively adjusting, according to World Bank, 1992c
†Data for 1989, not 1990
‡Data for 1988, not 1990

adjustment lending countries. But significant increases were achieved by Brazil, Chile and Panama. Brazil achieved its large increase by a considerable expansion in the expenditure ratio (partly financed by growing budget deficits), Chile by economic growth in the latter years and Panama by a significant increase in the social allocation ratio. The non-adjustment lending group suffered a universal large fall in per capita expenditure on health and education, mainly due to the poor macro-performance.

Changes in the priority ratio

Among Latin American countries for which evidence is available, it appears that the primary school sector is progressive, with the bottom 40 per cent of households receiving over 50 per cent of the benefits in six countries, although Brazil is an exception with the bottom 40 per cent receiving only 15 per cent of the benefits. The top 20 per cent received less than 10 per cent of the benefits from primary schooling, except for Venezuela.[13] Tertiary education is regressive, the bottom 40 per cent receiving significantly less than 40 per cent of the benefits and the top 20 per cent receiving much more than 20 per cent of the benefits.[14] Health expenditures as a whole appear progressive, with the bottom 40 per cent of the population receiving over 50 per cent of the benefits, and the top 20 per cent less than 10 per cent. Again Brazil is an exception, where the bottom 40 per cent receive 30 per cent of the benefits.[15] Within the health service, however, certain programmes, especially primary health care, seem likely to benefit the poor most.

Indications of changes in priority ratios in the 1980s (Tables 7.14 and 7.15) suggest a marked difference between the two sectors. In education, an increased priority ratio, as indicated by the proportion of total expenditure going to primary education, occurred in the majority of cases, with a worsening in only two cases. If secondary education is also included, then the situation looks less good, with a deterioration in four cases and an improvement in three, with little difference between the IAL countries and the rest. There is evidence that the worsening resource situation in education was translated into educational performance, as six out of seven of the IALs and a somewhat lower proportion of other countries showed some decline in enrolment ratios during the 1980s (Table 7.16). Only five out of twenty-three countries showed consistent increases in both primary and secondary enrolment rates before and after 1985.

Table 7.14 Indicators of priorities in the education sector, 1980s

	Share of total education expenditure (%)				
	Primary education		Change	Primary and secondary		Change
	1980	1986		1980	1986	
Argentina	46.2	10.0 (1985)	–	84.3	74.9	
Bolivia*	64.0	64.0 (1985)	0	90.0	82.0	–
Brazil*	18.4	49.0	+	68.0	78.0	+
Chile*	45.7	51.1	+	72.4	77.0	+
Costa Rica*	33.0	37.0	+	72.3	50.7	–
Dominican Republic	43.4	53.6 (1987)	+	77.8	81.1	+
Jamaica*	38.0	35.0 (1987)	–	81.0	76.0	–
Venezuela	28.3	43.5	+	n.a.	n.a.	

Share of benefits of bottom 30%:

	1983	1986	
Chile*	34.8	37.5	+
Costa Rica*	28.4	27.1	–

Source: Grosh, 1990a; World Bank, 1990b
*IAL countries

Table 7.15 Indicators of priorities in the health sector, 1980s

	1980	*1985*	*Change*
Argentina			
% hospitals	71.3	81.3	–
% environmental health	37.0	28.0	–
Belize			
% hospitals	81.3	88.3	–
Bolivia*			
% primary	27.0 (1984)	24.0 (1988)	–
Brazil*			
% hospitals	79.4	83.6	–
Chile*			
% hospitals	83.8	93.6 (1986)	–
Costa Rica*			
% share of benefits (health and nutrition) to bottom 20%	31.8 (1983)	27.7 (1986)	–
El Salvador			
% hospitals	93.9	99.9	–
% regional and other decentralised	24.0	25.0 (1987)	insignificant
Guyana			
% hospitals	67.8	63.7	–
Jamaica*			
% primary	20.0	21.0 (1986)	insignificant
Mexico*			
% programmes for poor and marginal groups	3.1	2.8 (1988)	–
% programmes serving general public	15.7	13.3	–
Panama			
% hospitals	90.1	90.8	insignificant
Uruguay			
% hospitals	89.0	79.5	+
Venezuela			
% preventative	23.0 (1983)	15.0 (1985)	–

Source: Grosh, 1990a; Rivero *et al.*, 1991, Albanez *et al.*, 1989
*IAL countries

The average length of years in school fell in six and rose in two countries in the second half of the 1980s compared with the first half, while school survival rates fell in half the countries over the same period.[16]

In contrast to some improvements in education, there was a near-universal deterioration in the priority ratio in the health sector. Of the thirteen countries for which there are some data, there was a significant worsening in ten and a significant improvement in only one (Uruguay). All the IALs showed a worsening. However, despite the cuts in expenditure, there was substantial progress in certain health measures, notably immunisation rates and the use of oral rehydration salts.

Table 7.16 Education indicators

	Recurrent expenditure per pupil, 1980–5 (% p.a.)	Gross primary enrolment rate		Secondary enrolment rate, 1980–90
		Increase (+), 1980–5	decrease (–), 1985 – last available date	
Argentina	0.0	+	+	+
Bolivia*	−11.0	+	n.a.	−
Brazil	−5.3	+	+	+
Chile*	+1.4	−	−	+
Colombia*	+10.7	−	+	+
Costa Rica*	−5.6	+	+	−
Cuba	+8.8	−	−	n.a.
Dominican Republic	0.0	−	+	+
Ecuador	+7.9	+	−	+
El Salvador	+2.1	−	n.a.	+
Guatemala	n.a.	+	+	+
Guyana	−10.5	−	n.a.	n.a.
Haiti	−12.9	−	n.a.	n.a.
Honduras	−1.7	+	+	+
Jamaica*	−5.7	−	+	+
Mexico*	−11.2	+	−	+
Nicaragua	−0.4	+	+	−
Panama	+0.5	+	+	−
Paraguay	n.a.	+	+	−
Peru	−12.4	+	+	−
Trinidad and Tobago	+3.2	+	+	+
Uruguay*	+7.6	+	−	+
Venezuela	+1.3	+	+	−

Source: Berstecher and Carr-Hill, 1990, Tables A3.2 (c) and A3.4; Carr-Hill, 1991; World Bank, *World Development Reports*, 1984; 1993
*IAL countries

Data deficiencies make it difficult to be confident about changes in infant mortality rates (IMRs): the Hill–Pebley data (1989), which cover a subset of countries, show a slowdown in improvements in seven countries and an acceleration in five countries in Latin America. A more detailed analysis of IMRs in Mexico found that the slowdown in reduction in the IMR was associated with an intensification of regional disparities and a rise in the rate of infant mortality caused specifically by malnutrition and peri-natal complications, both probably due to the economic crisis.[17]

Food and nutrition

The stabilisation and adjustment programmes had contradictory effects on nutrition. On the one hand, there were negative effects on food entitlements, especially among urban households; on the other, the programmes were intended to raise domestic food supplies. Negative effects on food entitlements came above all from the fall in incomes and rise in poverty, which reduced families' abilities to meet their food needs. Secondly, depreciation of the currency and movement of the internal terms of trade favouring the agricultural sector raised the relative price of food. Estimates of internal terms of trade indicate changes favouring agriculture in about half the cases, including Bolivia, Brazil and Venezuela. Countries which imported a significant amount of food (i.e. 10 per cent or more of total imports consisted of food, on average 1980 and 1989) and experienced significant real devaluation over this period included Bolivia, Chile, Colombia, Dominican Republic, Jamaica, Mexico, Paraguay and Venezuela. However, the 1980s, for the most part, saw falling international food prices, which partially offset the upward movement of domestic prices caused by devaluation.[18]

Thirdly, the adjustment policies frequently included abolition (or sharp reductions) of generalised food and/or agricultural subsidies. These subsidies had been sizeable in the early 1980s in Brazil, Ecuador, Jamaica, Mexico, Bolivia and Venezuela, accounting for around 1 per cent of GDP in Brazil, Mexico, Venezuela and Jamaica.[19] They were abolished or sharply reduced in each of these countries during the 1980s as a result of adjustment programmes. As noted in Chapter 4 in some cases they were partially replaced by targeted subsidies, but these tended to be associated with high F-errors.

The adjustment policies were intended to increase domestic food supplies, through improved incentives. There is some evidence that they did so successfully. Food availability per capita in 1989 was above the 1979–81 level in five of the IALs and unchanged in two; the performance in a number of the other countries was less good, with significant falls in food production per capita in five countries (Argentina, Honduras, Panama, El Salvador and Nicaragua). The course of food prices varied according to the country. There were sharp rises in the price of commodities whose subsidy was removed – bread in Brazil, Ecuador, Mexico and Bolivia, and maize in Mexico and Bolivia, partly offset by falls in the price of unsubsidised commodities. Exchange rate depreciation seems to have had less significant effects, being largely offset by falling international prices. Countries not undergoing adjustment and unaffected by depreciation or subsidy removal saw more consistent price falls.[20]

The rather sparse data for changes in nutrition in the 1980s show that the deteriorating conditions were translated into worsening nutrition in quite a number of cases, but generally for short periods. There is evidence of significant worsening nutrition among children over the 1980s in Peru and Nicaragua; a small increase, later reversed, in Chile and Jamaica; an increase, again reversed, in Venezuela; an increase in second- and third-degree malnutrition in the highlands of Guatemala and in Panama; and a rise in urban malnutrition, while rural improved, in Bolivia. In Uruguay the number of children admitted to the National Nutritional Programme almost doubled between 1982 and 1984. In most other countries for which there are data, malnutrition showed a continued decline, though where the data are differentiated between rural and urban, there appears to have been some slowdown in urban progress.[21] A rising incidence of the proportion of babies born with low birth weight was also found between 1979 and 1986 in Barbados, parts of Brazil, Colombia, Dominican Republic, El Salvador, Mexico and Surinam.[22]

ADJUSTMENT BY THE HOUSEHOLD

For households, all the changes reported on above, which occur as a result of changes in international conditions and macro- and meso-policy, are exogenous events to which they have to adjust to ensure the survival of the family. The well-being of individuals – especially children – depends critically on these adjustments. It is apparent from the observation that the human indicators – health, nutrition, especially – deteriorated far less (and in many cases not at all) despite the severe worsening in the objective conditions of poor households, and that households did manage to protect their members much more effectively than the market or the state. Detailed longitudinal micro-studies of poor urban households in the 1980s, one in Ecuador and two in Mexico, permit some analysis of how poor households adjusted in Latin America.[23] The studies came to similar conclusions:

- despite talk of 'household' adjustment, it is females, above all, who are responsible for most of the adjustments in work, child care and consumption patterns;
- one significant adjustment was an increase in household size, with fewer nuclear and more extended families emerging in each of the three studies;[24]
- women's pattern of work changed, with increased participation in both formal and informal economies;
- younger women (and girl children) played an increasing role in domestic tasks, especially child care; sometimes this meant that they had to leave school in order to do so;[25]
- the rise in the number of workers per household meant that household income declined less sharply than wage rates – for example, in Guadalajara real household income among those surveyed fell by 10 per cent, whereas the real earnings of male heads of household fell by 35 per cent;
- food expenditure per capita fell, and the pattern of food consumption changed; people ate fewer meals, less protein and fresh vegetables;
- non-food expenditures were also cut, including expenditure on health and education; water for washing clothes; expenditure on shelter and so on;
- savings stopped for many households in Queretaro; in Guayaquil, which was more badly affected by the crisis, households got into debt, pawning their possessions and borrowing from wealthier relations or neighbours.

The precise adjustments varied across the locations, but the major findings were very similar; in particular, that adjustment policies have been made tolerable for many through adjustments women have made; yet women are not infinitely elastic; ultimately a breaking point occurs; Moser observed that 'About 15 per cent of women are no longer coping, already casualties and *burnt out*' as a result of the pressures encountered.[26]

CONCLUSIONS

This review has shown that the situation worsened markedly for the poor in Latin America during the 1980s, as a result of falling per capita incomes, deteriorating income distribution and reduced provision of social services. The cause of this deterioration was a deflationary macro-situation, which neither structural nor meso-policies did anything to offset. Indeed, both contributed to the situation, as the policies were associated with worsening income distribution, and the share of health and education in the budget and in GNP was reduced in most countries. The main negative effects occurred in the first half of the decade for most countries when GNP per capita fell most sharply. After 1985, there was some recovery in some countries with consequent stabilisation of the poverty situation.

Deflation and recession were largely responses to the debt crisis of the early 1980s. The IMF, as the institution most concerned with macro-balance, was most closely associated with the deflationary policies. The data suggest, indeed, that for Latin America and the Caribbean, the macro-experience of those countries experiencing most intensive adjustment lending from the World Bank was significantly better than the other countries in the latter half of the decade. The most consistent positive macro-performance was that of Colombia which was relatively unaffected by the IFIs as it never experienced an acute debt crisis.

The basic cause of the weak macro-performance was the debt situation, and the need to transfer massive resources overseas, in a situation where exports were often rather sluggish and the release of resources had to come from cuts in imports. The major turnround – from being in receipt of foreign savings to supplying them – came in 1982 with the burden mounting to 1983 and staying very high to 1985. In 1985 almost 30 per cent of export earnings took the form of net negative transfer. Since then the burden has eased. The Brady plan and declines in international interest rates led to a significant reduction in the debt-servicing burden. Partly as a result, there was a resumption of private sector lending to a number of countries, which permitted rising imports and resumed growth. The movement in GNP per capita almost directly mirrors the changing debt burden and international capital flows.

Meso-policies in general failed to protect the poor over this period, since resources were switched away from the social sectors towards interest payments in adjusting countries. Real expenditure per head on health and education fell in most countries. General food subsidies were replaced by targeted ones, usually with less than comprehensive coverage of those in need. Experience with social funds was most successful in Bolivia, but even in this case only a small minority of those in need were covered as shown in Chapter 5. However, Chile's employment schemes achieved more comprehensive coverage. The most effective source of adjustment and protection for the poor was through change within the household, especially among women who bore much of the burden of adjustment.

Three success stories show that the adverse developments for the poor exhibited in the majority of countries were avoidable. Colombia provides the most successful example of combining adjustment, growth and equity, consequently experiencing a reduction in poverty. Costa Rica did less well in terms of economic growth, but improved income distribution and active meso-policies did much to protect the most vulnerable. Over the decade there was a reduction in poverty. The Chilean case showed that strongly targeted meso-policies could improve some of the human indicators – such as maternal mortality, child nutrition and infant mortality – despite the adverse effects of deflationary and regressive macro-policies which led to rising income poverty for much of the period.

NOTES

1 This chapter draws heavily on Stewart, 1992, and van der Hoeven and Stewart, 1993.
2 In this chapter, the term 'Latin America' should be understood to encompass the Caribbean.
3 Estimates of Psacharopoulos *et al.*, 1993; CEPALC estimates of poverty incidence are significantly higher, but the trends over time are similar.
4 As noted in Chapter 2 the fall in the investment ratio has been found to be worse among adjusting than non-adjusting countries – see Faini *et al.*, 1989; Mosley *et al.*, 1991; World Bank 1990a.
5 See ILO, 1992a.
6 This was the case in Mexico and Venezuela; for example, see Selowsky, 1991.
7 See, e.g. Jazairy *et al.*, 1992; El-Ghonemy, 1990.
8 ILO, 1991.
9 Measures of poverty incidence depend critically on methods of measurement. Some estimates use countries' own poverty lines, which may vary among countries; others attempt region-wide uniformity. While both CEPALC and Pscharapoulos use a region-wide line, the methodology differs and CEPALC's line is higher. In the text the estimates of Psacharopoulos *et al.* are used, unless otherwise noted. For a discussion of the methods used, and alternative measures, see Psacharopoulos *et al.*, 1980.
10 For example, in Brazil, poverty incidence jumped sharply from 1980–3, and has been falling, with fluctuations, since then. A similar pattern was shown by Costa Rica, but Venezuela showed steadily worsening poverty throughout the decade.
11 No data are available for Jamaica.
12 Social allocation ratios here include health and education expenditures only, since the 'housing and social security' category in general does not reach a high proportion of the poor in Latin America, as shown by Mesa-Lago (1983), while systematic aggregate cross-country data is lacking on food subsidies and employment schemes.

13 Grosh, 1990a, Table A.IV.2.
14 Grosh, 1990a, Table A.VI.3.
15 Ibid., Table A.VI.4.
16 Berstecher and Carr-Hill, 1990.
17 Rivero *et al.*, 1991.
18 For 1988, an UNCTAD index of the price of food was 83 per cent of 1979–81.
19 World Bank, 1989f.
20 Byerlee and Sain, 1991.
21 Evidence from World Bank, 1989f; United Nations, 1989; World Bank, 1990a; Raczynski, 1987; Albanez *et al.*, 1989.
22 Albanez *et al.*, 1989.
23 Moser, 1989, in Guayaquil, Ecuador; Gonzalez de la Rocha, 1988, in Guadalajara, western Mexico; and Chant, 1991, in Queretaro, Mexico.
24 This was less marked in the case of Queretaro.
25 Also a finding for two other Mexican cities studied by Chant, 1992.
26 Moser, 1989, p. 158 (original emphasis).

Chapter 8

Conclusions

During the 1980s poverty rose significantly in the two regions predominantly preoccupied with adjustment – sub-Saharan Africa and Latin America. The rise in poverty occurred both among countries adjusting with IFI assistance and 'non-adjustment lending' countries. But while increasing poverty is the norm for countries undergoing adjustment, *this is not necessary; poverty can be reduced during adjustment.* The main conclusion arising from the analysis in this book is that governments can make choices during adjustment which offset, or accentuate, any ill-effects of adjustment on the poor. This conclusion arises from both theoretical analysis and the large variety of experience observed over the 1980s with respect to policy choices during adjustment.

All developing countries were subject to the same rather hostile world environment in the 1980s – deteriorating terms of trade, slowdown in the growth of world trade, sharp reduction in voluntary capital flows and high interest rates. Yet in some areas growth and poverty reduction accelerated (much of Asia); while in others there was stagnation with falling per capita incomes and rising poverty (much of Africa and Latin America). Within the more stagnant areas, there was also variety, with some countries succeeding in growing and reducing poverty, others protecting the poor despite economic stagnation, and others experiencing sharp rises in poverty.

Differences in the poverty profile during adjustment can be traced to two types of cause. On the one hand, differences in prior conditions and the characteristics of an economy, interacting with the policy changes associated with adjustment, can affect outcomes, as explored in Chapter 2. On the other, differences may arise from the particular selection of policy instruments made during adjustment, including the combination of policies chosen, the weight given to each instrument, and the sequencing of policies. Governments can also protect the poor from the likely effects of the selected adjustment policies through conscious and specific use of meso-policies.

The aim of this chapter is to draw together policy conclusions about how best to reduce poverty during adjustment, on the basis of the earlier analysis of the effects of policies and experiences observed over the 1980s. The focus of the chapter is on those economies which experienced initial economic difficulties and were forced to adjust rather than those where initial problems were minor and growth accelerated, because it is in the former context that poverty reduction is most needed and most difficult to achieve. An obvious conclusion from analysis of the 1980s is that it is almost always better for the poor as well as others in society to be part of an economy which adjusts quickly and successfully, avoiding economic stagnation. It is beyond the scope of this book to provide a comprehensive and thorough investigation of why some countries were so much better at rapid and growth-accelerating adjustment than others, although some discussion of this issue arises in connection with the contrasting case studies to be discussed below.

The next section of the chapter provides an overview of developments in six countries, two from each region, representing contrasting experiences over the 1980s, so as to illustrate the alternative paths adopted at a country level. The three countries which were relatively successful in protecting the poor during adjustment whose experience is sketched here are Ghana, Chile and Indonesia and the less successful are Tanzania, Mexico and the Philippines. The subsequent section uses these experiences, together with the conclusions of earlier chapters, to arrive at some general policy lessons. The final section briefly reviews the performance of the international financial institutions on poverty and adjustment.

SIX COUNTRY OVERVIEWS

Tanzania

Tanzania is justly famous for her focus on human development in the first two decades after independence. Particular emphasis was placed on extending access to primary education and primary health care. The results were impressive: the infant mortality rate fell from 146 to 120, 1960–80; life expectancy rose from forty-one to fifty and the adult literacy rate from just 9.5 per cent of the population to 90 per cent over those twenty years.[1]

But economic performance was less good, and the country started the 1980s with massive imbalances. The reasons for this had accumulated since independence in 1960. Exports consisted almost entirely of primary commodities which were vulnerable to changes in the terms of trade. A combination of factors – including poor producer prices, the effects of villagisation, institutional deficiencies in the para-statal marketing and processing corporations, and defects in the transport and credit networks – led to declines in marketed produce, falling export volumes and rising food imports.[2] Industrial development was inefficient and heavily import-dependent.[3] Large inflows of aid in the 1970s led to a build-up in debt, while export earnings financed only a fraction of the imports needed for industrial development and other essential imports. By 1980, industrial capacity utilisation was at 30 per cent; the value of cash crop exports was 36 per cent below the 1970 level, the current account deficit amounted to 10.2 per cent of GDP and the fiscal deficit to 12.6 per cent.[4]

Adjustment fell into two phases, the first 1981–6, was marked by conflict with the IFIs, especially the Fund, and go-it-alone adjustment policies by the Tanzanian government. Policies emphasised growth in agricultural output and the reallocation of government spending to productive areas, social policies aimed to protect the vulnerable by rationing and price controls on essential items and protecting import allocations to the social sectors. Cuts in recurrent and defence spending and increases in indirect taxes reduced the budget deficit. After much hesitation the currency was devalued in 1983 and again in 1984/5 and producer prices were raised. This period of adjustment saw a sharp reduction in the major imbalances, with more than halving of both the budget and the current account deficits, but at the cost of a large fall in GDP and private consumption per capita. A basic problem was shortage of untied foreign exchange due to lack of access to IMF resources because of conflict with the Fund, and the government's inability to persuade bilateral donors to switch from project to balance of payments support.

The second phase of adjustment came with agreement with the IMF and a sharp reversal of Tanzania's previous policies of public ownership and control. The Economic Recovery Programme, initiated in 1986, was supported by a Stand-By Arrangement from the IMF. Policies included exchange rate adjustments, monetary restrictions, further rises in producer prices, some decontrol of consumer prices, increases in indirect taxes and a freeze on the hiring of civil servants (exempting doctors and teachers). Easing of the foreign exchange restrictions, partly responsible for agricultural recovery, led to positive growth in GDP per capita. However, a worsening of the terms of trade meant that despite a 50 per cent increase in cotton exports, there was no increase in foreign exchange earnings from cotton because of the fall in price. Export earnings as a whole fell by over 7 per cent per annum over the decade. The current account deficit worsened and debt grew dramatically, while the inflation rate remained above 30 per cent per annum.[5]

Incomes per capita fell by 0.7 per cent per annum over the 1980s while real per capita consumption was stagnant. The worst hit were urban households who suffered from restrictions on employment and cuts in formal sector wages. Seventy-five per cent of those entering employment in the 1980s joined the non-waged sector. The wage cuts in the public sector did slightly protect those at the lower end of the salary scale, whose wages fell by 47 per cent compared with cuts of over 60 per cent for top- and middle-level civil servants (1980–87). The minimum wage in 1989 was only 29 per cent of its 1980 value, less than a third of the estimated poverty line.[6] Farmers were less affected than urban dwellers because of rises in producer prices and because the urban–rural real income gap fell.[7]

Meso-policies were also adverse: government expenditure as a proportion of GDP fell dramatically from 33 per cent in 1981 to 21 per cent in 1990; there was also a significant fall in the share of government expenditure going to education and little change in the share going to health.[8] As a result, expenditure per head in education fell by 59 per cent (1978/9 to 1988/9) and in health by 49 per cent.[9]

The health outcome was mixed. The good record of infant mortality continued, with rates falling from 120 per 1,000 births in 1980 to 104 in 1991, while the percentage of the population with access to health services rose from 81 to 93 per cent although urban access fell. There was a rise in the proportion of one-year-olds immunised. The maternal mortality rate rose, however, and several other indicators of the human condition worsened, including access to safe water, which declined from 56 to 52 per cent, 1985/8 to 1988/90, and food availability per head, which fell sharply until 1985 but was restored to a bit above the 1981 level by 1988.[10]

Having been a point of national pride since the 1960s, educational attainment in Tanzania worsened in the 1980s. Increased financial burden on parents to cover current expenditure on wages and equipment discouraged enrolment: primary school enrolment fell by over a quarter through the decade and, even so the primary school pupil/teacher ratio rose (33 in 1986–8 to 35 in 1988–90). Funding for adult education and primary school construction was worst hit by budget cuts.[11]

In Tanzania's case, the poor macro-performance was mainly responsible for the worsening in human conditions. But the heavy emphasis on expenditure cuts to correct the fiscal deficit – the revenue ratio actually fell during the adjustment period – led to the large fall in the expenditure ratio, which was a major factor behind the substantial cuts in social expenditures.

Ghana

Adjustment began in Ghana in 1983, after fifteen years of economic misman-agement and very weak economic performance. The development strategy followed since independence had neglected cocoa producers, over-taxing them and providing agriculture with insufficient resources, while developing an inefficient pattern of import-substituting industrialisation, largely financed by short-term debt. Adverse commodity prices (cocoa prices fell over 60 per cent from 1970–83) dramatically reduced Ghana's earnings. The result was economic stagnation, with real gross GDP falling 11 per cent during the same period, and acute balance of payments problems, as well as large budget deficits due to reduced taxation (including lost revenue from cocoa). Inflation accelerated to over 100 per cent in 1983; the severe drought of 1982–4 exacerbated inflation and the current account deficit. Agricultural output fell and food prices and imports rose dramatically.

There was a dramatic fall in real expenditure on health and education by four-fifths between 1975/6 and 1982/3, reflecting both a fall in government expenditure as a percentage of GDP and a fall in GDP. The number of doctors fell by 50 per cent 1981–4 as skilled labour migrated in search of better pay, and both health and education suffered deterioration of infrastructure and equipment.[12]

Adjustment took the form of three Economic Recovery Programmes de-veloped in association with the IFIs. They included devaluation, improved prices and inputs for cash crop producers, consumer price liberalisation and revenue-raising tax reform, tariff reform and import liberalisation. The adjust-ment programme was generously financed – the inflow of aid amounted to between 4 and 7 per cent of GDP from 1980–7.[13] The third phase (1988–90) also included more social orientation of policy, following the claims that inadequate attention had been given to the social sectors or the vulnerable, especially by UNICEF.[14] These claims were one factor behind the initiation of PAMSCAD, described in Chapter 5. PAMSCAD was first proposed in 1987, but only got started in 1991.

The macro-economic outcome was remarkably successful. After three suc-cessive years of negative growth 1981–3, there was a turnaround with real GDP growing at over 5 per cent in all but two years between 1984 and 1990. Private consumption per capita rose (in constant 1987 dollars) from $270 in 1983 to $310 in 1986 and to $330 in 1990. The budget deficit was transformed into a small surplus by 1986 and gross domestic investment rose as a proportion of GDP from 5.6 to 15.0 per cent, from 1980 to 1990. Inflation fell to 10 per cent by 1985, but accelerated thereafter and was 27 per cent in 1990. Massive real depreciation of the exchange rate – by more than 450 per cent over the decade – together with rehabilitation of the export sectors led to a recovery of exports from only 6 per cent of GDP in 1983 to 10 per cent by 1987 and 15 per cent by 1991.[15]

Some of this success can be explained by independent forces: much of the rise and subsequent fall in prices was due to food supply conditions during and after the drought, while inflation accelerated again after 1985. Similarly, while the initial impact of a million Ghanaians returning from Nigeria in 1983 was to exacerbate conditions, they later provided plentiful agricultural labour, leading to greater output growth. A further important factor was the growth in imports, largely financed by aid.

Meso-outcomes were also positive: through reform and enforcement of tax collection, the tax ratio was raised from around 5 per cent of GDP in 1983 to 11.6 per cent by 1990. This permitted a rise in the expenditure ratio from a low of 8 per cent in 1983 to 13.4 per cent in 1985 and to 14 per cent in 1990. The social allocation ratio also rose from 29 per cent in 1981 to 34.7 per cent in 1990. As a consequence, real expenditure per head on education rose by 51 per cent and on health by 66 per cent over that period.

Charges were raised on public utilities and basic services during adjustment, with user charges introduced for health and education. In education, food and board subsidies for secondary school children were ended and charges were introduced for textbooks. As noted earlier, the charges introduced in the health services in 1985 had long-lasting negative effect on rural utilisation rates.

The economic reforms were especially directed at assisting the rural sector, which benefited from improved prices and resource access. However, the price increases were focused on cocoa, the real price of which rose three-fold, 1984–7, and remained high. In contrast, wholesale food prices in 1986 were below the 1980 level. Only 19 per cent of the poorest 30 per cent of the population participated in cocoa production. The rural poor – especially in the North where poverty is worst – were largely subsistence farmers with limited involvement in the monetised economy, and were not much affected by adjustment policies.

The urban poor were more directly affected – they benefited from the moderation in food price rises, and were hurt by the cutback in public sector employment. The real minimum wage rose from an index of 100 in 1982 to 169 in 1985 and fell to 129 by 1988, partly reflecting the changing inflation rate. The absolute level remained unacceptably low, however: in 1983 it was estimated that the minimum wage met less than 5 per cent of the requirements of a family of five.[16] A total of 45,000 civil servants were retrenched in a major shake out of public sector employment. Some of these benefited from PAMSCAD activities, directed towards the redeployed. While the majority found re-employment, many suffered a loss in living standards and poverty grew in this group.[17]

Quality of life indicators show deterioration in the first half of the 1980s, with some rather mixed recovery in the latter years. Ghana was one of the very few countries to record a rise in the under-fives mortality rate from 1978–82 to 1983–7. Worsening primary school enrolment was observed from 1980 to 1985 with recovery in the later years. Malnutrition in under-fives rose 1980–5 from 33 to 51 per cent and adult illiteracy was also increasing.[18] Calorie consumption as a percentage of requirements was only 76 per cent in 1985 but rose to 93 per cent by 1990; access to health services rose from 61 per cent of the population 1985–7 to 76 per cent 1987–90, but population per doctor also rose from around 15,000 in 1984 to 20,500 in 1989.[19] The percentage of one-year-olds immunised, having risen from 34 per cent in 1981 to 67 per cent by 1988/9, fell back to 64 per cent by 1991.[20]

PAMSCAD was intended to 'mitigate the social costs of adjustment'. But its long delays in getting started, complex and cumbersome system of administration and poor targeting, especially in terms of coverage of those in poverty, meant that despite quite generous financing (planned expenditure of $84 million or 6 to 8 per cent of the annual cost of international support for Ghana's adjustment effort), it had relatively insignificant effects on poverty. It made a contribution to the financing of retrenchment payments and to some social infrastructure.[21]

Both macro- and meso-policies in Ghana since 1983 have had positive effects on the poor, although not all the poor have benefited and for many the benefit has been small: the positive effects were mainly due to the fact that the recovery programme was expansionary, permitting rising incomes and government expenditure. There were two reasons why such an expansionary policy was possible: first, because the prolonged stagnation and mismanagement meant that reform could soon produce positive results; secondly, the programme was generously financed externally and net resources were not needed for debt repayments. But the longer run prognosis is not so good. The basic flaw in the programme is that it has depended heavily on increasing output of traditional commodities – whose prices have fallen, partly as a consequence of the success of this and similar programmes in other producing countries. From 1986 to 1990, volume of cocoa production increased by 30 per cent while dollar earnings declined by one-fifth.[22] There has been very little diversification of production or exports. In addition, there has been a build-up of debt, which will lead to a less favourable resource situation.

While macro-policies were expansionary and favoured the rural areas, the poor benefited by only a small amount from the recovery – from some extension and rehabilitation of social services; while some of the rural poor have benefited from improved prices and inputs, many do not produce cash crops and have been unaffected; PAMSCAD played a very minor, almost negligible, role.

Chile

Chile's adjustment policies go back to 1974 when Pinochet initiated strongly monetarist and pro-market policies. The policies led to a severe recession in 1974/5, greatly rising unemployment (from 5.7 per cent at the beginning of the 1970s to 13.9 per cent at the end) and cuts in real wages which fell dramatically in 1973 and never recovered their previous level. Per capita income in 1979 was just about at its 1970 level. In the 1980s Chile faced similar external shocks to other debt-laden and primary-producing nations. The large short-term capital inflows were suddenly reversed in 1982; the rise in the oil price together with the copper price fall led to a sharp deterioration in the terms of trade, 1979–83 – one of the worst in Latin America. Likewise, the debt ratio rose to one of the highest. The current account deficit amounted to 14.7 per cent of GDP in 1981.[23]

Macro-policies were initially deflationary and subsequently more expansionary. In the early 1980s, deflation was the main stabilisation measure, with large cuts in government expenditure in 1982 and 1983; stringent credit controls; cuts in trade tariffs and a small real depreciation. These measures were backed by an IMF Stand-By Agreement and a World Bank Structural Adjustment Loan. From 1984, more expansionary policies were adopted and growth in real government expenditure resumed. More emphasis was placed on expanding exports; the real exchange rate fell by 40 per cent between 1984 and 1988.

The adjustment measures were successful in reducing the current account deficit which fell to 11.3 per cent of GDP by 1988 and had been virtually eliminated by 1991.[24] In the early period, this was achieved by a drastic cut in incomes (GDP per capita fell by nearly 16 per cent in 1982); but in the latter part of the 1980s there was a strong expansion of non-traditional exports – exports in 1990 were 65 per cent above their 1980 level. After near-stagnation from 1980–5, GDP per capita recovered, growing by 5.3 per cent per annum

1985–90. Average real wages fell by nearly 11 per cent 1982–3 while minimum wages fell from an index of 100 in 1980 to 66.9 in 1984 and further to 58.7 in 1987. But by 1990, the average wage was 5 per cent above the 1980 level, although still significantly below the level of the early 1970s. The unemployment rate rose very steeply to over 20 per cent in 1982–3, recovering to 6.5 per cent by 1990.[25] Employment grew strongly in industry and agriculture for 1984–9 – the latter being particularly important for rural poverty which accounted for 60 per cent of total poverty in 1982. While incomes of lower income groups stagnated or fell through much of the decade, the incomes of the highest paid rose substantially. A wave of privatisations contributed to further concentration of wealth.[26] As a result, income distribution worsened, from a Gini coefficient of 0.52 in 1979 rising to an unprecedented level of 0.56 in 1984 and falling back to 0.53 in 1988.[27]

In the first half of the 1980s, weak economic growth and worsening distribution led to rising poverty: at the peak, in 1982, 45 per cent of households fell below the poverty line. Despite some improvements in the later years, 41 per cent of households were in poverty in 1989, compared with 36 per cent in 1979.[28]

Macro-policies showed a mixed performance from the perspective of protecting the poor: strongly negative in the first half of the decade, being very deflationary, with downward pressure on employment and real wages; and positive in the second half, with emphasis on switching as against deflation, leading to output and employment growth and wage recovery. Meso-policies did much to protect people from extreme destitution during the years when macro-policies were adverse. They achieved this by special programmes and by improving priority ratios, not by increasing social expenditure.

Incomes were sustained at minimal levels by very extensive public works schemes, which paid very low wages – one-fourth of the minimum wage for the main programme (as discussed in Chapter 5). By 1983, almost 13 per cent of the workforce participated in the employment programmes. These were largely phased out by 1989 as output recovered and unemployment fell.[29]

Expenditure on both health and education fell as a proportion of total government expenditure and of GDP, with interest payments taking a sharply rising share. From 1982 to 1987 per capita expenditure on education and health fell significantly, by 25 per cent on education and 15 per cent on health. However, improved intra-sectoral allocations did much to protect the most vulnerable. Tertiary education bore the brunt of the cuts in the education sector, falling by nearly 50 per cent, while non-university expenditure fell by 16 per cent, 1982–7. The percentage of the educational budget going to pre-school and primary education rose from 48.3 per cent in 1980 to 57.4 per cent in 1986 while the secondary education ratio remained broadly constant and the tertiary education share fell. As a result of the reforms, the distribution of overall public spending on education became considerably more progressive, with the poorest 30 per cent of the population receiving 37.5 per cent of the benefits in 1986, compared with 28.6 per cent in 1974 and the richest 40 per cent receiving 34.5

per cent in 1986, compared with 47.3 per cent in 1974.[30] However, there is some evidence of increasing inequities in the *quality* of education received.[31] Primary school enrolment ratios fell somewhat throughout the 1980s but pre-school and secondary enrolment rose consistently.

Available statistics do not permit a breakdown of the large expenditure cuts in health, 1982–3, between primary and curative care. Indirect evidence suggests that basic services were largely protected. Resources were shifted to mother–child care programmes and to curative activities after 1984. Fifty-five per cent of the cuts fell on wages. The share of expenditure devoted to supplies of drugs increased and a major cut was taken by investment. Evidence shows rising levels of medical visits per person and per mother and child, and a rising proportion of births attended by professionals, 1980–3. Immunisation rates were high throughout the decade. However, overall access to health services declined during the decade, as did access to safe water.[32]

A series of carefully targeted nutrition programmes did much to sustain nutrition during the recession, despite expenditure cuts. Total expenditure on the programme declined, by 8.5 per cent 1982–3, with a falling number of meals provided and halving of the milk distributed in schools programmes.[33]

While the improvement in priority ratios on the whole worked, despite macro-developments and worsening social allocation ratios, to protect the vulnerable during the 1982–3 recession, they were not sufficient in some respects as shown by the worsening primary school enrolments and access to health and safe water noted above. Most indicators of health continued to improve. Maternal mortality rates fell fast through the decade and infant mortality rates continued to decline, but not at the remarkable pace previously achieved. Thus from 1982 to 1986 the IMR fell by 18 per cent, compared with a fall of 40 per cent in the 1978–82 period. Moreover, several indicators did not perform well. There was a slight rise in malnutrition in 1983 but this fell back in later years. Reported cases of infectious diseases rose by 53 per cent, 1980–2 returning to the 1980 level by 1988.

Looking at the Chilean case over a longer time period, there was an unusual combination of almost stagnant incomes spanning the two decades, 1970–89, combined with tremendous advances in standards of health, education and nutrition. Over this period infant mortality fell from 79.3 (1970) per 1,000 to 19.4 (1986); there was a falling proportion of malnutrition (15.5 per cent in 1975 to 8.7 per cent in 1985 among under-fives); the proportion of low birth weight babies halved and other indicators of health (maternal mortality, diarrhoea mortality, bronchopneumonia mortality) greatly improved. Thus the twenty-year period was associated with an almost continuous effort to promote some aspects of human development during economic stagnation, which was, despite hiccups in 1982–3, broadly successful in terms of the social indicators, even though accompanied by a sharp increase in poverty as measured by incomes and falling real per capita public expenditure on social programmes. This was achieved mainly by effective targeting of public resources. But in a broader sense there was clearly a deterioration in important aspects of human well-being over these years, not only as a result of falling incomes; the improvements in health were narrowly focussed, targeted on mothers and children with less emphasis on the general population; there were also very high human costs in terms of suppressed civil liberties.

Mexico

Mexico grew fast from the 1950s to the 1970s, with an average annual growth of GDP of 6 per cent, based on import-substituting industrialisation. A major oil discovery in 1977 (taking oil from 22.3 per cent to 75 per cent of exports, 1977–81) sustained growth, but heavy foreign borrowing continued. In 1982, with the cessation of foreign lending, adjustment became essential.

The first IMF programme from 1983–5 consisted of tight financial control, devaluation and liberalisation of trade. The earthquake of 1985, involving emergency spending equivalent to 2.7 per cent of GDP, together with a fall in the price of oil from $25 to $12 per barrel, 1985–6, created the need for a new programme. In mid-1986, a second IMF arrangement continued the previous policies, introducing more extensive privatisation. In late 1988, a third programme began with a three-year IMF extended arrangement and a World Bank sectoral adjustment loan.

The negative impact of the 1980s recession on incomes was substantial; growth in GDP per capita was −2.0 per cent per annum, 1982–5, and −1.2 per cent per annum from 1986–9, only becoming positive again in the 1990s. Having grown at 1.2 per cent per annum 1970–80, earnings per employee fell 3.9 per cent per annum, 1980–9. By 1989, real earnings had fallen to 51 per cent of their 1980 level and the minimum urban wage had fallen further to just 44.3 per cent of its 1980 value. As a result of slow growth in formal sector employment and a cutback in the public sector, employment in the informal sector grew from 24.2 per cent to 36 per cent as a percentage of non-agricultural employment, 1980–90.[34]

Despite the stated aims of the Economic and Social Pact, introduced in the late 1980s to spread income losses evenly, the burden was highly regressive. The percentage change in real per capita income between 1984 and 1989 was: −3.2 per cent for the poor, +2.1 per cent for the middle-class and +27.7 per cent for the rich. As a result, the Gini coefficient rose from 0.43 to 0.47 over that period. The percentage of the population below the poverty line, having fallen from 34 to 29 per cent, 1970–81, rose dramatically to 51 per cent by 1984 – the worst such deterioration in Latin America.[35]

Macro policies were thus negative in their impact on the poor both as a result of negative growth effects and adverse distributional consequences for most of the 1980s.

Meso-policies were also negative. The revenue and expenditure ratios rose slightly over the 1980s, but the share of education and health fell sharply. The

National Plan for Education, launched in 1979, aimed to raise primary enrolment to 100 per cent, raise quality at all levels, prioritising pre-school education. Until the 1980s, the growth in enrolment rates was impressive, rising fast from a low level. This trend was challenged, however, by the cuts made in public spending in the adjustment programmes. Between 1981 and 1988, the education budget fell 29.9 per cent in real terms: with increased enrolment of 1.8 million students, this produced a fall in spending per student of 41 per cent over that period. Real spending on primary education fell 49.3 per cent and on research and new materials 94.4 per cent, partly offset by a 183 per cent rise in spending on vocational high schools.

The growth in primary and secondary enrolment rates fell sharply in the 1980s, compared with the 1970s; gross primary school enrolment rates fell from 1980–5 rising subsequently, while secondary ratios stagnated.[36] The rate of primary school desertion in the rural areas rose from 7.2 to 12.2 per cent, 1981–5, the worst period of the recession.[37] There was a fall in the percentage of students continuing from the first stage of education to the next with primary to secondary absorption falling from 86.8 to 82.2 per cent, 1981–8, due to rising poverty, the need to earn additional incomes and the lack of secondary schools in rural areas where primary education had expanded. Indicators suggest a decline in educational quality. With teachers' salaries falling approximately 50 per cent 1981–8, many sought secondary employment, thus devoting less time to their profession.[38]

In 1983, the Mexican constitution was amended to make access to health services a right for all citizens. The government also aimed to eliminate regional disparities and to strengthen the administrative structure. The record until 1980 had been good, with infant mortality falling from 73 per 1,000 in 1970 to 55.8 in 1980 and life expectancy at birth rising from 61.7 to 66.6 years over the same period. From 1976–81, the health budget had risen 70 per cent in real terms, but the cutbacks associated with the adjustment policies caused a budget slump 1982–7: in 1987, the real value of health expenditure per capita stood at just 41 per cent of the 1981 level.[39]

These cuts affected family health services especially and programmes for depressed areas, with a fall in budget allocations of about three-quarters 1981–7, hurting the most vulnerable in society. At the same time, the crisis prompted a restructuring of the health system, decentralising and improving coordination between sectors in an effort to raise productivity. Indicators of productivity appear encouraging: access to health services expanded in coverage from 81.2 to 91 per cent of the population 1982–7. The number of physicians grew by 53 per cent, 1976–88, hospital beds by 42 per cent and health care centres by 130 per cent despite the large cut in real expenditure per head. But indicators of outcomes suggest that service quality suffered. The percentage of births attended by medical personnel fell from 94 per cent (1983–8) to 45 per cent (1988–90) and maternal mortality rose from 82 per 100,000 (1980–7) to 150 (1988). Access to sanitation fell slightly between 1985/8 and 1988/90. While infant mortality rates continued to improve, falling from 55.8 per 1,000 births to 45.9, 1980–8, this statistic masks rural–urban disparities and changes in the cause of mortality. Mortality due to malnutrition rose 22 per cent in Mexico City and 56 per cent in the South as a result of rising poverty. Peri-natal complications as a cause of mortality rose in all regions except the Gulf, with the highest rise being in Mexico City. The child mortality rate (aged 1–5) rose by 114.3 per cent in the South, 1978–84, falling in all other regions. The link with the recession is likely since this region was hit particularly hard: here, diarrhoeal diseases as a cause of child mortality rose by 122 per cent.[40]

In Mexico both macro- and meso-policy choices led to a worsening in the position of the poor, resulting in a sharp rise in poverty as measured by incomes, and a worsening in some social indicators. One major reason that lay behind these policy choices was the early decision to respect debt obligations. This meant that GDP growth had to be tightly controlled in order to reduce imports and release resources for debt servicing; in addition, it required a huge shift in expenditure allocations with the share of government expenditure spent on the category including interest payments rising from 23.3 per cent (1981) to 61.1 per cent (1989), necessitating drastic cuts elsewhere, including the social sectors. It was only after the Brady plan had relaxed the debt servicing constraint (in 1990) that growth in GDP and social sector expenditure could resume.

The Philippines

The Philippines had high levels of poverty which were not reduced by the growth of the 1970s; 57 per cent of the population were estimated to fall below the poverty line in 1971. Following accumulation of debt during the 1970s largely to finance import-substituting industrialisation, the Philippines suffered a classic debt-crisis in the early 1980s, with adverse terms of trade and high interest rates leading to a large current account deficit (over 8 per cent of GDP in 1982) and the cessation of voluntary lending causing a foreign exchange crisis.

The Philippine adjustment process falls into three phases – a deflationary phase 1983–5, with substantial cuts in public expenditure and credit constraint and little change in the exchange rate; more expansionary policies from 1986, with exchange rate depreciation and growing government expenditure; and a further economic downturn, accelerating inflation and an unsustainable balance of payments, followed by exchange rate depreciation and contractionary fiscal and monetary policies in 1990. In the first phase there was negative growth (the cumulative cut in GDP per capita was 17 per cent 1982–7); the fiscal account was narrowed, entirely through expenditure cuts, and the current account narrowed through import cuts. In the second phase, there was positive growth in per capita incomes, exports grew, but imports grew faster and both fiscal and current account imbalances widened.[41] In the third phase, GDP per capita again contracted and imbalances were reduced.

There were strongly negative effects on the poor during the first phase, as a result of both macro- and meso-policies. There was little change in real wages, but unemployment and under-employment each increased by about a third. Government expenditure fell sharply – from 15.4 per cent of GDP in 1981 to 11.6 per cent in 1984. In real terms it fell by one-quarter, 1983–6. Real expenditures on health and education fell as a proportion of government expenditure, 83–5. Health expenditure per person fell by 50 per cent and education expenditure per student by 19 per cent, 1983–5. In the health sector, the priority ratio worsened, as the share of preventative health declined. There were falls in nurses, midwives, dentists, nutritionists and sanitary expenditures per patient (with a small increase in the doctor/patient ratio). In education, the priority ratio improved as primary expenditure per pupil was maintained, while falling by 40 per cent in secondary education and 20 per cent in tertiary.[42]

From 1986–90, macro-policies were more expansionary, with greater emphasis on switching and on structural reforms. Growth was above 5 per cent per annum, each year, 1986–9. The Aquino government implemented a number of programmes designed to improve social conditions. Government revenue rose as a percentage of GNP from 11.3 per cent 1983–5 to 14.6 per cent 1986–9, and the tax system became more progressive with income tax bringing in a greater per centage of the total. The expenditure ratio rose from 12.8 per cent in 1981 to 19.8 per cent in 1990, while health and education expenditure rose as a proportion of the total. Real expenditure per capita on health rose by 49 per cent between 1983–5 and 1989, while real education expenditure per capita rose by 88 per cent. The share of preventative medicine increased sharply from 1985 to 1987. The government introduced an emergency employment scheme – the Community Employment Development Programme – in 1986 designed to create employment opportunities for a million of the rural poor. In 1987, 182 million person-days of employment had been created (or jobs for about 100,000 people), roughly 2.5 per cent of the rural unemployed and under- employed population. Evidence suggests the jobs were mainly taken by the previously unemployed or under-employed.[43] Open unemployment fell from over 11 per cent in 1986 to 8.5 per cent in 1990.[44]

In the third phase, the adjustment programme included exchange rate depreciation and an improved budgetary position, both through raising revenue (the revenue ratio rising from 16.8 per cent to 17.6 per cent, 1990 to 1992) and curtailing expenditure – the expenditure ratio in 1992 was reduced to its 1989 level. Health expenditures were maintained but there was a cut of 8.5 per cent in per capita expenditure on education, 1989–92. The priority ratio in health worsened.

Data on poverty and social indicators show the social consequences of the different approaches to adjustment. In the first half of the decade the rate of poverty increased sharply, with the greatest increase being in the urban areas, but rural poverty also increased significantly.[45] The incidence of poverty fell by about a fifth from 1985 to 1988.[46] There was a rise in poverty during the third phase, with an increase of 2 per cent in the proportion of the population falling below the poverty line from 1988 to 1991. The rise in poverty was due to worsening distribution of consumption – much of it occurring within the agricultural sector.[47] Devaluation worsened distribution in agriculture, according to simulation results because the 'severity of poverty is greater among the disproportionately numerous landless and small farmers who are net buyers of staples' (Balisacan, forthcoming, p.23).[48] Open unemployment rose once more, increasing urban poverty.

Falling incomes and deteriorating health services in the first phase were reflected in a slowdown in the rate of improvement in infant mortality rates and in rising malnutrition. In 1984 there was a marked increase in the incidence of communicable diseases. There was also some worsening in enrolment ratios, cohort survival rates and pupil/teacher ratios in both primary and secondary schools.[49] Many of the social indicators show improvement in the second half of the decade, including primary and secondary school enrolment, the doctor and nurse/population ratios, access to drinking water and measures of child nutrition.[50] In the third phase, there was stagnation in social indicators, but no apparent reversals.

In the first phase of adjustment in the Philippine adjustment both macro- and meso-policies were negative from the perspective of the poor. The second phase reversed many of the adverse trends, with more favourable macro- and meso-policies, but imbalances widened necessitating a third phase. The third phase was intermediate with respect to both types of policy. Although poverty increased, the social indicators did not worsen in this phase.

Indonesia

Indonesia's adjustments started in 1983 with the fall in the oil price. Until then, Indonesia grew fast using her oil revenue to develop infrastructure in agriculture, education and transport. These efforts – and especially expansion of rice output – led to a rapid fall in poverty (the percentage of the population falling below the official poverty line declined from 60 per cent (1970) to 40 per cent (1984)). Income inequality also declined over this period, and human indicators (infant and child mortality rates, life expectancy, nutrition and educational attainment) improved.[51]

From 1983, a sharp adverse movement in the terms of trade necessitated adjustment. The adjustment package was self-imposed by the government but many of the policies were similar to those contained in IFI programmes, including severe public expenditure cuts (in real terms of 19 per cent, 1982/3 to 1986/7) and major currency devaluation, with the real effective exchange rate falling by 60 per cent from 1982 to 1987. The first World Bank loan was made only in 1987, incorporating trade policy conditions.[52]

The Indonesian adjustment was broadly successful in macro-economic terms: the current account deficit was reduced from a peak of over 6 per cent of GNP in 1983 to around 2 per cent in 1987 and 2.3 per cent in 1990; the value of exports fell sharply in 1985 and 1986, but then resumed a high growth rate and inflation fell significantly in the early 1980s rising again slightly at the end of the decade. However, the budget deficit rose as a percentage of GNP, from 1.7 per cent surplus in 1980 to a deficit of 3.0 per cent in 1985 as the revenue ratio fell more sharply than the expenditure ratio, but by 1990 it had improved to a surplus of 0.7 per cent.[53]

Unlike many countries, while growth slowed in Indonesia it remained positive during the adjustment period. Per capita GDP grew by 4.8 per cent per annum over the 1970s; growth was temporarily halted in 1980–2, but rose again by 3.0 per cent per annum 1983–87, accelerating to 4.9 per cent per annum 1987–90. Inequality lessened with a decline in the Gini coefficient for consumption expenditure (from 0.33 to 0.32, 1984–7 and a further slight decrease to 1990). According to official estimates of poverty, the percentage of poor continued to decline, from 21.6 per cent (1984) to 17.4 per cent (1987) and to 15.1 per cent in 1990, with a greater fall in the rural than urban areas largely due to rising incomes of self-employed farmers.[54]

Social indicators also continued to improve over the adjustment period. The average per capita calorie intake increased by 5.7 per cent, rising at every level of income; declining rates of protein-calorie malnutrition are reported in both urban and rural areas, 1978 to 1986/7; there was a significant increase in immunisation rates throughout the decade; declining infant mortality rates are recorded for 1980 to 1987, although progress stopped at the end of the decade. The percentage of births attended by medical personnel rose from an average of 31 per cent, 1983–8, to 44 per cent, 1988–90; maternal mortality rates fell significantly. The percentage of the poor who attended a clinic when ill rose substantially between 1978 and 1987, both in urban and rural areas – from 32 to 67 per cent in urban Java and from 35 to 51 per cent in the rural outer islands. Educational indicators improved in the first half of the 1980s, but there were signs of deterioration in primary and secondary enrolment ratios from 1986–8 to 1988–90, while indicators of educational quality showed some worsening over the 1980s.[55]

On the whole, the record shows that Indonesia was successful in combining adjustment, growth and human development.[56] How was this achieved? First, the considerable macro success in maintaining a significantly positive growth of GDP per capita was an important factor. This success was partly due to the balance of macro-policies adopted with considerable emphasis on switching as against disabsorption (associated with the big depreciation and the rising budget deficit from 1983–5); partly to the very favourable supply response – both in terms of expansion of cash crop exports (estate crops grew by 9 per cent per annum 1984–8, farm non-food crops by 4.3 per cent per annum – this was not greatly at the expense of other agricultural products, which continued to expand albeit at a slower rate), and of labour-intensive manufactured exports (manufactures had risen to 29 per cent of the value of exports in 1988 from 8 per cent

in 1983). The favourable supply response was in turn due to earlier developments, which had provided Indonesia with well-developed rural infrastructure,
extensive human capital and industrial and entrepreneurial experience. Secondly,
consumption growth was maintained at a much higher rate than income,
protecting consumption during the recessionary period. Thirdly, the growth was
relatively egalitarian so that the distribution of additional consumption was
favourable from the perspective of poverty reduction. As a result of the
changing terms of trade and rising agricultural output, rural consumption rose
faster than urban. Within the rural sector, relatively equal land distribution
meant that the poor participated in the increased output; while the poor were
not proportionately represented in cash crops, they did participate in their
expansion and in the sustained expansion of food crops, and non-agricultural
rural opportunities also expanded. Within the urban sector, the focus on
labour-intensive manufacturing led to growth in manufacturing employment,
which is estimated to have expanded by nearly 10 per cent per annum, 1985–8,
in enterprises with more than fifteen employees. In both rural and urban areas
there was a slight rise in real wages. In addition, a progressive tax reform – with
the introduction of a personal income tax – contributed to improving the
secondary income distribution.

Finally, while government expenditure was cut (the expenditure ratio fell from
26.4 per cent in 1981 to 20.9 per cent in 1990), the cuts in government
expenditure broadly protected the services of the poor over the period of severe
cuts (1983–6). First, the reductions fell most heavily on development expenditures, while routine expenditures were protected (central government routine
expenditure grew by over 7 per cent, 1982/3–1986 while development expenditure fell by 43 per cent); secondly, transfers to the provinces were protected,
growing despite the aggregate cuts; thirdly, development expenditures were
reallocated to priority areas – thus development expenditure on human resources rose from 16 per cent of the total, 1982/3 to 24 per cent, 1986/7. The
social allocation ratio remained constant over the 1980s, while the priority ratio
improved, when measured by the proportion of educational expenditure going
to primary and secondary schools and the proportion of health expenditure
going to basic health care.

In summary, both macro- and meso-policies supported adjustment with a
human face in Indonesia. But the process has been accompanied by rising
external debt and debt-service ratios. Total external debt as a percentage of
GDP almost doubled from 26.8 per cent (1980) to 50.1 per cent (1990) which
may cause future problems.[57]

Some conclusions from the six cases

The analysis of the six cases suggests the following conclusions.

1. Increasing poverty, as measured by the proportion of the population falling
below the poverty line, occurred when there was macro-economic stagnation or

decline, as happened in most of the countries at some point, including Tanzania, Ghana pre-adjustment, Chile until around 1986, Mexico for most of the 1980s and the Philippines up to 1985 and after 1989. Even extensive compensatory employment policies, such as those of Chile, were not sufficient to counter macro decline. Other employment/compensatory programmes (e.g. in Ghana and the Philippines) had much less significance.

2. Causes of such macro stagnation include economic mismanagement (as in Ghana pre-adjustment); deflationary macro-policies with little or no switching policies (Chile pre-1985, Philippines pre-1985; Mexico pre-1986); deflationary macro-policies combined with switching where the supply response was weak and/or switching was rendered ineffective by other policies (Tanzania).

3. Policies which promoted growth during adjustment contained a strong switching element in the form of real exchange rate depreciation, and, with the exception of Indonesia, were only mildly deflationary as indicated by minor expenditure cutting policies. This combination of policies could only be pursued if adequate external financing were available – as in Ghana through aid, in Mexico and the Philippines in the 1986–9 period because of more generous treatment of international debt after Brady, and in Chile in the later period because of renewed inflows of foreign capital. Only Indonesia succeeded in following deflationary stabilisation policies and yet achieved economic growth. This was due to the fact that in Indonesia deflation was accompanied by strong switching policies with a good supply response owing to prior investments.

4. While growth permitted poverty to be reduced, once again 'trickle-down' is seen to have had relatively small effects on the poor in economies where structures were inegalitarian, such as Ghana, Mexico and the Philippines (later period). While in each case, resumed growth halted the previous negative effects on poverty, the positive effects of growth for the poor were minor. Only in Indonesia, with a more egalitarian structure to start with and a more pro-poor pattern of growth did poverty fall rapidly. It is noteworthy that Indonesia was much more egalitarian at the beginning of the adjustment process than the other countries for which data are available: thus the Gini coefficient in Indonesia was estimated to be 0.33 in 1984 in contrast to 0.44 in Mexico (same year) and 0.52 in Chile in 1979. Moreover, Indonesia's adjustment involved an expansion of labour- intensive exports and rice output (a crop grown by farmers of all sizes).

5. A variety of meso-policies were observed – as one would expect from the earlier analysis in this book. The expenditure ratio fell significantly in Tanzania and Indonesia; it rose sharply in Ghana (from 1983) and in the Philippines in the expansionary phase, and changed only by a small amount elsewhere. The fall in Tanzania and the rise in Ghana were both important factors behind the fall/rise in expenditure on the social sectors. Raising the revenue and expenditure ratio can thus be an important element in pro-poor meso-policies, as argued in Chapter 3. But these measures are neither necessary nor sufficient, since the social allocation and priority ratios are also relevant and can offset changes in the expenditure ratio. In Tanzania, Chile and Mexico the social

allocation ratio declined significantly over the 1980s contributing to large declines in social expenditure per person. In Ghana, it rose significantly and elsewhere there was little change. It appears that in both Chile and Indonesia improvements in the priority ratios were the main way in which the poor were protected from cuts in government expenditure. Where education and health charges were introduced – as in Ghana and Tanzania – they appeared to have a negative effect on the use of services among the poor.

6. The evidence available on the distributional impact of government expenditure in Indonesia and the Philippines shows that government expenditure generally had a progressive impact on the distribution of secondary income. Expenditure in the health and education sectors were shown to be more progressive in these countries than government expenditure as a whole, and also highly progressive in Chile. No evidence on this was identified for the other countries.

7. The indicators of social service availability and use and the quality of life indicators, measuring changes in health outcomes and educational achievements, in general moved adversely as would be expected given the reduced incomes and social service expenditures, but the deterioration was less marked and less uniform than might have been expected. In terms of health outcomes, infant mortality rates continued to improve in most of the countries; Ghana was an exception in the middle 1980s and Indonesia at the end of the decade; there was a slowdown in the rate of improvement in Chile and the Philippines, and a worsening in a badly affected region in Mexico. One reason for the mostly good performance on infant mortality was that every country succeeded in increasing the immunisation rate, despite the health cuts. The rate of maternal mortality, however, worsened in Mexico, the Philippines and Tanzania. A rise in the incidence of various diseases was noted in the Philippines, Chile (first phase) and Mexico. Deterioration in health service availability (doctors, nurses, health attendance, etc.) was observed in Chile, Mexico, the Philippines and Ghana. Reduced access to safe water occurred in Tanzania, Chile and Indonesia (latter half). Average food availability, as measured by calories available in relation to needs (on average) worsened in the Philippines and Chile, over the decade, and Tanzania between 1982 and 1988/9, but improved significantly in Ghana, Mexico and Indonesia. There was evidence of deterioration in child nutrition in the Philippines (first phase), a temporary worsening in Chile (1982–3) and also a rise in the proportion of low birth-weight babies from 1984 to 1987. The most prevalent deterioration was in educational access and performance: primary and/or secondary enrolment worsened in Tanzania, Mexico, Indonesia and the Philippines, and signs of worsening attainments were noted in Chile, Mexico, Indonesia and the Philippines.

A SUMMARY OF POLICY CONCLUSIONS

While there was a variety of experience with respect to poverty over the adjustment era – as the contrasting case studies indicate – for most countries stabilisation and adjustment policies were associated with worsening poverty as measured by incomes, and with a slowdown and some reversals in improvements in social indicators. This was shown by the summary of experience in the two major adjusting regions. Adverse macro-developments are primarily responsible for the worsening income poverty, while adverse meso-policies are mainly responsible for the worsening social deprivation. Despite the worsening social deprivation, as measured by cuts in real resources going to the social sectors, some of the quality of life indicators have continued to improve – notably infant and child mortality rates in most countries. Full investigation of why this was possible is still needed. Potential explanations include the fact that the 1980s was a decade in which WHO and UNICEF were very successful in stimulating mass vaccination and some other improvements in child health. In addition, female education, which is a vital ingredient of improvements in child health, had made very major advances previously with continued positive effects.

The main elements of adjustment policies that protect the poor and may contribute to reduced poverty during adjustment should by now be apparent, and are briefly summarised below:[58]

1. *Expansionary macro-policies, i.e. adjustment with growth.* This is likely to mean more gradual attempts to reduce fiscal imbalances than in the normal policy set; more emphasis on switching than disabsorption and on promotion of exports than on cuts in imports. The cases of Ghana and Indonesia above are illustrative of expansionary adjustment policies, the first achieved by recovery from very low levels, partly due to generous external financing, the second to heavy emphasis on switching policies which were effective because of previous investments. Adequate external finance, either in the form of new aid flows, private flows, or reduced debt payments, may often be essential for expansionary adjustment.

2. *Structural changes may be necessary* in the case of economies with highly inegalitarian structures so that growth becomes pro-poor. This may require land reform, progressive taxation and credit reforms, including the development of new credit institutions for the poor.

3. *A review and reform of meso-policies is usually needed,* so that they support (and do not hurt) the poor. Pro-poor meso-policies include some combination of raising revenue (unless the revenue ratio is at least 25 per cent of GNP), raising the social allocation ratio and improving the priority ratio, with the aim of ensuring that social sector resource flows to the poor improve and do not, as is typical, worsen during adjustment.

4. *Food subsidies received by the poor should be maintained* (and, in cases where malnutrition is high, increased) in real value and in coverage. This may require use of universal subsidies, targeted by choice of commodity or region. The abolition of food subsidies, accompanied sometimes by narrow targeting – typical of most IFI adjustment packages – usually reduces the real value of the subsidies received and the coverage of the poor.[59]

5. There should be *no introduction of user charges on primary health and education.* Tertiary education and complex curative health care can be partially self-financed.

6. *Emergency support policies are needed* especially during stabilisation programmes to enable people to secure minimum incomes. There are three types of support schemes:

(a) Employment schemes have a valuable part to play; they must be open-ended, providing employment at minimum wages to anyone who wants a job. If well designed (which generally requires that they have been designed prior to the adjustment programmes) they can also contribute to social reconstruction and maintenance.

(b) Pensions for the incapacitated and old (these are usually needed to prevent destitution at all times, not only during adjustment).

(c) Nutrition interventions to provide supplementary food and medical support to malnourished children. They may be targeted individually (as in Chile) or by school/area according to average malnutrition (as in Botswana and Zimbabwe during drought).

7. *Careful monitoring of the condition of the poor* is essential with respect to income and access to and use of essential goods and services, so that policies may be appropriately designed and adapted in response to evidence on their effectiveness and changing conditions. The few countries with good monitoring systems generally also have good policies (e.g. Botswana, Chile, Costa Rica and Indonesia). Good monitoring need not be expensive or involve elaborate statistical machinery. It involves the selection of a few key indicators, regular collection of sample data, rapid processing and good communication of the results to policy-makers.[60]

8. *International policies:* countries have to make policy decisions in the light of actual and expected conditions internationally. They rarely have the power to change them, but the international community does have this power. Since international conditions were the prime cause of the need for adjustment, and further deterioration in these conditions has been a major factor inhibiting some countries' success in adjustment,[61] changes in these conditions are essential for sustained development and poverty reduction in the worst affected countries. Prime areas needing reform are commodity prices, interest rates and debt. Some improvement has occurred with respect to the last two – both primarily due to the changing situation and needs of the industrialised countries, with interest rates being reduced a little and significant progress being made on private sector debt for a few major debtors. Little progress has been made on public sector debt (which especially affects Africa) and no progress has been made at all on commodity prices.[62] Effective policies towards commodity prices – including international schemes for discouraging and controlling production, for example through agreed and comprehensive taxation of production by producer countries – are essential, especially for African countries.

THE PERFORMANCE OF THE FUND AND BANK ON ADJUSTMENT AND POVERTY

The analysis in this book has not shown (nor attempted to show) that the clearly adverse developments for the poor in many countries with IMF/World Bank policies in place were mainly *due* to these policies. Poverty has also worsened in countries without Bank/Fund programmes. Nonetheless, the IFIs have rightly been criticised for their actions and inaction in this area. The most telling criticism is that, though not primarily responsible, they were there and did little or nothing. Claiming innocence because of lack of responsibility for the initial causes is, in this context, akin to claiming no responsibility for not putting out a forest fire in the vicinity, or failing to call in the fire brigade, on the grounds that someone else started it.

The following more detailed criticisms may be made about the performance of the Fund and the World Bank (and/or the industrialised countries which determine their policies).

1. That the exogenous developments that necessitated adjustment were not tackled by these institutions – the major ones being falling commodity prices and exorbitant debt servicing. These events were taken as constraints to be accepted rather than challenged.

2. The policies of the institutions probably made these 'exogenous' developments worse. Encouragement of adjusting countries to promote expanded production of primary commodities contributed to the continued worsening in the commodity price situation. Flows of finance from the IFIs, which were given on condition that countries respected their debt obligations, tightened the debt straitjacket and delayed serious consideration of debt write-off.

3. The conventional stabilisation/adjustment package with heavy emphasis on expenditure cuts and deflation, together with abolition/reduction of food subsidies and introduction of user charges, directly contributed to the adverse developments at macro- and meso-levels. Most of the countries which avoided the adverse effects adopted unconventional packages (sometimes with and sometimes without IFI support) involving expansionary adjustment and revenue raising rather than expenditure cutting.

4. Both IFIs only acknowledged the need for a change towards policies in which protection of the poor became a central aim three-quarters through the adjustment decade (around 1987). Actual policy changes came even later – e.g. PAMSCAD only started effectively in 1991.

5. The IMF scarcely changed its policy even after the acknowledgement of the need for consideration to be given to the poor, the main change being to collect more information and do more research on the poor. The IMF claims that the existing policies are in fact those best suited to promote the interests of the poor.

These [Fund] programs involve, first and foremost, macroeconomic discipline, beginning with the reductions of fiscal deficits and monetary measures aimed at achieving price stability and realistic exchange rates.... Let me say outright: these policies serve the poor, and we must do our utmost to implement them if we are to be efficient in the fight against poverty.

(Statement by M. Camdessus, Managing Director of the IMF
to the UN Social and Economic Council, 11 July 1990)

The Fund has made a few additional moves in recent years.[63] Since 1991, some attempt has been made in SAFs/ESAFs to identify measures that 'can help cushion the possible adverse effects of certain policies on vulnerable groups';[64] some programmes contain safety nets for retrenched civil servants; and it was reported that food subsidies might be allowed in certain circumstances to offset some of the effects of devaluation.

In addition to research, the World Bank has made two major changes: reviews of public expenditure promoting reallocation to priority areas, and the introduction of social funds. The earlier analysis suggests neither has been very effective. Adjusting countries have not shown a greater switch to the social sectors than the non-adjusting – indeed in Latin America the reverse occurred as adjusting countries switched resources to debt payments. We have little systematic evidence on priority ratios, but what there is does not suggest any major positive effects there.[65] The analysis of social funds in Chapter 5 shows they have been of rather small significance, mainly directed at the 'new' poor, and doing little for the chronically poor. The World Bank has not accepted that there is any need to redesign the macro-package to protect the poor, nor to review meso-policies systematically as suggested here. 'Add-ons' in the form of social funds and similar measures are the normal way in which the 'social dimensions of adjustment' are incorporated.

In summary, the major criticism of the Fund and the Bank is not that their policies were the main cause of the adverse effects (nor even in some cases they were at all responsible for increasing poverty, this being due to prior events that led to the need for adjustment), but rather that adverse effects occurred while countries were undertaking adjustment policies for which the IFIs bore prime responsibility, and that many of these effects could have been avoided, but neither institution did much (and for many years anything) about it.

The 1990s seem likely to be better years for many of the adjusting countries – notably for much (but not all) of Latin America, and, possibly, for some countries in Africa. But this does not mean that we should simply forget the events of the 1980s, starting again as if the decade had not occurred. Many countries – especially in Africa – will continue to have adjustment policies in the coming decade. For these, and for the others, it is important to record the unnecessary burden for the poor and to identify the policy mistakes responsible so that similar errors can be avoided in the future.

NOTES

1 Data from Wagao in Cornia *et al.*, 1992; *Human Development Reports*.
2 See Stewart with Sharpley, 1986.

3 See Wangwe, 1992.
4 Wagao, 1990.
5 Ibid.
6 Derived from Jamal and Weeks, 1993.
7 Wagao, 1990; Jamal and Weeks, 1993.
8 Data from World Bank, *World Development Reports*.
9 Wagao, 1990.
10 Wagao, 1990; *Human Development Reports*.
11 Wagao, 1990.
12 UNICEF in Cornia *et al.*, 1987, Vol. 2.
13 Data from Toye in Mosley *et al.*, 1991.
14 See UNICEF in Cornia *et al.*, 1987, Vol. 2.
15 Toye, op. cit.
16 UNICEF in Cornia *et al.*, 1987.
17 Younger *et al.*, 1994.
18 Results of the Ghana Living Standards Survey, quoted in *The Africa Review*, 1991/2, p. 95.
19 UNDP, *Human Development Reports*, 1991 and 1993.
20 Ibid.
21 See Chapter 5.
22 Data from Kofi, 1993; this contains a devastating critique of this aspect of the adjustment programme.
23 Data from Castaneda, 1991.
24 The deficit widened again subsequently as foreign investment resumed.
25 Graham, 1994, Chapter 2.
26 Raczynski and Romaguera, 1992.
27 Psacharapulos *et al.*, 1993.
28 Graham, 1994, Chapter 2; Raczynski and Romaguera 1992.
29 Graham, 1994, Chapter 2.
30 Castaneda, 1991.
31 Espinola, 1991; Prawda, 1990.
32 Raczynski and Romaguera, 1992, and *Human Development Reports*.
33 Raczynski and Romaguera, 1992.
34 ILO, 1991.
35 Szekely, 1993.
36 Berstecher and Carr-Hill, 1990, for primary; UNDP *Human Development Reports*, for secondary.
37 Valerio, 1991.
38 Evidence from Valerio, 1991.
39 Cardoso and Helwege, 1992.
40 Health data from Rivero *et al.*, 1991.
41 Nuqui, 1991.
42 World Bank, 1988a.
43 NEDA, 1987.
44 de Dios and Associates, 1993.
45 World Bank, 1988a; Balisacan (forthcoming).
46 Nuqui, 1991.
47 Balisacan (forthcoming): he finds this deterioration mirrored an improvement that occurred in the 1986–8 upturn.
48 It is noteworthy that this finding conflicts with that of Blejer and Guerrero, 1990, that devaluation improves income distribution. This conflict is likely to be due to lesser disaggregation in the analysis of Blejer and Guerrero. Both agree that contraction is more regressive than devaluation.

49 UNICEF Philippines in Cornia *et al.*, 1987, Vol. 2; Manasan and Llanto, 1994.
50 Pante, 1990.
51 World Bank, 1990c.
52 World Bank, 1992b.
53 World Bank, 1992b.
54 See World Bank, 1990c; Ravallion and Huppi, 1989; World Bank 1993c.
55 World Bank, 1989e.
56 Thorbecke, 1991, on the basis of simulations using a computable general equilibrium model, finds that the policy set chosen produced better results for the combined objectives of growth, equity and stabilisation than any politically plausible alternatives.
57 World Bank, 1992b.
58 These policies are broadly the same as those we recommended in *Adjustment with a Human Face* (Cornia *et al.*, 1987) developed in the light of further analysis and experience.
59 See Cornia and Stewart, 1993.
60 See Cornia *et al.*, 1987, Vol. 1, Chapter 14, for much fuller analysis of data needs.
61 The role of adverse international conditions – especially terms of trade movements – in prolonging the adjustment crisis and reducing the success of adjustment programmes – is now acknowledged by both IFIs: see World Bank, 1990a, 1992a; and Schadler *et al.*, 1993.
62 For an excellent analysis of the commodity price question see Maizels, 1992.
63 Killick, 1994, p. 8.
64 IMF *Annual Report*, 1991, pp. 51–2.
65 A review of the implementation of ten World Bank loans between 1987 and 1990, which contained specific recommendations for reallocation of expenditure within the educational sector towards primary education, showed that there was no recorded success: project and supervision reports showed five cases of lack of success, with no assessments in the remaining cases (Stevenson, 1991).

Bibliography

Acharya, S., 1990, 'The Maharashtra Employment Guarantee Scheme: a study of labour market interventions', *ARTEP Working Paper*, (India: International Labour Organization).

ADB *et al.*, 1991, (African Development Bank, United Nations Development Programme, World Bank), 'Socio-economic development funds: A guideline for design and implementation', RAF/86/037/A/01/42, 1–85.

Adelman, I. and S. Robinson, 1988, 'Structural adjustment and income distribution', *Journal of Development Economics*, 29, 23–44.

Alaihima, P., 1984, 'Fiscal incidence in Sri Lanka 1973 and 1980', WEP Working Paper, WEP 2–32/WP 56 (Geneva: ILO).

Albanez, T., E. Bustelo, G.A. Cornia and E. Jespersen, 1989, 'Economic decline and child survival: the plight of Latin America in the Eighties', Innocenti Occasional Papers 1 (Florence: UNICEF).

Alderman, H., 1988, 'The twilight of flour rationing in Pakistan', *Food Policy*, 13/3 (August), 245–56.

Alderman, H., 1991, 'Downturn and economic recovery in Ghana: impact on the poor', Cornell Food and Nutrition Policy Program, Monograph 10, March.

Alderman, H. and J. von Braun, 1984, 'The effects of the Egyptian subsidy system on income distribution and consumption', International Food Policy Research Institute, July.

Alderman, H. and J. von Braun, 1986, 'Egypt's food subsidy policy: lessons and options', *Food Policy*, 11, 3, 223–37.

Amis, P., 1989, 'Structural adjustment, proletarianization and survival strategies: the urban working class in East Africa', processed (Bradford: Development and Project Planning Centre, University of Bradford).

Anand, S., 1983, *Inequality and Poverty in Malaysia* (Oxford: Oxford University Press).

Andrews, A.P., 1993, 'Employment schemes in Botswana', processed, Employment Strategies Branch, International Labour Organization, Geneva.

Angell, A. and C. Graham, 1994a, 'Why is social sector reform missing from the adjustment agenda?' processed (Oxford: St Antony's).

Angell, A. and C. Graham, 1994b, 'Adjustment in Venezuela: the political costs of neglecting social sector reform' processed (Oxford: St Antony's).

Ayako, A., 1990, 'Structural adjustment in the 1980s: Kenya case study', processed (Florence: UNICEF).

Azam, J.-P., C. Bonjean, G. Chambas and J. Mathonnat, 1993, 'Le Niger: la pauvrété en période ajustement' (Paris: L'Harmattan).

Babu, S.C. and J.A. Hallam, 1989, 'Socioeconomic impacts of school feeding programmes', *Food Policy*, 14, 1, 58–66.

Balisacan, A., forthcoming, 'Anatomy of poverty during adjustment: the case of the Philippines', *Economic Development and Cultural Change*.

Barrett, C. and P. Dorosh, 1994, 'Farmers' welfare and changing food prices: nonparametric evidence from rice in Madagascar', processed (University of Wisconsin-Madison and Cornell University Food and Nutrition Policy Program).

Basta, S., M.S. Koekerman, D. Karyadi and N.S. Scrimshaw, 1979, 'Iron deficiency anemia and the productivity of adult males in Indonesia', *American Journal of Clinical Nutrition*, 32, 4, 916–25.

Becker, G., 1981, *A Treatise on the Family* (Cambridge, MA: Harvard University Press).

Behrman, J., 1988, 'Intra-house household allocation of nutrients in rural India', *Oxford Economics Papers*, 40, 32–54.

Belavady, B., 1966, 'Nutrition and efficiency of agricultural labourers', *Indian Journal of Medical Research*, 54, 971–6.

Berry, A., 1990, 'Economic performance, income distribution and poverty in Latin America: the experience of the 1980s', Background Paper for World Bank *World Development Report 1990* processed (Washington DC: World Bank).

Berstecher, D. and R. Carr-Hill, 1990, *Primary Education and Economic Recession in the Developing World since 1980* (Paris: UNESCO).

Bethune, X. de, S. Alfani and P. Lahaye, 1989, 'The influence of an abrupt price increase on health resource utilisation: evidence from Zambia', *Health Policy and Planning*, 4, 76–81.

Blank, R. and A. Blinder, 1985, 'Macroeconomics, income distribution and poverty', National Bureau of Economic Research Working Paper 1567 (Cambridge, MA: NBER).

Blejer, M. and I. Guerrero, 1990, 'The impact of macroeconomic policies on income distribution: an empirical study of the Philippines', *Review of Economics and Statistics*, LXXXII, 3, 414–23.

Boateng, E.O., K. Ewusi, R. Kanbur and A. McKay, 1992, 'A poverty profile for Ghana 1987–88', *Journal of African Economics*, 1, 2, 25–58.

Bourguignon, F. and C. Morrisson, 1992, *Adjustment and Equity in Developing Countries – A New Approach*, (Paris: OECD).

Bourguignon, F., J. de Melo and A. Suwa, 1991a, 'Distributional effects of adjustment policies: simulations for archetype economies in Africa and Latin America', *The World Bank Economic Review*, 5, 2, 339–66.

Bourguignon, F., J. de Melo and C. Morrison, 1991b, 'Poverty and income distribution during adjustment: issues and evidence from the OECD project', *World Development*, 1485–508.

Byerlee, D. and G. Sain, 1991, 'Relative food prices under structural adjustment: preliminary findings from Latin America', *Food Policy*, 16, 74–84.

Cardoso, E. and A. Helwege, 1992, 'Below the line: poverty in Latin America', *World Development*, 20, 1.

Carr-Hill, R. A., 1991, 'Educational indicators during the 1980s', paper prepared for Commonwealth Secretariat, processed (London: Commonwealth Secretariat).

Castaneda, T., 1991, *Innovative Social Policies for Reducing Poverty: Chile in the 1980s* (Washington, DC: World Bank).

Chant, S., 1991, 'Women's work and household change in Mexico in the 1980s', in N. Harvey (ed.), *Mexico: The Dilemmas of Transition* (London: British Academic Press).

Chant, S., 1992, *Women and Survival in Mexican Cities: Perspectives on Gender, Labour Markets and Low-income Households* (Manchester: Manchester University Press).

Chen, M., E. Huq and S. D'Souza, 1981, 'Sex bias in the family allocation of food and health care in Bangladesh', *Population and Development Review*, 3, 435–74.

Chhibber, A. *et al.*, 1991, 'Supporting policy change: the interrelation between adjustment and sector/investment lending', processed (Washington DC: World Bank).

Chisvo, M., 1993, 'Government spending on social services and the impact of structural adjustment in Zimbabwe', processed (Harare: UNICEF).

Clark, G. and T. Manuh, 'Women traders in Ghana and the structural adjustment programme', in C. Gladwin (ed.), *Structural Adjustment and African Women Farmers* (Gainesville, Fla.; University of Florida Press).

Clark, J. with D. Keen, 1988, 'Debt and poverty: a case study of Zambia' (Oxford: Oxfam).

Colclough, C. and K. Lewin, 1991, *Educating all the Children, the Economic Challenge for the 1990s* (Oxford: Clarendon Press).

Connors, T., 1979, 'The apparent effects of recent IMF stabilization programs', International Finance Discussion Paper 135 (Washington DC: IMF).

Corbo, V. and P. Rojas, 1992, 'World Bank-supported adjustment programs, country performance and effectiveness', in V. Corbo, S. Fischer and S. Webb (eds), *Adjustment Lending Revisited* (Washington DC: World Bank).

Corden, W.M., 1960, 'The geometrical representation of policies to attain internal and external balance', *Review of Economic Studies*, 75, 1–22.

Cornia, G.A., 1987, 'Economic decline and human welfare in the first half of the 1980s', in Cornia *et al.*

Cornia, G.A. and F. Stewart, 1990, 'The fiscal system, adjustment and the poor', Innocenti Occasional Paper 11 (Florence: UNICEF).

Cornia, G.A. and F. Stewart, 1993, 'Two errors of targeting', *Journal of International Development*, 5, 2.

Cornia, G.A., R. Jolly and F. Stewart, 1987, *Adjustment with a Human Face*, 2 vols (Oxford: Oxford University Press).

Cornia, G.A., R. van der Hoeven and T. Mkandawire (eds), 1992, *Africa's Recovery in the 1990s* (New York: St Martin's Press).

Creese, A., 1990, 'User charges for health: a review of the recent experience', Strengthening Health Services Paper 1 (Geneva: WHO).

Dandekar, V. and M. Seth, 1980, 'Employment guarantee scheme and food for work programme', *Economic and Political Weekly*, 16 March.

Dasgupta, P., 1993, *An Inquiry into Well-being and Destitution* (Oxford: Oxford University Press).

Dasgupta, P. and D. Ray, 1987, 'Adapting to undernutrition: the clinical evidence and its implications', Working Paper No. 10 (April) (Helsinki: WIDER, World Institute for Development Economics Research, UN University).

Davies, R., D. Sanders and T. Shaw, 1991, 'Liberalisation for development: Zimbabwe's adjustment without the Fund', Innocenti Occasional Papers 16 (Florence: UNICEF).

Dawson, J., 1994, 'Responses to adjustment – the marginalisation of small enterprises in Nigeria', *Small Enterprise Development*, 5, 2, 18–23.

De Dios and Associates, 1993, *Poverty, Growth and the Fiscal Crisis* (Manila: Philippine Institute for Development Studies).

De Valk, P., 1993, 'A general framework for evaluating the performance of textile enterprises in LDCs: with an application to Tanzania under adjustment', PhD thesis (Amsterdam: Vrije Universiteit).

Deaton. A., 1987, 'The allocation of goods within the household adults, children and gender', Living Standards Measurement Study, Working Paper 39 (Washington DC: World Bank).

Dell, S., 1982, 'Stabilisation: the political economy of overkill', *World Development*, 10, 597–612.

Dell, S. and R. Lawrence, 1980, *The Balance of Payments Adjustment Process in Developing Countries* (New York: Pergamon).

Demery, L. and T. Addison, 1987, 'Stabilisation policy and income distribution in developing countries', *World Development*, 15, 12, 1483–98.

Deolalikar, A., 1988, 'Nutrition and labor productivity in agriculture: estimates for rural South India', *Review of Economics and Statistics*, 70, 406–13.

Dhatt, G. and M. Ravallion, 1994, 'Income gains for the poor from public works employment', Living Standards Measurement Study, Working Paper 100 (Washington DC: World Bank).

Donovan, D.J. , 1981, 'Real responses associated with exchange rate action in selected upper tranche stabilization programs', *IMF Staff Papers*, 28, 698–727.

Donovan, D.J., 1982, 'Macroeconomic performance and adjustment under Fund-supported programs: the experience of the 1970s', *IMF Staff Papers*, 29, 171–203.

Dorosh, P.A. and D.E. Sahn, 1993, 'A general equilibrium analysis of the effect of macroeconomic adjustment on poverty in Africa', processed (Washington DC: Cornell University Food and Nutrition Policy Program).

Dorosh, P., R.E. Bernier and A. Sarris, 1990, 'Macroeconomic adjustment and the poor: the case of Madagascar', Cornell Food and Nutrition Program, Monograph 9 (Washington DC: Cornell Food and Nutrition Program).

Dougna, K.D., 1987, 'Crise economique et crise de "Education en Afrique"', IIEP/KD/87–06 (Paris: International Institute for Educational Planning).

Echeverri-Gent, J., 1988, 'Guaranteed employment in an Indian state: the Maharashtra experience', *Asian Survey*, 28, 1294–310.

ECLAC, 1989, *Preliminary Overview of the Economy of Latin America and the Caribbean 1989* (Santiago: United Nations).

ECLAC, 1990, *Preliminary Overview of the Economy of Latin America and the Caribbean 1990* (Santiago: United Nations).

ECLAC, 1991, *Preliminary Overview of the Economy of Latin America and the Caribbean 1991* (Santiago: United Nations).

ECLAC, 1992a, *Preliminary Overview of the Economy of Latin America and the Caribbean 1992* (Santiago: United Nations).

ECLAC, 1992b, *Stabilization, Structural Adjustment and Social Policies in Costa Rica: The Role of Compensatory Programmes*, Occasional Paper No. 1 (Geneva: Interdepartmental Project on Structural Adjustment).

ECLAC, 1993, *Preliminary Overview of the Economy of Latin America and the Caribbean 1993* (Santiago: United Nations).

Edirisinghe, N., 1987, 'The food stamp scheme in Sri Lanka: costs, benefits and options for modification', International Food Policy Research Institute, Research Report 58 (Washington DC: IFPRI).

Edirisinghe, N., 1988, 'Recent targeting attempts in Sri Lanka's food stamp schemes', *Food Policy*, 12, 4, 401–2.

Egger, P., P. Garnier and J. Gaude, 1993, 'Ajustement structurel et compensation sociale: étude de cas en Honduras, Madagascar et Sénégal', *Interdepartmental Project on Structural Adjustment Occasional Paper* No. 11 (Geneva: International Labour Office).

El-Ghonemy, M., 1990, *The Political Economy of Rural Poverty* (London: Routledge).

Elbadawi, I.A., 1992, 'World Bank adjustment lending and economic performance in sub-Saharan Africa in the 1980s', Policy Research Working Papers, WPS 1001 (Washington DC: World Bank).

Elbadawi, I., D. Ghura and G. Uwujaren, 1992, 'World Bank adjustment lending and economic performance in sub-Saharan Africa in the 1980s', Policy Research Working Paper 1000 (Washington DC: World Bank).

Espinola, V., 1991, *Decentralizacion del Sistema Escolar en Chile* (Santiago: Centro de Investigacion y Desarrollo de la Educacion).

Faini, R., J. de Melo, A. Senhadji-Semlali and J. Stanton, 1989, 'Growth-oriented adjustment programs, a statistical analysis', Luca D'Agliano and Queen Elizabeth House, Development Studies Working Papers, 14 (Oxford: Queen Elizabeth House).

Ffrench-Davis, R. and D. Raczynski, 1990, 'The impact of global recession and national policies on living standards: Chile, 1973–89', *Corporacion de Investigaciones Economicas para Latin America* (Santiago de Chile: CIEPLAN).

Folbre, N., 1984, 'Household production in the Philippines: a non-neoclassical approach', *Economic Development and Cultural Change*, 32, 2, 303–30.

Folbre, N., 1986, 'Hearts and spades: paradigms of household economics', *World Development*, 14, 2, 245–256.

Foster, J., J. Greer and E. Thorbecke, 1984, 'A class of decomposable poverty measures', *Econometrica*, 52, 761–5.

Fox, M. and S. Morley, 1991, 'Who paid the bill? Adjustment and poverty in Brazil 1980–85', Policy Research and External Affairs Working Paper, WPS 648 (Washington DC: World Bank).

Gallagher, M., 1990, 'Fiscal duress and the social sectors in developing countries', Background Paper for *1990 World Development Report* (Washington DC: World Bank).

Galler, J.R., F. Ramsey, G. Solimano and W.E. Lowell, 1983, 'The influence of early malnutrition on subsequent behavioral development. II. Classroom Behavior', *Journal of the American Academy of Child Psychiatry*, 22, 1, 16–22.

Garcia, M.H. and P. Pinstrup-Andersen, 1987, 'The pilot food price subsidy scheme in the Philippines: its impact on income and food consumption', Research Report, No. 61 (Washington DC: International Food Policy Research Institute).

Gaude, J., 1993, 'Système de compensation sociale et ajustement structurel: étude de cas en Honduras', *Interdepartmental Project on Structural Adjustment*, Occasional Paper No. 5, March (Geneva), 1–48.

George, M., R. Hay and F. Stewart, 1994, 'Health sector financing in SubSaharan Africa', processed (Oxford: Queen Elizabeth House).

Gertler, P., L. Locay and W. Sanderson, 1987, 'Are user charges regressive? The welfare implications of health care financing proposals in Peru', *Journal of Econometrics*, 36 (supp.), 67–88.

Gindling, T.H. and A. Berry, 1992, 'The performance of the labor market during recession and structural adjustment: Costa Rica', *World Development*, 20, 11, 1599–616.

Goldstein, M. and P. Montiel, 1986, 'Evaluating Fund stabilization programs with multicountry data: some methodological pitfalls', *IMF Staff Papers*, 33, 304–44.

Gonzalez de la Rocha, M., 1988, 'Economic crisis, domestic reorganisation and women's work in Guadalajara, Mexico', *Bulletin of Latin American Research*, 7, 207–33.

Gorringer, A.A., M. Guevera and J. Gracia, 1994, 'A study of the incidence of the Philippine fiscal system', processed (Manila: Philippine Institute of Development Studies).

GOZ (Government of Zimbabwe), 1991, *A Programme of Actions to Mitigate the Social Costs of Adjustment* (Harare: GOZ).

Graham, C., 1994, *Safety Nets, Politics and the Poor, Transitions to Market Economies* (Washington DC: The Brookings Institution).

Griffin, K., 1989, *Alternative Strategies for Economic Development* (London: Macmillan).

Grootaert, C., 1993, 'The evolution of welfare and poverty under structural change and economic recession in the case of Côte d'Ivoire, 1985–88', World Bank Policy Research Working Paper 1078 (Washington DC: World Bank).

Grosh, M., 1990a, *Social Spending in Latin America: The Story of the 1980s,* World Bank Discussion Papers, 106 (Washington, DC: World Bank).

Grosh, M., 1990b, 'What should social funds finance: portfolio mix, targeting and efficiency criteria', processed (Washington DC: Human Resource Division, Latin America and the Caribbean, World Bank).

Grosh, M., 1992a, 'The Jamaican food stamps program: a case study in targeting', *Food Policy*, 17, 1, 23–40.

Grosh, M., 1992b, 'Towards quantifying the tradeoff: administrative costs and targeting accuracy', paper prepared for World Bank Conference on Public Expenditures and the Poor: Incidence and Targeting (Washington DC: World Bank).

Guyer, J., 1980, 'Household budgets and women's incomes', Working Paper No. 28 (Boston: African Studies Centre, Boston University).

Gylfason, T., 1987, 'Credit policy and economic activity in developing countries with IMF stabilization programs', *Princeton Studies in International Finance* 60 (Princeton: Princeton University).

Haaga, J. and J. Mason, 1987, 'Food distribution within the family: evidence and implications for research and programmes', *Food Policy*, 12, 146–60.

Hackman, E., I. Emanuel, G. van Belle and J. Daling, 1983, 'Maternal birth weight and subsequent pregnancy outcome', *Journal of the American Medical Association*, 250, 15, 2016–19.

Harrell, M.W., C. Parillon and R. Franlin, 1989, 'Nutritional classification study of Peru', *Food Policy*, 14, 4, 313–29.

Harriss, B., 1992, *Child Nutrition and Poverty in South India* (New Delhi: Concept Publishing Co.).

Helleiner, G.K., 1987, 'Stabilisation, adjustment and the poor', *World Development*, 15, 12, 1499–514.

Helleiner, G.K., 1993, 'UNICEF paper on sub-Saharan African debt relief', processed (New York: UNICEF).

Heller, P., A.L. Bovenber, T. Catsambas, K. Chu and P. Shome, 1988, 'The implications of Fund-supported programs for poverty', IMF Occasional Paper 58 (Washington DC: IMF).

Hicks, N., 1991, 'Expenditure reductions in developing countries revisited', *Journal of International Development*, 3, 1.

Hicks, N. and A. Kubish, 1984, 'Recent experience in cutting government expenditures', *Finance and Development*, 21, 37–9.

Hill, K. and A. Pebley, 1989, 'Child mortality in the developing world', *Population and Development Review*, 15, 657–87.

Hoddinott, J. and L. Haddad, 1991, 'Household expenditures, child anthropometric status and the intrahousehold division of income: evidence for the Côte d'Ivoire', September (Princeton, NJ: Research Program in Development Studies).

Horton, S. and T. King, 1981, *Labor Productivity: Un Tour d'Horizon*, Staff Working Paper No. 497 (Washington DC: World Bank).

Horton, S., *et al.*, 1994, 'Labor markets in an era of adjustment: an overview', in S. Horton, R. Kanbur and D. Mazumdar (eds), *Labor Markets in an Era of Adjustment* (Washington DC: World Bank).

Hussein, I., 1993, 'Does structural adjustment help or hurt the poor?', paper prepared for International Seminar on Structural Adjustment and Long-term Development on sub-Saharan Africa: Research and Policy Issues (The Hague: Netherlands Ministry of Foreign Affairs), 1–3 June.

Hussein, I. and R. Faruqee (eds), 1994, *Adjustment in Africa: Lessons from Country Case Studies* (Washington DC: World Bank).

IADB, 1993, 'Growth and poverty: assessment and reforms', processed, 1 (Washington DC: IADB).

Illif, P., 1992, 'A case for exempting maternity patients from health services charges', processed (Harare: University of Zimbabwe).

ILO, 1988, *African Employment Report 1988* (Addis Ababa: JASPA, ILO).

ILO, 1991, *Employment Policies in the Economic Restructuring of Latin America and the Caribbean* (Geneva: 1991).

ILO, 1992a, 'Stabilization, structural adjustment and social policies in Costa Rica: the role of compensatory programmes', Occasional Paper No. 1 (Geneva, Interdepartmental Project on Structural Adjustment).

ILO, 1992b, *African Employment Report* (Addis Ababa: JASPA, ILO).

ILO, 1993, 'Structural change and adjustment in Zimbabwe', Occasional Paper 16 (Geneva: ILO).

Infante, R. and E. Klein, 1992, 'Chile, transformaciones del mercade laboral y sus effectos sociales, 1965–1990' (Santiago: PREALC).

International Monetary Fund, 1987, 'Theoretical aspects of Fund-supported adjustment programs', Occasional Paper 55 (Washington DC: IMF).

International Monetary Fund, Fiscal Affairs Dept., 1986, 'Fund-supported programs, fiscal policy and income distribution', IMF Occasional Paper 46 (Washington DC: IMF).

International Monetary Fund, 1990, *Government Financial Statistics* (Washington DC: IMF).

International Monetary Fund/World Bank, 1989, *Strengthening Efforts to Reduce Poverty* (Washington DC: World Bank).

Jabara, C.L., 1990, 'Economic reform and poverty in the Gambia: a survey of pre- and post-ERP experience', Cornell Food and Nutrition Policy Program, Monograph 8, December.

Jamal, V. and J. Weeks, 1993, *Africa Misunderstood or Whatever Happened to the Rural–Urban Wage Gap?* (London: Macmillan and ILO).

Jazairy, I., M. Alamgir and T. Pannucio, 1992, *The State of World Rural Poverty* (New York: New York University Press).

Jebuni, C. and W. Seini, 1993, 'Agricultural input policies under structural adjustment: their distributional implications', Cornell Food and Nutrition Policy Program, Working Paper 31 (Ithaca: Cornell).

Jespersen, E., 1992, 'External shocks, adjustment policies and economic and social performance', in Cornia *et al.*

Johnson, O. and J. Salop, 1980, 'Distributional aspects of stabilization programs in developing countries', *IMF Staff Papers*, 27, 1–23.

Jolly, R., 1988, 'Poverty and adjustment in the 1990s' in John Lewis (ed.), *Strengthening the Poor: What Have We Learned?* (Washington DC: Overseas Development Council).

Jolly, R. and G.A. Cornia, 1984, *The Impact of World Recession on Children* (Oxford: Pergamon Press).

Jones, S., 1994, 'Structural adjustment in Zambia', in van der Geest.

Jorgensen, S., M. Grosh and M. Schachter, 1991, 'Easing the poor through economic crisis and adjustment: the story of Bolivia's Emergency Social Fund', processed (Washington DC: World Bank).

Kakwani, N., E. Makonnen and J. van der Gaag, 1989, 'Structural adjustment and living conditions in developing countries', processed (Washington DC: World Bank).

Kaldor, N., 1983, 'Devaluation and adjustment in developing countries', *Finance and Development*, June, 35–7.

Kamara, S., M.T. Dahniya and P. Greene, 1990, 'The effect of structural adjustment policies on human welfare in Africa south of the Sahara: Sierra Leone', processed (Florence: UNICEF).

Kanbur, R., 1987, 'Structural adjustment, macroeconomic adjustment and poverty: a methodology for analysis', *World Development*, 15, 12, 1515–26.

Kanbur, R., 1990, 'Poverty and the social dimensions of structural adjustment in Côte d'Ivoire', SDA Working Paper Series (Washington DC: World Bank).

Kanji, N. and N. Jazdowska, 1993, 'Seminar on the gender-specific effects of ESAP on households in Kambuza', Summary presentation of findings, processed (Harare: IDRC/NUCI).

Kennedy, E. and T. Alderman, 1987, 'Comparative analyses of nutritional effectiveness of food subsidies and other food-related interventions' (Washington DC: Joint World Health Organization–UNICEF Nutrition Support Programme, International Food Policy Research Institute).

Kesselman, J.R., 1982, 'Taxation behavior and the design of a credit income tax', in I. Garfinkel (ed.), *Income-Tested Programs: The Case For and Against* (New York: Academic Press).

Keys, A., J. Brozek, A. Henschel, O. Mickelson and H.L. Taylor, 1950, *The Biology of Human Starvation*, 2 vols (Minneapolis: University of Minnesota Press).

Khan, M., 1990, 'The macroeconomic effects of Fund-supported programs', *IMF Staff Papers*, 37, 2, 195–231.

Khan, M. and M. Knight, 1985, 'Fund-supported adjustment programs and economic growth', Occasional Paper 41 (Washington DC: IMF).

Killick, T., 1984, *The Quest for Economic Stabilisation: The IMF and the Third World* (London: Heinemann).

Killick, T., 1992, 'Explaining Africa's post-independence development experiences', Overseas Development Institute Working Paper 60 (London: ODI).

Killick, T., 1994, 'Low-income countries and the IMF – a case of structural incompatibility?', paper prepared for a Colloquium in Honour of G. K. Helleiner, 22–4 June (Ottawa: North–South Institute).

Killick, T., M. Malik and M. Manuel, 1991, 'What can we know about the effects of IMF programmes?', ODI Working Paper 47 (London: ODI).

Kingsbury, D., 1992, 'Programs for mitigating adverse social impacts during adjustment: the AID experience' (Bethesda, MD: Development Alternatives Inc.).

Klugman, J., 1990, 'Adjustment with a human face – rhetoric or reality', MSc Essay Development Economics, processed, University of Oxford.

Knight, J.B., 1976, 'Devaluation and income distribution in less developed economies', *Oxford Economic Papers*, 28, 2, 208–27.

Knight, J. and R. Sabot, 1990, *Education, Productivity and Inequality. The East African Natural Experiment* (Washington DC: World Bank and Oxford University Press).

Kofi, T., 1993, 'Structural adjustment in Africa: a performance review of World Bank policies under uncertainty in commodity price trends: the case of Ghana' (Helsinki: WIDER).

Kozel, V., 1990, 'The composition and distribution of income in Côte D'Ivoire', LSMS Working Paper 68 (Washington DC: World Bank).

Kraut, H. A. and E. A. Muller, 1946, 'Calorie intake and industrial output', *Science*, 104, 495–7.

Krugman, P. and L. Taylor, 1978, 'Contractionary effects of devaluation', *Journal of International Economics*, 8, 445–56.

Lambert, S., H. Schneider and A. Suwa, 1991, 'Adjustment and equity in Côte d'Ivoire: 1980–86', *World Development*, 19, 11, 1563–76.

Lee, E., M. Loutfi, L. Goreux, B. Fall, M. Sidibé and D. Diop, 1992, *Ajustement, Emploi et Développement en Sénégal* (Geneva: International Labour Office).

Liedholm, C. and D. Mead, 1993, 'The structure and growth of microenterprises in Southern and Eastern Africa: evidence from recent surveys', GEMINI Working Paper 36 (Bethesda, MD: Development Alternatives).

Lipton, M., 1983, 'Poverty, undernutrition and hunger', World Bank Staff Working Paper 597 (Washington DC: World Bank).

Litvack, J., 1992, 'The effects of user fees and improved quality on health facility utilization and household expenditure: a field experiment in the Adamaoua Province in Cameroon', PhD dissertation, Fletcher School (Medfor, MA: Tufts University).

Londono, J. L., 1989, 'Income distribution in Colombia: turning points, catching up and other Kuznetsian tales', processed (Cambridge, MA: Harvard University).

Lowenson, R., 1993, 'Survey of clothing and textile industry', processed (Harare).

Loxley, J., 1984, 'The IMF and the poorest countries' (Toronto: North–South Institute).

Loxley, J., 1990, 'Structural adjustment and rural labour markets in Zambia', WEP Working Paper (Geneva: ILO).

Lyngstadt, J., 1993, 'Geographical distribution of poverty in Zambia: an analysis of data from the Priority Survey 1', processed (Oslo: Statistics Norway).

Maasland, A., 1990, 'Distributional implications of adjustment policies: a review of methodologies', processed (Washington DC: World Bank).

McElroy, M., 1990, 'The empirical content of Nash-bargained household behaviour', *Journal of Human Resources*, 25.

McElroy, M. and M. Horney, 1981, 'Nash-bargained household decisions: toward a generalization of the theory of demand', *International Economic Review*, 22, 333–50.

McGuire, J. and J. Austin, 1987, 'Beyond survival: children's growth for national development', *Assignment Children*, 2 (New York: UNICEF).

Mahendra Dev, S. and M. Suryanarayana, 1991, 'Is PDS urban biased and pro-rich?', *Economic and Political Weekly*, XXVI, 41 (12 October) 2357–66.

Maizels, A., 1992, *Commodities in Crisis* (Oxford: Clarendon Press).

Manasan, R. and G. Llanto, 1994, 'Financing social programs in the Philippines: public policy and budget restructuring', processed (Manila: Philippine Institute of Development Studies).

Mans, D., 1994, 'Tanzania: resolute action' in I. Hussein and R. Faruqee (eds), *Adjustment in Africa: Lessons from Country Case Studies* (Washington DC: World Bank).

Manser, M. and M. Brown, 1980, 'Marriage and household decision making: a bargaining analysis', *International Economic Review*, 21, 31–44.

Martorell, R. and T. Gonzalez-Cossio, 1987, 'Maternal nutrition and birth weight', *Yearbook of Physical Anthropology*, 30, 195–220 (New York: Alan R. Liss, Inc.).

Mateus, A., 1983, 'Targeting food subsidies for the needy: the use of cost–benefit analysis and institutional design', World Bank Staff Working Paper 617 (Washington DC: World Bank).

Meerman, J., 1979, *Public Expenditure in Malaysia: Who Benefits and Why?* (New York: Oxford University Press).

Meller, P., 1992, 'Adjustment and equity in Chile', *OECD Development Centre Studies*, (Paris) 99pp.

Mesa-Lago, C., 1983, 'Social security and extreme poverty in Latin America', *Journal of Development Economics*, 12, 83–110.

Miller, B., 1981, *The Endangered Sex: Neglect of Female Children in Rural North India* (Ithaca, NY: Cornell University Press).

Morales, J.A., 1990, 'The transition to sustained growth in Bolivia', processed (Bolivia: Universidad Catolica Boliviana).

Moreno de Padilla, C., 1993a, 'El Fondo Hondureno de inversion social antecendentes de su creacion y funcionamiento (version préliminar)', mimeo, 25pp. (Geneva: International Labour Office).

Moreno de Padilla, C., 1993b, 'Costa Rica: el fondo de desarollo social y asignocaiones familiares: documento complementario al informe del proyecto interdepartamental sobre ajuste estructural', processed, 19pp. (Geneva: International Labour Office).

Moser, C., 1989, 'The impact of recession and structural adjustment policies at the micro-level: low-income households in Guayaquil, Ecuador', in UNICEF (ed.), *Invisible Adjustment* (New York: UNICEF).

Mosley, P., 1987, 'Conditionality as bargaining process: structural adjustment lending 1980–86', *Princeton Essays in International Finance*, 168 (Princeton).

Mosley, P., 1994, 'Decomposing the effects of structural adjustment: the case of Sub-Saharan Africa' in R. van der Hoeven and F. Vender Kraaij (eds), *Structural Adjustment and Beyond in Sub-Saharan Africa* (London: James Currey).

Mosley, P. and J. Weeks, 1993, 'Has recovery begun? Africa's adjustment in the 1980s revisited', *World Development*, 21, 10.

Mosley, P., J. Harrigan and J. Toye, 1991, *Aid and Power*, 2 vols (London: Routledge).

Musgrove, P., 1987, 'The economic crisis and its impact on health and health care in Latin America and the Caribbean', *International Journal of Health Services*, 17, 3.

Mustapha, A., 1990, 'Structural adjustment and multiple modes of social livelihood in Nigeria', paper prepared for UNRISD/SIAS/CMI Joint Symposium on the 'Social and political context of structural adjustment programmes in SubSaharan Africa', Bergen, Norway, 17–19 October.

National Economic and Development Authority (NEDA), 1987, 'The results of the CEDP workers' profile survey', processed (Manila: NEDA, Government of Philippines).

Newman, J., S. Jorgensen and M. Pradhan, 1990, 'How did workers benefit from Bolivia's Emergency Social Fund?', processed (Washington, DC: World Bank).

Nolan, B. and V. Turbat, 1993, 'Cost recovery in public health services in sub-Saharan Africa', Human Resources Division, World Bank (Washington DC: World Bank).

Noss, A., 1991, 'Education and adjustment: a review of the literature', processed Education and Employment Division, Population and Human Resources Dept, World Bank (Washington DC: World Bank).

Nuqui, W., 1991, 'The health sector and social policy reform in the Philippines since 1985', Innocenti Occasional Papers, EPS 12 (Florence: UNICEF, International Child Development Centre).

Osmani, S., 1988, 'Social security in South Asia', Development Economics Research Programme, Working Paper 18 (London: London School of Economics).

PAMSCAD Secretariat, 1990, 'Proposed review of PAMSCAD', processed (Accra: Ministry of Local Government).

PAMSCAD Secretariat, 1992, 'PAMSCAD report as at 31 December', mimeo (Accra: Ministry of Local Government).

Pante, F., 1990, 'Health policy research and development in the Philippines', processed (Manila).

Pastor, M., 1987, 'The effects of IMF programs in the Third World: debate and evidence from Latin America', *World Development*, 15, 249–62.

Pastor, M., 1991, 'Debt, stabilization and distribution in Latin America', processed (Los Angeles: Occidental College).

Pearce, R., 1990, 'Food consumption and adjustment in Zambia', Food Studies Group, International Development Centre, Working Paper 2 (Oxford: Queen Elizabeth House).

Pearce, R., 1994, 'Food consumption and adjustment in Zambia', in van der Geest.

Pfefferman, G. and C. Griffin, 1989, *Nutrition and Health Programs in Latin America: Targeting Social Expenditures* (Washington DC: World Bank).

Pinstrup-Andersen, P., 1988, *Consumer-Oriented Food Subsidies: Costs, Benefits and Policy Options* (Baltimore, MD: Johns Hopkins University Press).

Pinstrup-Andersen, P., 1991, 'Targeted nutrition interventions', *Food and Nutrition Bulletin*, 13, 3, 161–9.

Pinstrup-Andersen, P., M. Jaramillo and F. Stewart, 1987, 'The impact on government expenditure' in G. A. Cornia *et al.*

Polak, K., 1991, 'The changing nature of IMF conditionality', *Essays in International Finance*, 184, (Princeton, NJ: Princeton University).

Pollittt, E., 1984, 'Nutrition and education achievement', *UNESCO Nutrition Education Series*, 9, ED. 84/WS/66 (Paris: UNESCO).

Prawda, J., 1990, 'Decentralisation and educational bureaucracies', A view from LATHR 2, Human Resources Division, World Bank (Washington DC: World Bank).

Psacharopoulos, G., 1980, 'Returns to education: an updated international comparison', in *Education and Income*, World Bank Staff Working Paper 402 (Washington DC: World Bank).

Psacharopoulos, G., in collaboration with S. Morley, A. Fiszbein, H. Lee, A. Penagides, B. Wood, F. Castro, Y. Ng and H. Yang, 1993, *Poverty and income distribution in Latin America: The story of the 1980s*, Latin America and the Caribbean Technical Department Report No. 27 (Washington DC: World Bank).

Quinn, V., M. Cohen, J. Mason and B. Kgosidintsi, 1987, 'Crisis proofing the economy: the response of Botswana to economic recession and drought', in Cornia *et al.*, 2.

Raczynski, D., 1987, 'Social policy, poverty and vulnerable groups: children in Chile', in G.A. Cornia *et al.*

Raczynski, D. and P. Romaguera, 1992, 'Chile: poverty, adjustment and social policies in the 1980s', Paper prepared for the Conference, 'Confronting the Challenges of

Poverty and Inequality in Latin America', The Brookings Institution and Inter-American Dialogue, 16–17 July, Washington DC (Santiago: Cieplan).

Ravallion, M., 1991, 'Reaching the poor through public employment: arguments, evidence, and lessons from South Asia', *The World Bank Research Observer*, 6, 2, 153–75.

Ravallion, M. and M. Huppi, 1989, 'Poverty and undernutrition in Indonesia during the 1980s', Policy, Planning and Research Working Papers (Washington DC: World Bank).

Ravallion, M., G. Datt and S. Chen, 1992, 'New estimates of aggregate poverty in the developing world, 1985–90', in World Bank, Population and Human Resources Dept (Washington DC: World Bank).

Reichmann, T., 1978, 'The Fund's conditional assistance and the problems of adjustment: 1973–75', *Finance and Development*, 15, 38–41.

Reichmann, T. and R. Stillson, 1978, 'Experience with programs of balance of payments adjustment: standby arrangements in the higher credit tranches, 1963–72' *IMF Staff Papers*, 25, 293–309.

Ribe, H. and S. Carvalho, 1990, 'World Bank treatment of the social impact of adjustment programs', World Bank PRE Working Paper WPS 521 (Washington DC: World Bank).

Ribe, H., S. Carvalho, R. Liebenthal, P. Nicholas and E. Zuckerman, 1991, 'How adjustment programs can help the poor; The World Bank's experience', World Bank Discussion Papers, 71 (Washington DC: World Bank).

Rivero, C.C., R. L. Ascencio and J.Q. Vinagre, 1991, 'The impact of economic crisis and adjustment on health care in Mexico', Innocenti Occasional Papers 13 (Florence: UNICEF).

Robinson, S., 1991, 'Macroeconomics, financial variables and computable general equilibrium models', *World Development*, 19, 1509–25.

Rodrik, D., 1990, 'How should structural adjustment programs be designed?' *World Development*, 18, 7, 947–93.

Rosenzweig, M., 1986, 'Program interventions, intrahousehold distribution and the welfare of households; modelling household behavior', *World Development*, 14, 2, 233–44.

Roy, S., 1993, 'Aspects of structural adjustment in West Africa and South-East Asia', *Economic and Political Weekly*, 11 September, 1937–49.

Sahn, D., 1989, 'Fiscal and exchange rate reforms in Africa: considering the impact upon the poor', processed (Washington DC: Cornell University Food and Nutrition Policy Program).

Sahn, D., 1990, 'Fiscal and exchange rate reforms in Africa: considering the impact upon the poor', Cornell Food and Nutrition Policy Program, Monograph 4.

Sahn, D. and H. Alderman, 1988, 'The effects of human capital on wages, and the determinants of labor supply in a developing country', *Journal of Development Economics*, 29, 2, 157–84.

Sahn, D.E. and A. Sarris, 1991, 'Structural adjustment and the welfare of rural smallholders: a comparative analysis from sub-Saharan Africa', *The World Bank Economic Review*, 5, 2, 259–89.

Sahn, D. and R. Bernier, 1994, 'Evidence from Africa on the intra-sectoral allocation of social sector expenditures', Cornell Food and Nutrition Policy Program, Working Paper 45 (Ithaca: Cornell).

Salter, W.E.G., 1959, 'Internal and external balance – the role of price and expenditure effects', *The Economic Record*, 00, 226–38.

Satyanarayana, K., A. Naidu, B. Chatterjee and B. Narasinga Rao, 1977, 'Body size and work output', *American Journal of Clinical Nutrition*, 30, 322–5.

Schacter, M., 1989, 'Bolivia's "Emergency Social Fund": historical notes and impressions', processed (Washington DC: World Bank).

Schadler, S., F. Rozwadowski, S. Tiwari and D. Robinson, 1993, 'Economic adjustment in low-income countries, experience under the Enhanced Structural Adjustment Facility', International Monetary Fund Occasional Paper 106 (Washington DC: IMF).

Schultz, T.P., 1989, 'Women and development: objectives, frameworks and policy interventions', PPR Working Papers, WPS 200 (Washington DC: World Bank).

Scrimshaw, N., 1986, 'Nutritional and health consequences of economic adjustment policies that increase poverty', Paper for the North–South Round Table on Development, Salzburg, September.

Selowsky, M., 1981, 'Nutrition, health and education: the economic significance of complementarities at early age', *Journal of Development Economics*, 9, 331–46.

Selowsky, M., 1991, 'Protecting nutrition status in adjustment programs: recent World Bank activities and projects in Latin America', paper prepared for the 18th Session of the United Nations subcommittee on Nutrition, processed (Washington DC: World Bank).

Selowsky, M. and L. Taylor, 1973, 'The economics of malnourished children: an example of disinvestment in human capital', *Economic Development and Cultural Change*, 22, 1, 17–30.

Sen, A.K., 1977, 'Rational fools: a critique of the behavioural foundations of economic theory', *Philosophy and Public Affairs*, 6, reprinted in A.K. Sen, 1982, *Choice, Welfare and Measurement* (Oxford: Blackwell).

Sen, A.K., 1981, *Poverty and Famines: An Essay on Entitlement and Deprivation* (Oxford: Clarendon Press).

Sen, A.K., 1984, *Resources, Values and Development* (Oxford: Blackwell)

Seshamani, V., 1990, 'Towards structural transformation with a human face', Innocenti Occasional Papers, Economic Policy Series, 7 (Florence: UNICEF).

Seshamani, V., O.S. Saasa, G.J. Bhat, G. Lungwangwa, M.C. Milimo and C. Osborne, 1993, 'Zambia: constraints to social service delivery' (Lusaka: World Bank).

Siegel, P.B. and J. Alwang, 1993, 'Rural poverty in Zambia: an analysis of causes and policy recommendations', processed (Tennessee: University of Tennessee).

Singer, H., 1989, 'Relationship between debt pressures, adjustment policies and deterioration of terms of trade for developing countries (with special reference to Latin America)', Institute of Social Studies, Working Paper 59 (The Hague: ISS).

Singer, H., 1991, 'Does the World Bank Structural Adjustment Programme in sub-Saharan Africa work?', processed (Sussex: Institute of Development Studies).

Srinivasan, T.N., 1988, 'Structural adjustment, stabilisation and the poor', Economic Development Institute, World Bank (EDI: Catalogue No. 400/056).

Steel, W. and L. Webster, 1992, 'How small enterprises in Ghana have responded to adjustment', *The World Bank Economic Review*, 6, 3, 423–38.

Stein, H., 1992, 'Deindustrialization, adjustment, the World Bank and the IMF in Africa', *World Development*, 20, 1, 83–95.

Stevenson, G., 1991, 'Adjustment lending and the education sector: the Bank's experience', mimeo (Washington DC: World Bank).

Stewart, F., 1991, 'The many faces of adjustment', *World Development*, 19, 12.

Stewart, F., 1992, 'Protecting the poor during adjustment in Latin America and the Caribbean in the 1980s: how adequate was the World Bank response?', Luca D'Agliano and Queen Elizabeth House Working Papers 44.

Stewart, F., 1993, 'Compensatory and support programmes in Zimbabwe during adjustment', processed (Oxford: Queen Elizabeth House).

Stewart, F., 1994, 'Education and adjustment: the experience of the 1980s' in R. Prendergast and F. Stewart (eds), *Market Forces and World Development* (London: Macmillan).

Stewart, F., 1995, 'Why we need a structured market', in G.K. Helleiner, S Abrahamian, E. Bacha, R. Lawrence and P. Malan (eds), *Poverty, Prosperity and the World Economy, Essays in Memory of Sidney Dell* (London: Macmillan).

Stewart, F., with J. Sharpley, 1986, *Economic Policies and Agricultural Performance: The Case of Tanzania* (Paris: OECD).

Strauss, J., 1986, 'Does better nutrition raise farm productivity?', *Journal of Political Economy*, 94, 2.

Streeten, P., 1987, 'Structural adjustment: a survey of the issues and the options', *World Development*, 15, 12, 1469–82.

Sukhatme, P.V., 1977, 'Malnutrition and poverty', Ninth Lal Bhaduri Shastri Memorial Lecture (New Delhi: Indian Agricultural Research Institute).

Summers, R. and A. Heston, 1988, 'A new set of estimates of real product and prices: estimates for 130 countries, 1950–85', *The Review of Income and Wealth*, 34, 1, 1–26.

Svedberg, P., 1990, 'Undernourishment in SubSaharan Africa: is there a gender bias?', *Journal of Development Studies*, 26, 3, 469–86.

Szekely, M.E., 1993, 'El programa nacional de solidaridad en Mexico' (paper presented at Seminar on Social Funds, Santiago, November).

Tabatabai, H. and M. Fouad, 1993, *The Incidence of Poverty in Developing Countries: An ILO Compendium of Data* (Geneva: International Labour Office).

Taylor, L., 1983, *Structuralist Macroeconomics, Applicable Models for the Third World* (New York: Basic Books).

Thorbecke, E., 1991, 'Adjustment, growth and income distribution in Indonesia', *World Development*, 19, 1595–614.

Tinguiri, K. L., 1992, 'Stabilisation without structural adjustment: the case of Niger, 1982–9', in Cornia *et al.*

Toye, J., 1991, 'Ghana' in P. Mosley *et al.*

Tripp, R., 1981, 'Farmers and traders – some economic determinants of nutritional status in Northern Ghana', *Journal of Tropical Paediatrics*, 27, 1, 15–22.

Tyler, G., and O. Akinboade, 1992, 'Structural adjustment and the poor: a computable general equilibrium model of the Kenyan economy', *Oxford Agrarian Studies*, 20, 1, 51–61.

UNCTAD, 1992, *The Least Developed Countries 1991 Report*, (New York: United Nations).

UNDP, 1990, *Human Development Report 1990* (New York: Oxford University Press).

UNDP, 1991, *Human Development Report 1991* (New York: Oxford University Press).

UNDP, 1992, *Human Development Report 1992* (New York: Oxford University Press).

UNDP, 1993, *Human Development Report 1993* (New York: Oxford University Press).

UNDP, 1994, *Human Development Report 1994* (New York: Oxford University Press).

UNICEF, 1987, 'Adjustment policies and programmes to protect children and other vulnerable groups in Ghana', in Cornia *et al.*, Vol. 2.

UNICEF, 1990, 'Protecting the poor and vulnerable during adjustment: the case of Ghana', processed (Accra: UNICEF).

UNICEF, 1991, *State of the World's Children* (New York: United Nations).

UNICEF, 1992, *The State of the World's Children 1992* (New York: United Nations).

United Nations, 1989, Administrative Committee on Coordination (ACC/SCN), 'Update on the nutrition situation. Recent trends in 33 countries' (New York: United Nations).

Valentine, T.R., 1993, 'Drought, transfer entitlements, and income distribution: the Botswana experience', *World Development*, 21, 1, 109–26.

Valerio, F., 1991, 'Fiscal shock, wage compression and structural reform: Mexican adjustment and educational policy in the 1980s', Innocenti Occasional Papers, EPS 17 (Florence: UNICEF, International Child Development Centre).

Van der Geest, W., 1994, *Negotiating Structural Adjustment in Africa* (London: James Currey Ltd).

Van der Hoeven, R. and F. Stewart, 1993, 'Social development during periods of structural adjustment in Latin America', paper prepared for a CEPAL/CEDLA seminar on the 'Transformation of Industrialisation Policies in Latin America', 12–13 July, processed (Geneva: ILO).

Van der Walle, D., 1990, 'Poverty and inequality in Latin America and the Caribbean during the 70s and 80s: an overview of the evidence', processed (Washington DC.: Human Resources Division, World Bank).

Vandermoortele, J., 1991, 'Labour market informalisation in SubSaharan Africa', in G. Standing and V. Tokman (eds.), *Towards Social Adjustment: Labour Market Issues in Structural Adjustment* (Geneva: ILO).

Villasenor Fabella, R., 1982, 'Economies of scale in the household production model and intra-family allocation of resources', PhD, Yale (New Haven: Yale University).

Viteri, F.E., B. Troun and M.D.C. Immink, 1975, 'Interaction between nutrition and productivity of agricultural labourers', Paper prepared for the 14th meeting of the Advisory Committee on Medical Research of the Pan-American Health Organization.

Waddington, C.J. and K.A. Enyimayew, 1989, 'A price to pay: the impact of user charges in Ashanti-Akim District, Ghana', *International Journal of Health Planning and Management*, 4, 17–47.

Wagao, J.H., 1990, 'Adjustment policies in Tanzania, 1981–89: the impact on growth, structure and human welfare', Innocenti Occasional Papers, 9 (Florence: UNICEF).

Wangwe, S., 1992, 'Building indigenous technological capacity: a study of selected industries in Tanzania' in F. Stewart, S. Lall and S. Wangwe (eds), *Alternative Development Strategies in SubSaharan Africa* (London: Macmillan).

Wheeler, D., 1984, 'Sources of stagnation in SubSaharan Africa', *World Development*, 12, 1, 1–23.

Williamson, J. (ed.), 1983, *IMF Conditionality* (Cambridge, MA: MIT Press).

Williamson, J., 1990, *Latin American Adjustment: How has this Happened?* (Washington DC: Institute for International Economics).

Winnick, M., K.K. Meyer and R.C. Harris, 1979, 'Malnutrition and environmental enrichment by early adoption', *Science*, 190, 1173–5.

Wolgemuth, J.C., M.C. Latham, A. Hall, A. Cheser and D.W.T. Crompton, 1982, 'Worker productivity and nutritional status of Kenyan road construction laborers', *American Journal of Clinical Nutrition*, 36, 68–78.

World Bank, 1981 (Berg Report), *Accelerated Development in Sub-Saharan Africa* (Washington DC: World Bank).

World Bank, 1987, *Funding Health Services in Developing Countries: An Agenda for Reform* (Washington DC: World Bank).

World Bank, 1988a, *The Philippines: The Challenge of Poverty*, October (Washington DC: World Bank).

World Bank, 1988b, *Adjustment Lending: An Evaluation of Ten Years of Experience* (RAL I), Working Paper Policy and Research Series No. 1 (Washington DC: World Bank).

World Bank, 1989a, *Sub-Saharan Africa: From Crisis to Sustainable Growth* (Washington DC: World Bank).

World Bank, 1989b, *Poverty Alleviation in Madagascar: Country Assessment and Policy Issues* (Washington DC: World Bank).

World Bank, 1989c, *African Economic and Financial Data* (Washington DC: World Bank).

World Bank, 1989d, *Bolivia, Country Economic Memorandum* (Chapter IV and Annex III) (Washington DC: World Bank).

World Bank, 1989e, *Indonesia: Basic Education Study,* Population and Human Resources Dept (Washington DC: World Bank).

World Bank, 1989f, *Latin America's Children*, Report No. IDP-0049, 'Latin America and the Caribbean Region', Human Resources Dept, 1989 (Washington DC: World Bank).

World Bank, 1990a, *Report on Adjustment Lending II: Policies for the Recovery of Growth*, RAL II (Washington, DC, World Bank).

World Bank, 1990b, *Costa Rica: Public Sector Social Spending* (Washington DC: World Bank).

World Bank, 1990c, *Indonesia: Poverty Assessment and Strategy Report* (Washington DC: World Bank).

World Bank, 1990d, *Venezuela Poverty Study: From Generalized Subsidies to Targeted Programs,* processed (Washington DC: Human Resources Division, Latin America and the Caribbean, World Bank).

World Bank, 1991, *Report and Recommendation of the President of the IBRD to Executive Directors on a Proposed Agricultural Adjustment Loan II,* Report No. P-5520-ME (May) (Washington DC: World Bank).

World Bank, 1992a, *Adjustment Lending and Mobilization of Private and Public Resources for Growth* (RAL III), World Bank Country Economics Dept, Policy Research Series 22 (Washington DC: World Bank).

World Bank, 1992b, *Structural and Sectoral Operations* (Washington DC: World Bank).

World Bank, 1993a, *Implementing the World Bank's Strategy to Reduce Poverty* (Washington DC: World Bank).

World Bank, 1993b, *Better Health in Africa,* Human Resource and Poverty Division (Washington DC: World Bank).

World Bank, 1993c, *Indonesia Public Expenditures, Prices and the Poor* (Washington DC: World Bank).

World Bank, 1993d, *Social Recovery Project Zambia: Annual Implementation Report* (Washington DC: World Bank).

World Bank, 1994, *Adjustment in Africa, Reform, Results and the Road Ahead* (Washington DC: World Bank).

World Bank, various years, *World Development Report* (Washington DC: World Bank).

World Bank and UNDP, 1989, *Africa's Adjustment and Growth in the 1980s* (Washington DC: World Bank).

Wurgraft, J.B., 1993, 'Fondo de solidaridad e inversion social', processed (Santiago: PREALC).

Younger, S., 1994, Presentation to Cornell University/USAID Conference on Adjustment and Poverty in sub-Saharan Africa, Accra, Ghana, 18–20 March.

Younger, S., S. Conagarajah and H. Alderman, 1994, 'Labor market consequences of retrenchment for civil servants in Ghana', Cornell Food and Nutrition Program Working Paper 64 (Washington DC: Cornell Food and Nutrition Program).

Yusuf, M.D., 1989, 'On reforming Tunisia's food subsidy program', processed (Washington DC: World Bank).

Zuckerman, E., 1989, 'Adjustment programs and social welfare', World Bank Discussion Papers, 44 (Washington DC: World Bank).

Zulu, J. and S. Nsouli, 1985, 'Adjustment programs in Africa: the recent experience', IMF Occasional Paper 34 (Washington DC: IMF).

Index

Note: Page numbers in bold print refer to diagrams, charts and tables